BULLETPROOF VEST

BULLETPROOF VEST

*The Ballad of an Outlaw
and His Daughter*

◆

MARIA VENEGAS

FARRAR, STRAUS AND GIROUX ◆ NEW YORK

Farrar, Straus and Giroux
18 West 18th Street, New York 10011

Printed in the United States of America
First edition, 2014

Some portions of this book are adapted from material previously published in *Granta*.

Library of Congress Cataloging-in-Publication Data
Venegas, Maria, 1973–
    Bulletproof vest : the ballad of an outlaw and his daughter / Maria
Venegas. — First edition.
      pages cm
    ISBN 978-0-374-11731-3 (hardcover) — ISBN 978-1-4299-4416-8 (ebook)
      1. Venegas, Maria, 1973–   2. Children of criminals—Family relationships—
Mexico.   3. Criminals—Family relationships—Mexico.   4. Fathers and
daughters—Mexico. I. Title.

HV6248.V455 A3 2014
364.1092—dc23
[B]

2013038777

Designed by Abby Kagan

Farrar, Straus and Giroux books may be purchased for educational, business, or
promotional use. For information on bulk purchases, please contact the Macmillan
Corporate and Premium Sales Department at 1-800-221-7945, extension 5442, or
write to specialmarkets@macmillan.com.

www.fsgbooks.com
www.twitter.com/fsgbooks • www.facebook.com/fsgbooks

10 9 8 7 6 5 4 3 2 1

Some names and identifying details of certain people and places have been changed to
protect the privacy of individuals.

PARA MI QUERIDO VIEJO

It's no wonder that I had no father and that I had already died one night twenty years before I saw light. And that my only salvation must be to return to the place . . . where my life had already ceased before it began.

—WILLIAM FAULKNER, *Light in August*

CONTENTS

BULLETPROOF
VEST

JOSE MANUEL VENEGAS
Zacatecas, Mexico, 1967

◆ PROLOGUE: AMBUSH
(Zacatecas, Mexico, 1998)

MEXICO'S RURAL 44 IS THE ONLY ROAD that leads from the taverns of Valparaíso back to his ranch. Unless he decides to spend the night in a bordello, eventually he will be on that road. But there he is, standing at the bar, one foot propped on the chrome rail, the heel of his cowboy boot wedged against it, his hand wrapped around a beer, the músicos playing a corrido just for him.

He takes a cold one for the road, settles his tab. The tires of his gray Chevy grip the concrete, the truck jerks with every shift of the gears. The lights of Valparaíso fade in the distance while he drives into the stillness of the desert night. The stench of a decomposing carcass fills the cabin as he pushes a tape into the deck and cranks up the volume. Drums and horns come thundering from the large speaker he rigged behind his seat, each note blasting through him as he listens to one corrido after another—to ballads of long-ago heroes, outlaws, and bandits.

His music and the stars above are his only companions. His truck swerves freely. The headlights slice through the pitch dark and bugs fly in and out of the beams. Some hit the windshield, leaving milky streaks on the glass. He drives past the ditch where he and his buddy recently drove off the road; the truck rolled twice before hitting a mesquite, his arm pinned under the hood for six hours before anyone found them. Best to take it nice and easy, he thinks. Take it right down the middle of the road, wouldn't want to end up kissing a tree again.

The beams catch the taillights of a stalled blue car on the side of the road in front of the slaughterhouse. Pobre pendejo, he thinks. He idles past, noticing the car is empty. He takes a swig, and in the rearview mirror he sees the headlights of an approaching truck. And then it's upon him, flashing its high beams in rapid succession, practically pushing him out of the way. He pulls slightly onto the gravel to let it pass. The truck flies by in a fury, and soon it has vanished around the only curve on the road between town and his home. Must be in a hurry. He reaches for his beer, but before the can touches his lips, his truck is lit up in a hail of bullets. Every muscle in his body contracts, pulling him toward the steering wheel. Hot pressure pierces his body, bullets skid across his scalp, singeing his hair. All around him glass shatters as the truck slows to a halt. The music has stopped. The speaker behind his seat is pumped full of lead.

The sound of his breathing fills the cabin and a warm stream runs down his face and neck. Through the cracked side mirror he sees the headlights of the blue car flick on. Two men with machine guns emerge from the ditches on either side of the road, run through the beams, and jump in. Tires screech as they speed off in the opposite direction. Pinches culeros, he thinks, watching their red taillights vanish in the distance.

He prays to the Virgen de Guadalupe, to the Santo Niño de Atocha, to San Francisco de Asís, to any saint who will listen. It might be hours before another car comes down the road and already the blood is collecting inside his shirt, his right arm growing numb. He stares at the keys, still in the ignition, reaches for them, turns them slowly and, to his surprise, the truck fires right up. It's a goddamn miracle. He reaches for the scorpion gear knob, manages to shift into drive, and soon he's clearing the curve and drifting home.

The sounds of creaking metal and shattered glass fill the truck's cabin. He turns left onto the dirt road that leads to La Peña. The truck picks up momentum on the downward slope and wobbles violently as it rolls over gullies left behind by the flash floods of the rainy season. It flies past the Virgen de Guadalupe shrine and, in his mind, he makes the sign of the cross: up, down, left, right. His truck glides into the river, crawls up the slight incline on the other side, and clears the entrance to La Peña. But he's lost speed on the ascent and his focus is fading while the pool collecting in his shirt keeps growing.

The truck inches past the small limestone church; the bell sits quietly in its tower above. The entrance to his courtyard comes into view. His right arm slips off the steering wheel, and the truck veers off the dirt road, crashing into a cinder-block wall. The hood flies open and sends hot steam hissing into the cold night. He drifts off, comes to; he pushes the door open and slips into unconsciousness.

There is a distant barking, which seems to be traveling through a long tunnel toward him, then claws are digging into his shoulder, wet tongues sliding over his face and neck. He opens his eyes and his two dogs are standing on their hind legs; he swings at them and falls out of the truck. A cloud of dust envelops him when he hits the ground. He pushes himself up and leans into the truck. It takes all his might to pull the weight of his body toward the house. Staggering, he goes up the dirt road, past the two eucalyptus trees where the chickens sleep, past the encino woodpile he recently chopped, and then he's at the courtyard gate, pushing it open and stumbling past the parakeet cage, the propane tank, the half rubber tire filled with drinking water for the dogs, the plants arranged in large rusty tin cans along the cinder-block wall, until he reaches the blue metal door of the house and collapses.

In the early hours of dawn, while the chickens are still tucked away in their trees and the chill of night lingers in the air, Doña Consuelo, the elderly woman who lives on the other side of the dirt road, goes out for her morning walk. She adjusts her headscarf and leans on her cane as she makes her way toward the small church, her Chihuahua prancing alongside her. She turns the corner and there it is, pressed up against the wall, like a metallic bird shot down from the night sky, its carcass riddled with bullets. In the driver's-side door alone, there are over forty holes. The windows are shattered, the door still ajar, the seat slick with blood, and the rumors start circulating: *Jose is dead. Pumped full of lead. His truck completely destroyed.* By the time the news sweeps across the desert, crosses barbed-wire fences, travels north, and makes it to the other side, there are conflicting stories.

"Hey, did you hear about Dad?" my sister Sonia asks when she calls me.

"No," I say. I'm at work, trying to decide on what to order for lunch. "What happened?"

"He got ambushed," she says. "Apparently there were two guys with machine guns."

"Oh." I continue browsing through the menu. "So, is he dead?"

BOOK ONE

1. BULLETPROOF VEST
(Chicago suburbs, 1987)

THE FIRST GUNSHOT snaps me out of my sleep. I lie in bed and stare at the two blinking red dots of my alarm clock: 12:35 a.m. It's Thursday night and my father has been playing cards with the neighbors. I can almost see the eye of the gun following its target, and then the second and third shots ring out. Something is different. Whenever he drinks and fires his .45, it's always in rapid succession, four or five bullets following one another into our front lawn or out at the night sky.

My sister Sonia is the first out of bed. She hears someone coughing, as if choking, outside her bedroom window. She goes outside and walks around the side of the house, follows the red streak along the white aluminum siding. My father is leaning into the wall, just below her bedroom window. He's covered in blood, his gun still in his hand.

"Escóndela," he says, handing his gun to her. The gun is still hot to the touch. She takes it and helps him inside.

By the time I step out of my bedroom, he's standing in the middle of the living room, slightly swaying forward and back. He's looking right at me but his gaze feels as if he's looking at me from a distant mountaintop. My mother is next to him, in her white slip, pressing a towel under his chin.

"You're bleeding to death. You're bleeding to death. You're bleeding to death," she says as the towel becomes saturated and thin red lines stream down her arm and onto her white slip. She pulls the towel away and readjusts it.

There is a gash under his chin that's about two inches long. Thick blood flows from it and runs down his neck. His white undershirt is already soaked. On the hardwood floor beneath him, there is a dark pool forming and inching closer to my bare feet. He's mumbling something about that pinche pendejo—how he knows someone put him up to this. But with him, all those culeros go in circles, like dogs chasing their tails. How he's not going to rot in jail because of that son of a bitch.

"Salvador!" he yells for my brother as he pushes past my mother and stumbles through the dining room, bumping into the china cabinet and making everything inside tremble. He disappears into his bedroom, shouting orders for Salvador to pull his car around the back.

Salvador does as he's told, and by the time my father emerges from his bedroom, red and blue lights are already flashing through every window in the house and dancing across his face. He goes out the back door, climbs over the chain-link fence, and crouches through the neighbor's backyard. Salvador is waiting on the next street over, sitting in the car, engine running, lights off. My father climbs into the backseat, lies down, and Salvador drives off. There is a flurry of screeching car tires and police sirens all around our house.

"Dios nos tenga de su santa mano," my mother prays out loud.

Soon, the sirens are fading in the distance, while out there on Route 45, Salvador is flooring the car, speeding through red lights, and swerving around traffic as a swarm of flashing lights and sirens is closing in on him. My father yelling the whole way for him to step on it, telling him not to stop, no matter what. But up ahead, a row of police cars is blocking the road, and officers stand behind open doors with their guns drawn. Salvador hits the brakes, throws the car into reverse, but before he hits the gas, a police car skids to a halt behind him. There's a voice bellowing from a megaphone, demanding that he put his hands where they can see them. He lifts his hands from the steering wheel and raises them slowly, watching as four officers with guns pointing at him move in, shouting for him to step out of the car.

"I need to get my father to the hospital," Salvador says, motioning to the backseat with his head. "He's bleeding to death." An officer shines his flashlight on my father, who is lying unconscious, his clothes soaked with blood. A police escort takes them to the nearest hospital, fifteen minutes away.

An hour later, my younger brother and sister and I are outside, leaning into the chain-link fence next to Rocky's doghouse. Even though it's nearly two in the morning, it feels like the middle of the day. Police cars with flashing lights sprawl from our driveway, lighting up the entire block, and all the neighbors are out. The Colombian woman who lives across the street stands on her stoop with her hands resting on her daughter's shoulders. The elderly white woman who lives alone in the three-story house next to the Colombians' watches from behind her screen door. The five little blonde girls who live next door are on the other side of the chain-link fence, still in their pajamas, lined up beside their mother, their fingers gripping the fence, and staring wide-eyed at us. A few officers scan our front yard with their flashlights, searching under the picnic table and around the mulberry tree near the driveway. Mateo and Julio, who live up the street and are in my class at school, stand on the other side of the yellow tape. Mateo waves at me, I wave back. Salvador ducks under the yellow tape and is stopped in our driveway by a man who has a camera strapped around his neck.

One of the officers makes his way over to us, pointing his flashlight along my mother's zucchini and tomato garden, which sprouts along the chain-link fence that separates our house from the small blue house next door where six Mexican men live. The men are questioned by police, and we watch as they reenact the scene around their picnic table: how Joaquín lunged at my father with a knife, was pushed away, came at him again, swinging from left to right, finally lodging the knife under my father's chin. My father pulled out his gun and shot him once. Joaquín stumbled back, fell down, got up, and lunged at him again. He was shot two more times.

"Hola," the officer says when he reaches us. He gets down on one knee and points his flashlight into Rocky's doghouse and peeks inside. Rocky starts growling. "What kind of a dog is it?" he asks.

"A Doberman," Jorge says.

"Is he friendly?"

"Sometimes."

He turns off his flashlight and stands up.

"What's his name?"

"Rocky."

He picks grass particles off his pants.

"Is Jose your father?"

"Yeah," we nod our heads.

He looks at us, presses his lips tight, and draws a deep breath. His nostrils flare.

"Is he *nice* to you?"

"Yeah," we shrug.

"Except when he's drunk," Yesenia says.

"Yeah, then he can be kind of mean," says Jorge.

The officer glances at him, at Yesenia, then back at me.

"Does he ever *hit* you?"

"No . . . yeah . . . sometimes," we overlap.

"Only when we're bad," Yesenia says.

He looks at her, crosses his arms, and throws his head back, as if he's counting stars.

"You wouldn't happen to know where his gun is, would you?"

My brother and I both shrug.

"Sonia took it," Yesenia says, "and . . ." I reach behind her and pinch her arm. She falls silent. The officer looks at her, then at me, and says that if we know where the gun is and don't tell them, we could all be in big trouble. He follows us into the house, where other officers are in the living room, looking under couch cushions, behind the television, inside the china cabinet, and under the dining room table.

"No vayan a decir en dónde está la pistola," my mother mumbles when we come into the house.

"Amá, ya saben," I say.

"Ni se les ocurra decir nada de las otras pistolas," she says under her breath.

"What did she say?" the officer asks.

"Nothing," we say, making our way to Sonia's bedroom.

He picks up her pillow and there is my father's .45, black and heavy and resting on the paisley sheet. He pulls out his walkie-talkie.

"Murder weapon has been located," he says into it.

Soon there are more officers in the room. One of them is wearing white latex gloves. She picks up the gun and drops it into a clear plastic bag. We follow them back into the living room, where other officers are standing around. "Murder weapon has been located" is leaping between the static of their walkie-talkies.

"Does your father keep any other weapons in the house?" one of them asks.

We tell him no, though inside the closet, behind the dining room table, there is a steel trunk filled with rifles, handguns, and machine guns.

The following day, Salvador is quoted in one newspaper and described as a neighbor, not related to Jose Venegas. The headlines read: ARGUMENT OVER BEER LEAVES ONE MAN DEAD, ANOTHER CRITICALLY WOUNDED. According to the papers, the whole thing had started over an argument about who would drink the last beer. I never trust anything I read in the papers after that. We knew it had nothing to do with beer. Joaquín probably hadn't even finished unpacking his belongings in the house next door when already men at the local taverns were warning my father to watch his back, to not let his guard down with his new neighbor. Even one of the men at my mother's church warned her. He was the manager at a photo-framing factory, and he had overheard the workers, who were mostly Mexican men, talking about how someone had hired Joaquín to kill my father.

Hard to know who or why as my father had left a handful of enemies back in Mexico. For all we knew, it may even have been the three brothers who had killed Chemel, my eldest brother, six months before. They must have known it was only a matter of time before my father went back down to Mexico looking to avenge his son, and so perhaps they thought they should strike first. Or maybe they had heard about the phone calls my father had been making, offering to trade one head for another—you do this one for me, and I'll do one for you.

My father spends two weeks in the hospital in intensive care, and we go visit him after school.

"Your father is lucky to be alive," the doctor says, explaining how the blade missed his jugular vein by a hair, and had that been severed, my father would have bled to death within minutes. I sit next to his bed watching dark fluids drain through the blue plastic tube that is attached to the gash under his chin, and I think that maybe he will die, that maybe he deserves to die. If I could trade heads, I would give his up to have my brother back. By then, there were rumors that my brother being killed had something to do with my father, an old vendetta or something. We heard that someone had paid to have Jose Manuel Venegas killed, and they had killed the wrong one. Even my mother claimed that it was my father's fault. According to her, God had taken my brother in order to "deal" with my father—this would be the thing that would make my father surrender at the Lord's feet, once and for all. My mother had already surrendered, had given up Catholicism and become a born-again Christian a few years back.

Not long after my father is released from the hospital, we start hearing new rumors. Joaquín has two brothers in the area and they have been asking questions around town: Where does Jose live? How many kids does he have? How many sons? Daughters? My father buys himself a bulletproof vest, and before leaving the house in the evening, he slips the heavy black vest over his undershirt and snaps the Velcro side straps in place. Then he throws on his cowboy shirt, and tucks it into his jeans.

"Can you tell I'm wearing a vest?" he asks us as he turns to one side, then the other.

"Sort of," we say, pointing to his horseshoe belt buckle, which appears to be pressing on the bottom edge of the vest. "Maybe you should pull your shirt out a bit," we say.

He retucks his shirt, making it a bit looser, and throws on a black leather vest over it.

"Now can you tell?"

"Not really," we say.

He slips one of his guns into the back of his Wranglers, grabs his black cowboy hat and goes out the door: metal, leather, bulletproof—indestructible.

In early October he starts preparing for his annual trip to Mexico. He buys linens and a blender for his mother, Hanes undershirts, socks, and a small television for his father. We go through our closets and throw anything we no longer wear into the growing pile in the corner of the dining room. On the day before he leaves, he takes his guns from the trunks in the closet and lays them out on the living room floor. He covers each one in several layers of tin foil, then swathes each with a towel from the factory where my mother works. Each towel has a different bright design on it—yellow butterflies, red roses, or pink flamingos, and they all smell of the same chemical dye that my mother smells like when she comes home from work. Finally, he wraps each contraption tight with duct tape. He arranges most of the bundles inside the steel trunks, along the bottom, and covers them with clothes from the pile in the dining room.

His two friends come over that night and help him rig his gray truck. They drive it onto two red metal ramps in the driveway, pop the hood, remove the spare from the back, split the doors open by pulling away the inside panels, and load up whatever contraptions didn't fit in the trunks. Carlos, the Puerto Rican man who is helping him drive down, shows up a few hours later with a duffel bag and a big grin. He's excited, has never been to Mexico. He also has no idea that—on paper—he's the legal owner of the gray truck with the red leather seats. They pull out of the driveway in the dark hours of pre-dawn, and by the time we wake up and start getting ready for school, he's long gone.

"Your father is never coming back," my mother tells us, a few days later.

"How do you know?" we ask.

"Because God showed me in a vision that He has taken him away for good," she says. "Plus he took all of his things."

"He did?"

"Yes," she says. "He didn't leave a single thing, not in the closet or the dresser or anywhere. Nothing."

What a coward, I think. He's the one who created this mess, and what had he done? He had bought himself a bulletproof vest and left. He had run away, had saved himself, and hadn't even had the guts to say goodbye.

After he leaves we begin noticing things, like the two men who park their black car and sit across the street from our house in the morning. We go out the back door, hop the fence, cross the neighbor's yard, and catch the bus on a different street. At night we start hearing noises. Whenever I hear something outside my window, I roll out of bed onto the carpet and then drag myself by the elbows into the living room where, close to the cool hardwood floor, I usually bump into one of my sisters. They heard a noise too. We crawl to the phone, reach up and pull it off its ledge and onto the floor, dial 911.

"Nine one one, what is your emergency?" the operator asks.

"Someone is trying to break into our house," we whisper.

Soon we hear police cars whizzing by on the back street, the front street, speeding around the house with their lights and sirens off. We watch flashlights make their way from the kitchen windows to the living room windows while we sit under the ledge, breathing into the receiver.

"Miss? Hello, miss, you there?" the operator asks.

"Yes," we whisper.

"It appears the coast is clear," she says. "There is an officer at your front door, please let him in."

My mother wakes when she hears the knock at the door.

"¿Qué andan haciendo?" she says, stepping out of her bedroom in her white slip, bra straps hanging halfway down her arms. "You called the police again?" she asks, yawning. "Ay, no, no, no, next thing you know they're going to want to charge us."

"Mom, it's nine one one. It's free," we say as we open the front door and the officer comes in.

"Where exactly did you hear the noise?" he asks.

"Outside that window," I say, pointing toward the bedroom I share with Yesenia.

"What did it sound like?" He takes a few steps toward the bedroom door, shines his flashlight between the bunks. "Did it sound like someone was trying to open the window?"

"Yeah," Yesenia says. "It was like a scratching noise."

Other times, there had been a shadow standing outside the living room window, a gentle tapping at the back door, a strange noise on the front porch. He glances at my mother, then back at us.

"Where's Jose?" he asks.

"In Mexico," we say.

"When is he coming back?"

"He's not."

"Doesn't he have a court date?" he asks. Even though it was proven to be self-defense, my father was out on bail and still had to appear before a judge for possession of an unregistered weapon.

We shrug.

The officer is looking at us as if contemplating something, and years from now Sonia will run into a retired officer from that town. "Oh, you Venegas kids," he will say, "we used to talk about you at the station, we worried about what would become of you." Perhaps what they worried about was that, once we grew up, we might keep them busy for years to come.

"Can you park a police car in our driveway and leave it there?" I ask, though we've made this request before, have told them about Joaquín's brothers. But since they haven't threatened us directly, since we don't know their names, don't even know what they look like—there's nothing the police can do to protect us.

"Maybe you should move," he says.

After my father leaves, news of his whereabouts always reaches us, and I'm certain it's only a matter of time before he turns up dead—shot by the federales, killed in a bar brawl, in prison, or crushed under the weight of his truck after going off the road for the umpteenth time. I know that sooner or later we will get that phone call, and I assume I'll be prepared for it. We hear he's back in Mexico, then in Colorado, then back in Mexico, in prison. When he's released from prison, he returns to La Peña, the old hacienda where he was born and raised. The house has been abandoned for several years and I imagine he arrives with nothing but the clothes on his back, a few pesos in his pocket, and the rope he made in prison slung over his shoulder. Perhaps he draws a bucket of cold water from the well and splashes some on his face before going inside to open the metal shutters, dust off the horse saddles, and reclaim his place among the scorpions that had infested the house.

This is where he is living when I go back to visit him fourteen years later. After the first visit, eventually, I return and spend summers and holidays with him, and between herding cattle and fixing barbed-wire fence posts together, he begins sharing stories. A lasso will remind him of one of the final conversations he had with his father. From there he will follow the rope further back in time to when he was extradited for murder from the United States. Then he'll go further still, to when he was a newlywed and the federales sliced him open at a rodeo. Over the years, I realize that he keeps going back to the same stories, as if they had been prerecorded and he was the needle, stuck in a groove, running over the same old ground. He had identified the defining moments in his life, and though he could pinpoint the twists and turns that had shaped him along the way, he was powerless to free himself of his past.

In sharing his stories with me, perhaps he's trying to explain why he lived such a violent and self-destructive life, or maybe he's trying to make sense of what road led him back to the same dusty corner of the world where his life began, and so, too, would come to end. Twelve years after the ambush, the feds will find him near the same curve, at the foot of a huisache, his skull crushed in.

After he dies, his neighbors, relatives, and even my mother seem eager to share stories about him and, other than slight variations, they are the same stories he had been telling. It was as though he had already written his own corrido—the ballad of his life.

2 ◆ HANDICAPPED BASTARD

"WHAT DID YOU SAY was your relationship to the patient, sir?" the woman behind the counter asks, looking up from her chart.

"I'm his second cousin," he says, clearing his throat, and perhaps the way he's fidgeting with his coat, or the way his gaze keeps darting around the lobby, is giving him away. The very thought of being face-to-face with that handicapped bastard sends the blood boiling in his veins. One of the first things he did upon returning to Mexico was go to the prison in the plaza to pay the handicapped bastard a visit, but he was informed that the man he was looking for had been transferred to a higher-security prison in the next, larger town over. A two-hour drive and he arrived at the prison, where they informed him that said inmate had been deemed mentally unstable, and thus was transferred to a mental institution in the next, even larger town over. A six-hour bus ride later and there he is standing in the brightly lit lobby, his gun weighing heavy in his coat pocket. "He probably doesn't remember me," he says to the woman. "It's been a few years, but I happened to be passing through and, well, I thought I'd pay him a visit." He flashes her a winning smile and watches as she goes through the files, aware of the line forming behind him, the shuffling of feet, the occasional impatient cough.

She pulls out a manila folder and looks through the papers in it.

"That patient was discharged three months ago," she says.

"Discharged?" he forces through his teeth. He knows exactly how things work in Mexico—a country where people have more time than money, and those who have money can buy themselves all the time they need. He wants to ask the woman how much was paid and who took the bribe—who was the cabrón that gave the order to set the bastard that killed his son free. He feels the hot flush under his skin, feels his hands trembling and draws them into a tight fist. "Discharged. That's. Great." He bites down on that word. "Well, how about that? My cousin is out there somewhere," he says, motioning toward the window with his hand, "and I'm in here looking for him." Though he's overcome with the urge to laugh hysterically, he stifles it because he knows that if he starts laughing, his laughter may turn on him. He draws a deep breath, forces a smile. "You wouldn't happen to know who it was that gave the order for his release, would you?"

Again she's searching through the file.

"La licenciada Barcena," she says looking up at him.

It had to be a woman, he thinks as he steps back out into the hot afternoon sun and makes his way to the bus station. Had it been a man, he would have tracked him down, just to see his reaction when he looked him in the eye and reminded him that, in those parts, taking bribes was as easy as trading heads. By the time he boards the next bus out of that town, his mind is already racing. If the handicapped bastard is no longer behind the protective gates of the system, then he is out there somewhere. He watches the nopales and huisaches come and go. That bastard may have feigned insanity, but if that son of a bitch was so mentally unstable, how was it he remembered to run after he pulled the trigger? It had been a year, almost to the day, since his son had been killed, and he didn't need to think back to that cold winter night to remember it. The events of that evening played on in his mind like a relentless reel. He and his son were in La Peña preparing for their trip back to Chicago. It was Christmas Eve, and the women were in the kitchen making buñuelos, their laughter and the scent of cinnamon drifted through the house. He was in the spare bedroom, polishing his boots, when Chemel came through the courtyard and stopped in the doorway.

"I'll be right back," he had said, reaching up and resting his hands on the doorframe. "I'm going over to Las Cruces to say goodbye to some friends." He looked up and saw his son's silhouette in the doorway, the light of the sinking sun already setting the sky ablaze behind

him. He knew the real reason why Chemel was going to Las Cruces—
to say goodbye to his sweetheart. "Are we still leaving in the morning?"
Chemel asked.

"Before the first cock sings out," he said. Everything was pretty
much ready to go, the crates and suitcases packed.

"Está bien," Chemel said, giving the doorframe above him a solid
tap, as if testing the structure, as if making sure it was strong enough
to withstand the test of time. It was the largest room in the house—
an addition to his grandparents' house that he himself had just completed. At the foot of the doorframe that led to the storage room, he
had etched the year of its construction into the wet cement: 1986.
"See you in a bit," he said, and then turned and walked away.

"See you in a bit." This was the last thing his son ever said to him.
Had he known then what his boy was about to walk into, he would
have tried to stop the sun in its tracks, because not only did he know
where Chemel was going, the three brothers also knew where his son
was going, and they were already waiting for him. Not even two hours
had passed when there was a knock at the door. It was already dark
out and he had just finished packing the last of the suitcases. The
knock came again, and the women fell silent. They weren't expecting
any guests, but then again, it was Christmas Eve, so it could be just
about anyone, a relative or a neighbor coming over to drop off some
tamales or atole. He went to the door and stepped out into the cold
December night.

"Who was at the door, Jose?" his mother asked, when he appeared
in the kitchen's doorway, the pigment already receding from his face.
The grease hissed in the frying pan on the stove as the raw dough
bubbled and churned in the heat. He looked at his mother, but was
unable to utter a single word.

"Are you all right, Jose?" his sister asked, commenting on how
pale he looked. Another buñuelo was dropped into the boiling grease
and instantly curled in on itself.

He turned from the doorway, and back in his bedroom he went
through a string of motions, without stopping to think about what he
was doing, without breaking his momentum. He reached under his
pillow, pulled out his gun, made sure it was loaded, slipped it into the
back of his jeans, grabbed his truck keys off the dresser, and before he
knew it, he was clearing the entrance of La Peña. When he reached

the main road, he turned right instead of left, thinking he'd go into town to get the feds, to make sure whoever was responsible would be brought to justice, but by the time he reached the curve, he thought better of it, and so he turned around and headed out to Las Cruces.

When he arrived, there were cars and trucks parked haphazardly near the wall that ran along the river, and men with kerosene lanterns were milling about by the water's edge where a crowd had gathered. He climbed out of the truck and made his way toward the crowd, the red glow from their lanterns reflecting off the thorny branches of a mesquite above. They parted to let him pass, and when he got to the center, there was his son, facedown in the river. That was a moment he didn't so much see as hear like a deafening clap. No one had touched his son. They were waiting for the feds to arrive. He dropped down to his knees and turned him over. His eyes were still open, and his face was scraped and bruised where it had hit against the stones on the river's floor.

Later, all the eyewitnesses gave the same account. They had been standing around near their trucks, next to the river, sharing a laugh, a final farewell with Che, as everyone knew that he would be leaving for the other side before the first light of morning. It had just grown dark out, when they saw what looked like a human grasshopper moving along the wall. They watched the man approaching slowly, steadying himself on his cane as he thrust the weight of his body forward and up before slumping back down. There was something almost mechanical about his walk.

"Do you have any vino?" he asked, when he reached the circle, alcohol fumes already exuding from his nostrils. They told him no, they didn't have any vino, and he stood there sizing up the group in a way that seemed off, though they thought nothing of it. They all knew who he was: El Cojo from Las Cruces. He was always hitchhiking in and out of town, and at some point, they had all given him a lift—even Che had picked him up along the main road several times, had driven past La Peña and all the way out to Las Cruces to drop him off at his front door, practically.

"Come on, one of you must have a bottle, no?" he said, and again they assured him they didn't have anything. "Well, I do have a bottle," he said, reaching into his coat pocket and pulling out a .357 Magnum.

He aimed it at Che and fired three times. The circle scattered. Some ran up the hill, others took for the road or jumped behind their trucks, and Che ran toward the water. His sweetheart's house sat on a boulder just on the other side of the river, and perhaps he thought he could make it to her front door. But he never reached her house, and though she must have heard the three blasts, and maybe even heard someone struggling in the river below her bedroom window, how was she to know that it was he? That at that very moment her sweetheart's life was draining from him, his blood being carried in the current like a long red ribbon, which flowed through the fields, around the mountains, along the ridges, and goodbye, goodbye, the ribbon unfurled until it spilled into the ocean. One of the bullets had gone astray, another had hit the young man standing next to Che in the arm, and the third had buried itself deep within his chest, just above his heart.

El Cojo had tried to make a run for it. His two brothers were waiting in a car nearby, engine running, lights off. But the feds had caught up to them that same night. They arrested El Cojo and threw him in prison, and now, not even a year later, he was already a free man. So be it, Jose thinks as the bus pulls into the station. If he's no longer behind the protective gates of the system, then he's out there somewhere. He will keep the word on the street. Knows it's only a matter of time before that handicapped bastard turns up.

The first thing he does upon returning to town is track down la licenciada Barcena. He hires an attorney and files a lawsuit against her. His photo appears in the papers the following day, and in it he's wearing a white cowboy hat and sporting a full black beard. The caption reads: *Jose Manuel Venegas, forty-five years of age, files a lawsuit against la licenciada Guadalupe Barcena for having aided in the escape of a murderer.*

3. WITNESS PROTECTION PROGRAM

"SO, WHAT'S GOING ON?" Norma asks as she slides onto the bench next to Fabiola and adjusts her orange tray in front of her. I considered not saying anything. Let them figure it out when Monday morning rolled around and I didn't show up for school, not that day—or ever again. But it's too late now, I've already told my friends I have something to tell them, and now they're all sitting across the lunchroom table from me, waiting.

"I'm moving," I say.

"What? Why?" they ask, in unison, practically. They're all here: Frida Chávez, Mirna Escobar, Fabiola Huertas, Maribel Torres, Juana Moreno, Norma García, and Araceli Ortega—this is my group of friends, or my "gang" as Mr. Kauffman, the principal, had referred to them on the day he called me down to his office. He sat eyeing me from behind his wide, wooden desk, his plump fingers crossed and resting on the smooth surface. "What's the name of your gang?" he asked. "What gang?" I said, thinking, what a jerk. I can't believe he called me out of class to ask me this. "Don't play games with me, Venegas. I know you're in a gang. I know you're the leader. I want the name."

Even though I wasn't the leader of a gang, in the four years I'd been at his school—fifth through eighth grades—I probably had spent more time serving in-school suspensions and detentions than in the classroom. At one point, the school had even placed me in a program for "at risk" kids, though I never understood what exactly we were at risk for. I was assigned to a mentor, a retired professional football player. "What do you want to be when you grow up?" he asked at our first meeting. "A famous fashion designer," I said. "Okaaay," he said, "and just in case that doesn't work out, is there anything else you might want to be?" he asked. "A supermodel," I said, without thinking twice.

"Is it because of your neighbor?" Frida asks.

"Yeah," I say.

They all know about the neighbor and his two brothers. Frida, Mirna, and Fabiola all live on my street, had heard the gunshots on that night, and every other night, when my father came home in the wee hours, blaring his music and unloading his gun into our front yard. At first, the neighbors used to call the police and report that they had heard gunshots, but eventually, they got used to it, and no one bothered calling the police anymore. I had once gotten into an argument in the library with Marcos, one of the boys who lived up the street. "Well, at least my father doesn't come home in the middle of the night, shooting his gun and waking up the entire neighborhood," he said. "Well, at least my brothers aren't drug dealers," I shouted, because word around the neighborhood was that the high school kids bought weed from his older brothers. The librarian shushed us, but still, the sting of his words lingered. Why did we have to end up with a lunatic for a father? Why couldn't we have had a normal dad like my friends and cousins had? It was a relief that he was gone, and gone for good.

"Where you moving to?" Mirna asks.

"I can't tell you," I say. My mother had warned us not to breathe a word to anyone—it was our own makeshift witness protection program.

"When?" Norma asks.

"This weekend," I say.

I pull out a notebook, have them write down their addresses and phone numbers, and promise to call and write. Over the next year, I keep in touch with several of them, though eventually we stop corresponding, except Frida and I. She'll keep me updated on everyone: Maribel was not going to high school because she had gotten pregnant, and soon after high school began, Araceli had also gotten pregnant and dropped out. After high school, Norma had landed in rehab. Eventually, I lost track of all of them, including Frida, though years later, I heard that she had gotten into drugs and that one day she had driven her car deep into the forest and slit her wrists.

My mother isn't there when we move. She's in Mexico taking advantage of our recent status as temporary residents to visit her mother. We had been granted temporary residency under President Reagan's amnesty act—except for my father, who had already had one too many run-ins with the law; his application was the only one denied. Though he was still allowed to stay in the United States with his work permit.

Between Friday night and Sunday afternoon, my siblings and I take what seems like fifty truckloads from our old house to the new one. We strap chairs, tables, mattresses, and bicycles down with rope in the back of a borrowed truck, and load boxes packed with dishes and garbage bags filled with linens and clothing into my eldest sister Mary's car. Back and forth we go all day Saturday and all day Sunday, until our final trip on Sunday afternoon. We step outside and Mary closes the front door—the sound of it hitting the frame sends an echo through the empty house. It's a relief to be leaving that house for good, not only because of the threat of the two brothers, but also because it feels like by moving away we are leaving the past behind us. The last time I ever saw my brother he had been standing in that doorway, one hand resting on the doorknob, the other holding a duffel bag. He was wearing a light blue Windbreaker, jeans, and a brand-new pair of white leather Nike sneakers.

"I'm leaving," he said, pausing at the door and looking at me. I was sitting on the couch, under a blanket, watching a rerun of *The Greatest American Hero*. My father had asked Chemel if he'd go back to Mexico to help my grandfather—who had recently been diagnosed with diabetes—with the livestock. It would only be for a month or two, just long enough for him to find and train a responsible cattle hand to stay on permanently.

"You promised to pay for my gymnastics lessons," I said, crossing my arms tight, even though I had already taught myself how to do just about everything from a back walkover to the splits. A few years back, we had lived near a gymnastics studio, and I used to ride my dirt bike to the studio and stand in the doorway, observing the classes. Then I'd ride home and practice in our front yard until it grew dark. The following day, I'd practice during recess, doing countless backbends over the blue rubber seat of a swing, pulling my right knee up and over the way I'd seen the girls in the class doing, until eventually I no longer needed the swing to spot me.

"I will," he said. "When I come back." He lingered in the doorway, waiting. He was the one who had told me to observe the classes and practice on my own, because that way, when I did start lessons, I'd be at a more advanced level. That's what he had done with karate. He had watched back-to-back Bruce Lee movies, observing and practicing before enrolling in classes, and he'd become a black belt in no time. "Aren't you going to give me a hug?" he said, his hand still resting on the doorknob.

"Why?" I said. "It's not like you're going to be gone forever." He stood in the doorway for a bit longer before turning and walking away, the light of the television reflecting off his white sneakers as he went.

Mary locks the door and we make our way to her car. It's spring and the icicles that hang from the white gutter in front of the house are melting in the afternoon sun, dripping and sending small streams down the driveway. I climb into the passenger seat, wedge myself next to a pillow, and place the box I'm carrying on my lap. Inside the box are my alarm clock radio, my coin collection, and the letters Chemel had written me from Mexico. After he'd been gone for six months, I had sat down and written him a letter, asking when was he coming back, and what was taking so long. I had already memorized the three chords he had left me practicing on the guitar and was sick of playing "Twinkle Twinkle Little Star." Also, I told him that his ex-girlfriend Leticia Jiménez had gotten married, and so had Anna Sánchez from down the street, and Lucy Hurtado from my mother's church said to say hello to him. I signed my name, licked the envelope, and placed four stamps on the upper right-hand corner. I wrote the address my mother had given me on it. There was no zip code, no street number—not even a street name—how was it possible that he was living in a place where the streets had no names? I sent the letter, convinced it would never reach him. Still, I checked the mailbox every day after getting off the school bus, until finally, about a month later, there was a letter from him.

For the next year, we wrote a few letters. He always inquired about how I was doing in school, and always asked me to say hello to the gang, which is how he referred to my siblings. He asked me to give my parents a hug and kiss on his behalf, but I never did, as I never gave my parents hugs or kisses even on my own behalf. Both my parents kept him busy that year. My father wired him money so that he could add on a new room to my grandparents' house in La Peña, and my mother sent him enough money for him to build her a house on a small plot of land she had purchased. The plot sat on a low hill in the outskirts of town, next to the cemetery. When he had completed the jobs, he called my father and asked him to wire the money he would need in order to get back to Chicago, but my father convinced him to stay, just a little longer. The holidays were only five months away, and since my father would be going to Mexico in December, they could drive back together. He agreed to wait for my father, to wait until the holidays.

I felt like one of the lucky ones because I had not gone to Mexico for the holidays to witness any of the things I'd later hear about from my two older sisters who had been down there. After my father pulled Chemel from the river, a few men had helped him hoist the body onto the back of his truck. My brother had been wearing his white sneakers and his feet dangled over the back of the truck bed, bouncing along as his body absorbed every bump on the dirt roads. Back in La Peña, they had laid him out on the limestone floor on top of a wooden plank, and while they waited for the coffin to arrive, my grandmother had cleaned away the mud that had dried around his hairline, ears, and nostrils. By the time my mother arrived from Chicago, they had already placed him inside the coffin, which was a simple wooden box.

"Where is your God now?" my father asked, taunting her. Wasn't He the God of miracles? The one who brought people back from the dead? Why didn't she pray to him now and ask him for a miracle. But there would be no miracle, and on the morning they were to take the body to the cemetery, in a sudden fit of desperation, my father had thrown himself on top of the coffin, opened it, grabbed my brother by the shirt and practically pulled him from it, demanding that he get up, get up, get up.

My father had had a corrido composed for Chemel, and when he returned to Chicago, he spent countless hours kneeling in front of the speaker, his back shaking violently as he listened to that corrido over and over again, as if the music might deliver his firstborn back into his arms. My brother seemed forever trapped inside that song, caught somewhere between the drums and the wailing horns. If I was lying in bed, the minute I heard the first note I pressed my pillow to my ears, cranked up my alarm clock radio, and soon either Madonna or Prince were drowning out the story of how my brother had been killed. I refused to shed a single tear, convinced myself that my brother was still alive, still in Mexico, forever riding his horse on that distant mountainside. Though at night when the house was dark and everyone was asleep, he started showing up in my dreams. I'd see him standing on the edge of the woods that lined the school's playground, and I'd run to him, desperate to throw my arms around him, but before I could reach him, he'd turn, walk into the woods, and vanish.

Mary hits the radio switch before reversing out of the driveway, and the beats of a cumbia fill the car as we make our way down the street. It feels good to be leaving that house for good, to be leaving the past in the past. Soon we are flying down Silver Lake Road, the lake on one side and Paradise on the other. Paradise is a wooded hill at the end of an asphalt parking lot, and when I was younger, my friends and I used to ride our dirt bikes to the hill and play in the woods, pretending that we had discovered paradise. We drive past Shady Lane, the street where we lived when we first arrived from Mexico. My parents had come first. They had left us with Tito, my maternal grandmother, and had crossed the border, found jobs, and saved money, and two years later they had sent for us.

My tío Manuel, my mother's older brother, had taken the three-day bus ride to the Arizona border with us. When we arrived at the border, three days later, he met up with a woman who would go through customs with us four younger kids—we all had loaned birth certificates. But Chemel, who was fourteen, and Mary, who was twelve, had no documents, and so my uncle had taken them across the river with a coyote. My father was waiting on the other side, in Yuma, Arizona. He had driven out from Chicago, and in the camper of his blue pickup truck he had packed a foam mattress, pillows, blankets, and a cooler filled with soda, packages of bologna, American cheese slices, a jar of mayonnaise, and two loaves of white bread.

It was a cold October day when we arrived in the Chicago suburbs. The sky hovered low and gray over the two-story brick house, which sat on a small hill and was surrounded by tall evergreens. My mother was not there when we arrived. She was at the hotel where she worked cleaning rooms. Eventually she came home, though I have no memory of that reunion. I had been two years old when they left, was four years old when we were reunited, and went straight into kindergarten.

"So, have you learned English yet?" my uncle asked me a month later, while we were all sitting around the kitchen table. I nodded. "Let's see," he said, looking around, eyeing my father at the head of the table. "How do you say papá in English?" I looked at my father and everyone fell silent. I stared at his beard, at his fingers wrapped around his fork, as if the word might suddenly appear. "Well?" my uncle said. They were all waiting, and my eyes finally came to rest on my father's white T-shirt, on his gut. It was round and hard and pressing against the edge of the table like a balloon.

"Pues, el inflado," I said, and everyone burst into laughter, including my father.

"The inflated one?" my uncle roared, and told me that I best start paying attention in class. I don't remember learning English. It was like I had fallen asleep dreaming in one language, and had awoken speaking in another.

By the time I was in first grade, it was clear that I was having trouble focusing in class. Whenever I didn't understand something, I blurred my vision until I could almost see the empty playground beyond the cinder-block walls, and I imagined myself on one of the swings, the wind in my hair as I gained momentum, until the chains were jerking in my hands. I could practically smell the rust coming off them while the tips of my sneakers almost touched the blue sky above.

"Maria, what is two plus two?" The teacher was pointing at the numbers on the board, and I imagined that if I were to let go of the chains, I'd go soaring over the distant treetops and vanish. "Maria!" She was then leaning over my desk, the scent of coffee emanating from her. "What is two plus two?" I was aware of how the other kids were all looking at me, and though I could hear her, I was unable to utter a single word. I felt so overwhelmed that I shut down, had gone, momentarily, mute.

"When was the last time you had your ears checked?" she asked. A few giggles erupted in the classroom, and I stared at my shoelaces and shrugged. She sent me to the nurse's office with a note. The nurse sent me home with a different note. One of my sisters translated it for my parents. The note stated that I might be hard of hearing and that they should take me to see a doctor as soon as possible.

That Saturday morning, after dropping my sisters off at the Laundromat with what seemed like sixty loads of laundry, my parents took me to a doctor. I sat on a blue leather cot, feet dangling, while they stood in the doorway watching as the doctor inserted a cold metal funnel in my ears, and then placed a large dry Popsicle stick on my tongue and told me to say "ah." He shone a light onto the back of my throat, as if the problem with my ears might be somewhere on the inside. My ears were fine, he concluded, but maybe the muscles behind my eardrums needed to be strengthened, and the best way to do that, according to him, was by chewing gum.

On Monday morning I returned to school with my doctor's note and a full week's supply of Wrigley's, Hubba Bubba, and Juicy Fruit. Whenever the teacher made other kids spit their gum out, they always pointed at me.

"She's chewing gum too," they complained.

"She has a medical condition," the teacher always replied.

Medical condition or not, I ended up being held back in the first grade, and years later I found out that chewing gum is often prescribed to kids with attention deficit disorder. Though it would be longer still before I learned exactly where my deficit stemmed from.

We lived in that house on Shady Lane for nearly three years before it started slanting to one side and was condemned to be demolished. We were given a month's notice to move out, and since then, we had continued to move. Every three to four years, it seemed, we were packing. This being the fourth and, hopefully, last time we'd be moving. We drive over the railroad tracks and turn right onto Route 145, where the speed limit is higher and the road stretches long and smooth for miles. Rolling fields give way to apple orchards until, finally, in the distance, the outdoor movie theater comes into view, like a beacon.

It sits at a four-way intersection on the outskirts of town, and is the highest structure for miles around. After clearing the intersection, we drive past the marina and across the one-lane bridge that stretches over the Somerset River and leads right into the heart of town. We make our way down Main Street, go past Mancini Brother's Pizza, the Custard Ice Cream Shack, O'Brien's Bar and Grill, Aunt Tillie's Pancake House, and the Somerset Savings Bank before turning left at a Catholic church on the corner of Berry—our new street.

It's been five months since my father left, and if he were to change his mind and return to the old house, thinking he'd walk through the front door and reclaim his seat at the head of the table, he would not find the table or a single chair to sit in. The only evidence that he and his family had ever lived in that house may be a splintered floorboard in the living room, where one of the bullets he had shot off in the house had ripped through the grain before ricocheting and vanishing into the drywall.

On Monday morning, I show up for school and almost immediately notice how other students stare at me. They come to the doorway of the classroom, necks craning over and around each other as they try to catch a glimpse of the new girl.

"Stop staring at her," the teacher says. "She's not an animal at the zoo."

I'm the only Mexican girl in the entire grade. There is one Mexican boy and one Puerto Rican boy, but other than that, everyone else is white. I don't know if I'll get along with these white girls, have never had a white friend before, am not even sure I like them. A few days later, I find out there's one other Mexican girl in my grade. Her name is Rosalba, but she only attends school half the day, has classes with the special ed kids, and she won't be going to high school, because she's pregnant.

We are lining up after recess one day, shortest to tallest, and I'm still at the back of the line where I've always been. Natalie Miller, the girl who stands in front of me, flicks her hair back and squints at me through her glasses.

"Oh my God," she says. "You're so sophisticated."

Sophisticated—I have no idea what that word means, but there's something about the way she says it that makes it feel like an insult. I don't really like Natalie Miller, because not long ago, she had pointed out that I talked funny, saying "it's Shicago, not Cheecago." When I get home from school that day, I pull out the dictionary and look up the word, thinking, if it's a cut down, I'm going to go back to school tomorrow and kick that girl's ass.

> Sophisticated: Having acquired worldly knowledge or refinement, a person who lacks natural simplicity or naiveté, someone who has been altered by experience, education or circumstance.

I read the definition several times trying to decide what she meant by it. I would have never let anyone offend me and get away with it. Especially not since the warning my father had given me when I was in sixth grade and he had caught Frida and me skipping school. We were sitting on the couch watching television when he came through the front door and surprised us. His yellow construction helmet was tucked under his arm, the green stainless steel thermos dangling from his index finger, and there were wet specks of rain on his jeans and Timberland boots. "Why aren't you at school?" he grunted over the blaring television. The minute I opened my mouth, I was already lying, telling him how Ramona, the big fat girl at our bus stop, had started picking on me, and that I was afraid of her, so I had run back home, and since Frida didn't want to go to school without me, she had run after me. "What do you mean you ran away?" he said, the door slamming shut behind him.

"She's a lot bigger than I am," I said.

"I don't care how big she is," he said. "Next time someone picks on you, even if you know you're going to get your ass kicked, you stay and you fight like a man," he said, taking two steps toward me. "Never again do I want to hear that you are running away from anybody, do you understand?" I nodded, though I was utterly confused by his anger, and it would be years, still, before I found out where that warning stemmed from.

He made us get ready and drove us to school, but after that day, if anyone so much as looked at me the wrong way, it was enough to instigate a fight. A few weeks later, I had just gotten on the bus after school and settled into my seat when a backpack came flying and landed next to me. Even before I picked it up, the whole bus was already chanting: "Throw it back, throw it back." I picked it up and flung it back, watched it soar through the air and hit against the emergency exit door on the back of the bus before landing on the ground.

I hadn't even turned all the way around when I felt the immense sting of an open hand smacking against my face. Everything went gray, and once I regained focus, my upper lip was throbbing, and a hot stream was running from my nose and filling my mouth with the taste of aluminum.

Through the haze, I could see Mike González taking his usual seat at the very back of the bus. His mouth was agape with laughter, and I wanted to reach into that black hole and rip out his tonsils. He was in eighth grade, two years older than me, and though he had never picked on me, he was always picking on my friends, slamming their lockers shut, pushing them down on the ice, or punching their books out of their hands. He didn't see me coming, and perhaps I didn't even realize that I was running toward him, until we were both flying backward onto his seat and before he had a chance to react, I had pinned both his arms under my knees and was throwing wild punches. The blood from my nose rained down on his face as the entire bus vibrated in unison: "Fight, fight, fight, fight."

The bus driver pulled me off him and made us both go to the principal's office, but since it was self-defense, and there were eyewitnesses, I was allowed back on the bus. When I got home from school my father was in the driveway, the upper half of his body leaning into the open hood of his truck.

"What happened to you?" he asked, when he saw my bloodstained clothes.

"You should have seen her, Mr. Venegas," Frida blurted out. "She beat up Mike González, and he's a lot bigger than her." I opened my mouth to say something, but before I managed a single word, I burst into tears. My father looked at Frida, back at me, at my bloodshot eye, my swollen lip, and grimaced. "Go get cleaned up," he said, leaning back into the hood of his truck.

Sophisticated. I can't decide whether Natalie meant it as an insult or a compliment, so I let it go, and she and I end up being friends, though it's a short-lived friendship. Eighth grade graduation is upon us, and in the fall we will be going to different high schools.

That summer, we receive a letter from the immigration office in Chicago. We've been given an appointment to appear in person and take a civics exam. How well we do on the exam will determine whether we'll be granted permanent residency or not. Since I've just taken the Constitution test at school, I answer every question the im-migration agent asks, almost before he has finished asking it.

When high school registration comes around, my mother is in Mexico visiting her mother again. Sonia and I go to registration, pick up the forms, sign my mother's name, and drop them off on the first day of classes. There is a three-minute intermission between classes, and even though I switch rooms and teachers for each subject, the students in my class are always the same. Each time the bell rings at the end of intermission, the same sixteen students come clamoring into the classroom. The guys with their shoulder-length hair, ripped jeans, black Metallica or Skid Row T-shirts, and the girls with a freshly applied coat of electric-blue eye shadow. A cloud that reeks of cigarette smoke and Aqua Net hairspray following in their wake.

There are three levels in each grade, level one, two, and three—we are level three, which is the lowest. Physical education is the only period where there is any crossover between our level and the other two. The girls in my gym class wear silk blouses tucked into designer jeans, chunky sweaters, and a lot less makeup. The guys wear baseball caps and T-shirts with their favorite sports team logo, or the logo of whatever college they plan to attend.

"What do you plan on doing after high school?" Ms. Flint, my English teacher, asks me after class one day.

"I don't know. Work, I guess."

"Don't you plan on going to college?"

"We can't afford it," I say, though going to college has never even crossed my mind.

"What does your father do for work?" she asks.

My father? How to say that it doesn't matter what he does for work, because he is no longer a part of our lives. By then, we had heard that he was living back in La Peña with a younger woman.

"He doesn't live with us," I say.

"What about your mother, what does she do?"

"She and her friend own a grocery store," I say. Not long after my father had left, my mother quit her job at the towel factory where she had worked for ten years, and she and one of her church friends had opened a small Mexican grocery store in the next town over.

"Oh, that's wonderful, your mother owns her own business," she says. "And how does it do?"

"Not good." I shrug, though I know that the store is barely break-ing even. That if it wasn't for Mary's beauty salon business suddenly booming, we probably wouldn't have a roof over our heads.

"It doesn't matter," she says, and explains that if I want to go to college and I keep my grades up, I will probably qualify for financial aid—government grants, loans, and scholarships. "How are you doing in your other classes?"

"Good," I say. "I'm getting straight A's." I had never been a straight-A student, but without "my gang" to distract me, I had ac-tually started paying attention in class—taking notes and asking questions even. I had always been more of a high-D or a low-C student—not a complete lost cause, but always hovering just below average. Only once had I tried for straight A's, when I was in third grade and had decided that I wanted a pet monkey. I waited for Chemel to come home from work, and the minute I heard his truck on the gravel driveway, I went running out to meet him, already ask-ing if he would buy me a pet monkey before he was even out of his truck.

"What do you want a monkey for?" he asked, picking me up and carrying me back into the house. I told him that I was going to teach it to do tricks and make it sit on my shoulder, like the one I had seen on television. He made a deal with me—if by the end of the school year I had straight A's, he would buy me a monkey. I applied myself, and when classes ended, I had all A's and one B.

"Straight A's, that's great," Ms. Flint says, as a smile flashes across her face, gone before it has fully formed. She explains how the classes I'm in are not really preparing me for college, and that if in a year or two I decide that I do want to go to college it will be too late. She sug-gests that I meet with my counselor, see about switching up a level, and offers to stay after school and tutor me.

After that day, going away to college is the only thing that mat-ters. I had no idea that financial aid was an option, that college was a real possibility. Not only is college my ticket out of my mother's house, but it's also a way to keep running; if I keep moving, go even farther away, I just might be able to outrun my past—especially my brother, who always finds me in my dreams. Each time I see him, I run to him, and though there are so many things I want to say, each word I utter is trapped inside a bubble, and I watch everything I will never be able to say to him float away, forming a long strand, like a pearl necklace unfurling from my throat to the stars.

A few days later, I finally work up the courage to go talk to Mr. Nelson, my counselor.

"Switch up a level? Why would you want to do that?" he asks. "You're getting straight A's."

"I know, but the classes I'm in are not preparing me for college," I say.

"You want to go to college?" he asks, furrowing his brow. "Remind me, what is it that your parents do for a living?"

Oh, come on, not again, I want to say. Who cares what my parents do for a living, because they won't be paying for my college. I will get a job, take out a loan—take out ten loans if I have to—but I'm determined to go away. I explain that my father is gone, and that my mother owns a small grocery store.

"I see," he says. "And how much revenue does your mother's store generate?"

"Not much."

"Not much," he says, glancing behind me, where other students are waiting for their turn to speak with him. "This is what I think you should do," he says. "I think you should stay in the classes you're in now, and then after you graduate, if you still want to go to college, you can enroll at the community college for two years, take whatever other courses you need, get your electives out of the way, and then transfer to a four-year university. That would be more economical."

"I don't want to go to a community college," I say. "I want to go away."

He removes his glasses and presses the tips of his fingers against his eyelids.

"Why don't we do this," he says, readjusting his glasses back onto his nose. "If by the end of the semester you still have straight A's, and if you can get me a letter of recommendation from two of your teachers, I'll let you move up one level across the board."

We are about halfway through the semester when one of the older guys comes up to my locker. I've noticed the way a group of them huddle around their lockers, whispering and staring as they watch me pass.

"Hi," he says, pulling down on his baseball cap. "So, are you a foreign exchange student?"

"No," I say. "I'm a freshman."

"Holy shit, you're only a freshman?" he says, glancing back at his buddies. "We kept trying to figure out where you were from. We thought for sure you were an exchange student from Spain or Brazil, or some strange place like that." He stands there, watching me switch my books out. "So, where are you from, anyway?"

"Mexico," I say.

"You're a Mexican?" He wrinkles his nose as if he just caught a whiff of something unpleasant. "No way. You're too tall to be a Mexican."

I probably give him the same blank look I gave Natalie when she called me sophisticated. "Too tall to be a Mexican"—what did that mean? Was there a height limit for Mexicans? A line drawn on a wall, which we best not surpass?

I close my locker and walk away.

It's probably close to midnight and outside a few flakes are free-falling onto the frozen ground. It's midterm week, and I'm sitting at my usual spot at the head of the dining room table, next to the large bay window. My book, calculator, pencils, and scrap pieces of paper are strewn about the table. Math is the only midterm I have left, and how I do on the exam will determine whether I keep my A in the class, whether I will be allowed to switch up a level across the board—to have or have not. Why can't everything be as easy as my literature class? I've never been a math person.

What was two plus two anyway? I had been two years old when my parents left us in Mexico. Two years later they had sent for us when I was four—that was two plus two. My brother had been back in Mexico for two years before he was killed. Dead at twenty-two— was that two plus two? Two years was not such a long time, and yet it was eternal. So many problems staring back at me, so many formulas waiting to be memorized: fractions, equations, decimals, and radicals. How does one isolate the radical? Is that similar to capturing the criminal and placing him in solitary confinement? *Isolate the radical.* We'd already heard that the thirty-nine-year-old guy who killed my brother had been released from prison. He had pleaded insanity, was transferred to a mental institution somewhere in Guadalajara, and was later released. Nine months is all the time he had served.

The headlights from my mother's station wagon come shining through the bay window. The beams send the shadow of our Christmas tree across the living room and onto the wall where my brother's guitar now hangs next to my mother's china cabinet. He had bought her that china cabinet, her bedroom set, and the dining room set where I'm now sitting before he left for Mexico. It had all belonged to one of the couples that went to her church. "When will I ever be able to afford something so beautiful," my mother said when she heard the couple was moving and selling the furniture. Chemel had made them an offer, brought the furniture home, and surprised her.

A thin layer of dust has settled on his guitar and stayed there. Each time it's my turn to dust the living room, I dust around his guitar, afraid of knocking it off the wall. Soon it will be Christmas. It will come and go as the others have come and gone and we will go to my mother's church, witness the birth of baby Jesus, and then stay up until midnight to open our presents, as we've always done, and none of us will breathe his name—it's almost like he had never been.

"You haven't gone to bed yet?" my mother asks when she comes through the door that leads from our garage into the kitchen.

"I have an exam tomorrow," I say.

"I don't know why you're wasting your time with those books," she says, making her way over to the dining room table and setting her heavy black purse down. "You should be reading the Bible, that's what you should be doing." She pulls out a chair and takes a seat. "If Jesus were to come back tonight, what good would all of this studying do you?" she asks, raising her brow and looking at me. I don't say anything. I go back to plugging in numbers, hoping she'll get the hint and leave me alone. "What good will all of this studying do you if you lose your soul, huh?"

"Ya amá," I say, because I know that if I don't stop her, she'll keep going, she'll pull out her Bible and start preaching to me, and I'm sick of being preached to.

"Ya amá," she mumbles under her breath as she reaches over and grabs an orange from the fruit bowl that sits on the center of the table. She starts peeling it, and I go back to my problems. "So, have you heard the latest news?" she asks.

"What happened?" I ask, looking up from my notebook, already knowing that whatever it is must have something to do with my father.

"Your father will soon have a new family," she says, glancing over at me. "The vieja he's living with is pregnant." She places the orange peels in a neat pile on the table in front of her. "He always told me that any time he wanted to, he could go off and start a new family," she says. "That man never cared about anyone but himself. He never loved you guys."

This is something she's been saying since the day he left, practically. *Your father never loved you guys.* I always knew that I wasn't one of his favorites. Assumed it was because I was the only one with dark skin in the family—la negra. He had never taken me on the secret runs to McDonald's that he used to take with Jorge and Yesenia, and though he'd tell them not to say anything, inevitably one of them would end up bragging about it, and after one of their trips my mother had found me lying in bed with my pillow over my head. She asked what was wrong, and between gasping for air and wiping the tears away I had managed to tell her that mi apá didn't love me because he never took me to McDonald's. A few days later, he ushered me out of the house and into his truck and we went to McDonald's—just the two of us. On the way home, my feet were dangling off the seat, and my hand was in my pocket, rubbing the toy from my Happy Meal. When we pulled into the driveway, I reached for the door handle, and he reached for my bony knee. "Now don't be telling people that I don't love you," he said, giving my knee a slight squeeze, and I clutched the toy in my pocket until something snapped.

Let him have a baby, let him have ten babies for all I care. The more kids he has, the less likely he'll be to ever come back. As far as I'm concerned, his having left is the best thing that ever happened to us. There are no more sleepless school nights, or the fear that he will come home in the middle of the night, blaring his music, shooting his gun, and waking the entire neighborhood. Though our new neighbors, who are all white, would probably not put up with his antics.

After Christmas break, we go back to school and there's a new girl. I hear about her before I actually see her, because everyone says that she looks like me, looks like she could be my sister. That's impossible, I think, as I'm the only brown person in the entire grade, my skin a few shades darker than everyone else's. The new girl is smart—really smart. Though I was allowed to move up one level in all my subjects, except math, physical education is the only class we have together. When she walks into the locker room on that first day, I know it's her. She's tall, slim, and has long, dark, straight hair. She's wearing a denim miniskirt, an oversized forest green sweater, and a pair of brown leather Frye boots—no one in that town wears tall leather boots. I want her outfit—the sweater, the skirt, and the boots—all of it.

"Hi," she says when she notices me staring at her boots. I'm standing there in my black polyester gym shorts and my black padded bra that is so worn out the stitching is coming undone. "I'm Sophia."

"I'm Maria," I say, as I let my white turtleneck drop onto the bench between us.

"I have that exact same shirt," she says, looking at my turtleneck. "Except mine is green. My mother bought it for me at J.Crew," she says. "Where is yours from?"

"I'm not sure," I say, because I'm not about to tell her it's from Kmart. I reach into my locker and pull out my stinky yellow gym tee. She picks my shirt up off the bench and looks at the label. It's black and has *Jazz* written across it in silver stitching.

"Oh, it's not from J.Crew," she says, letting my shirt drop back onto the bench.

I decide I don't like her.

A week later, a sign is posted in the girls' locker room. Cheerleading tryouts are coming up. I think I'll give it a shot, figuring it might be a good way to meet people. A few days after tryouts, the list goes up in the locker room and a crowd of girls gathers in front of it. I scan it, reading every name from top to bottom: Rachel Burns, Melissa Cunningham, Gina Mancini, Liz McCarthy, Trisha Shultz, until I get to the very bottom of the list and there is my name—Maria Venegas. Though I haven't practiced gymnastics in years, it's amazing how much my body still remembers.

Right before classes let out for summer, we hear that the guy who killed my brother has turned up dead. His body was found in the desert in Mexico, in Mexicali, somewhere near the Tijuana border. He had been stabbed over fifty times.

"Do you think it was mi apá?" I ask my mother.

"Probably," she says. "Your father is capable of anything."

That summer, we take a road trip to Texas, a family vacation of sorts—the one and only. There is a Christian youth convention in Brownsville and we caravan down with other members of my mother's church. When we return, we haven't even finished unloading the car yet when the phone rings.

"Hello?" I say.

"Where were you guys?" he asks. Though I haven't talked to him since he left, I recognize his voice immediately, and I find myself wishing I hadn't been the one who picked up the phone.

"Texas," I say.

"Who gave you permission?"

"No one."

"Were you with the hallelujahs?"

"Yeah."

"Who drove?"

"Mi amá and Maria Elena."

"Let me talk to your mother."

I set the phone down on the kitchen counter and go outside. Jorge is dragging a duffel bag that easily weighs more than him up the driveway. My mother is pulling soda cans and empty potato chip bags from the back of her station wagon.

"Guess who's on the phone?" I say, when I reach her.

"Who?" she says, standing straight up, "your father?"

"Yeah," I say. "He wants to talk to you."

"Did you tell him where we were?"

"He already knew," I say, scanning the electrical wires across the street, almost expecting to see him perched there like a blackbird, watching us.

"I have nothing to say to that viejo," she says, and goes back to collecting candy wrappers and trash from the backseat. "You should just hang up."

I make my way back through the garage. Jorge is in the kitchen, pouring himself a glass of ice-cold water from the fridge. I pick up the phone, even think about hanging up, because I don't necessarily want to talk to him either.

"She doesn't want to talk to you," I say.

There's a long silence.

"Y Jorge?" he asks.

I wave my free hand at Jorge and point to the phone.

"He wants to talk to you," I whisper.

"Tell him that as far as I'm concerned, he's dead," Jorge says, setting down the glass and heading back out to the garage.

"He doesn't want to talk to you either," I say, wondering if he heard that.

Again there's a long silence.

"Y La Poderosa?"

"Hang on," I say, and go looking for La Poderosa. This is one of the nicknames he had given Yesenia, the baby of the family. I find her in the bathroom.

"Hey," I call out from the other side of the door. "Dad is on the phone and he wants to talk to you."

"Why?" she says.

"Do you want to talk to him or not?"

"Not really," she says.

I make my way back through the living room, the dining room, and into the kitchen.

"She doesn't want to talk to you either," I say.

There's a silence that feels thousands of miles long, and I try to imagine where he's calling from, probably from some public caseta in Valparaíso or, for all we know, he could be calling from a pay phone just up the road.

"So," he says, clearing his throat. "How are you?"

"Me? I'm fine."

"Do you guys need any money?"

"No, we're fine," I say, though I really want to say we don't need your stinking money, we don't need anything from you, and we certainly don't need for you to ever come back.

"So you guys bought that house you live in, huh?"

"Yeah," I say, getting the sinking feeling that he's closer than we think, wouldn't be surprised if he showed up at our front door next.

"Where did you get the money for it?"

None of your goddamn business, I want to say. You're the one who left, started a new family, and you still have the audacity to call and question us?

"I'm not sure," I say, though I know that Mary, Salvador, and my mother pooled their incomes and qualified for a mortgage.

He lingers on the phone for a bit, before hanging up.

4 ◆ THE HALLELUJAHS

HE STAYS IN THE BOOTH for a while, his hand still gripping the receiver as if the phone might ring, as if the operator herself might call back and apologize—tell him it was a bad connection—a terrible misunderstanding. Maybe she'd even offer to pay him for his troubles, refund his call. The going rate to call the United States is thirty pesos for the first two minutes, and though those long moments of silence felt like an eternity, it probably hadn't even been two minutes. Ninety seconds is what the call lasted—ninety seconds is all the time it has taken to prove something he already suspected.

He fumbles around in his shirt pocket, pulls out his aviators, and puts them on before leaving the booth. He pays for the call and steps out into the glare of the afternoon sun. The last time he talked to his wife, she had told him none of his kids wanted anything to do with him, and though he hadn't believed her, now he'd heard it for himself—not one of them came to the phone. He makes his way along the dusty streets of Valparaíso, his mind already racing ahead, looking for the excuse—for a way to justify something he doesn't even know he's going to do yet.

He could have dealt with being rejected by his wife and by that country, even. His application was the only one denied, and if he ever wanted to step foot on American soil again, he had two options: cross illegally or use an alias. If he were to cross illegally and they caught him at the border and ran a background check, they would see that he was wanted by the authorities in Illinois for having skipped out on bail, and the last thing he needed was to land in prison on the wrong side of the border.

His safest bet for crossing was to go under an alias, and when his wife had been in Mexico about a year ago, he had told her about a man that he knew, a man who fixed documents for people. If she were to wait a few more weeks, he could have a crooked passport made and they could drive up to the border and cross together. But she had not wanted to wait, and besides, she had told him, the business with a crooked passport sounded too risky. What if the name he was given turned out to be that of a criminal, then what? It would be best if she went ahead, borrowed a birth certificate from one of the brothers at her church, and then sent it to him. He could then have a passport made with it.

"What about that birth certificate?" he asked, when he called her after she'd been back in Chicago for a week.

"Mire, Jose," she said, "I don't think it's a good idea for you to come back right now. The police are looking for you. There is a warrant out for your arrest, and they keep sending letters and stopping by the house. Besides, everyone knows that you are living with that woman. Why don't you stay with her, start a new life for yourself, and leave us alone."

So that had been it. Though she had known about the other woman all along, she had waited until she was safely back on the other side to say to him, from ten thousand miles away, what she would have never said to his face. All along she must have known that there would be no borrowed birth certificate, not from this brother, or any brother.

"What about the kids?" he asked. "Let me talk to them."

"They don't want anything to do with you," she said.

Back then, he had not believed her, but now he had witnessed it for himself, and the sting of that rejection pulls him into the cool darkness of the first tavern he stumbles upon. He wedges the heel of his boot against the chrome rail and orders a stiff one—anything to help douse the rage that is already gnawing at him. Not one of them had come to the phone—not even his baby girl, La Poderosa. This was the nickname he had given her when she was five years old and used to make him close his eyes before placing her hands on his aching head to pray for him, to ask God to take his headache away. When she was finished, she always asked, "Now do you feel better, Papi? Did your headache go away?" He always told her yes. Yes, he felt better. Yes, his headache had gone away. He promised he would never drink again. She had cured him. She was the powerful one—La Poderosa.

But the day came when she refused to pray for him, refused to touch him, even. She was afraid that if she placed her hands on his head, some evil spirit from his never-ending hangover might slip through her fingertips—use them as a portal, and invade her soul. Even back then, the brainwashery had begun. He knew that his baby girl was afraid because her mother had made her afraid, had warned her that whatever evil spirit was in him could be transferred to her, and so La Poderosa stopped praying for him. But now, for her to refuse to even talk to him? He polishes off his drink and orders another.

The hallelujahs had brainwashed his wife years ago. Their marriage troubles had begun on that hot summer day when she had found her way to a service that was held in the basement of a house. Ever since that day, there had been an almost imperceptible shift in her mood. There was a new ease about her, like she had relinquished some cumbersome load that had been bogging her down for years. He knew this could mean only one thing, because even though she was his wife, he was aware that her heart had always been shut against him, that the day might come when some cabrón would walk into the place that had been denied to him.

"You don't fool me, Pascuala," he said, eyeing her from across the kitchen table one night. "You have fallen in love, haven't you?"

She did not deny it. She told him yes. Yes, she had fallen in love. She had asked Jesus to come live in her heart, and he should do the same, so that he too could feel the same peace and joy that she felt. He agreed to join her at a service, and on the following Sunday, the two of them stepped into the dank basement. He removed his hat, same as he would have done had he stepped into a Catholic church. Rows of foldout metal chairs sat under the humming lights. They took a seat in the back row, near the entrance, and while she bounced their baby on her knee, he took in the mayhem. Men and women spilled into the aisles, jerking about with their eyes closed and bumping into the walls and chairs—to him, they looked like blind chickens clucking about.

The only thing that place had in common with the Catholic church was the wooden pulpit from where a minister delivered a sermon. He carried on and on, shouting about hell and damnation one minute and practically weeping the next as he spoke of a place where the streets were paved with gold and the seas shimmered like crystals, a place where there would be no more suffering and no more pain. His wife sat next to him, staring at the minister with an unflinching gaze. The minister went on, saying that the only way to get to the Promised Land was through Jesus, by asking Him to come live in your heart. And then the minister was extending an open hand to him, asking if their visitor would like to ask Jesus to come live in his heart. He told them no, thank you. No, he would not like to ask Jesus to come live in his heart. He had seen enough, his suspicions confirmed. It was so obvious—his wife had fallen in love with the minister. He forbade her to ever return to that church.

Ever since she gave her heart to Jesus, she stopped cutting her hair, stopped wearing jeans, makeup, and jewelry—she had stopped doing all kinds of things. Such was her devotion to Jesus that she did not make any decisions, no matter how great or small, without consulting Him first. The holier she became, the more damned she made him feel. Damned for drinking too much and damned for being a Catholic— for worshipping plaster statues that could not possibly hear his prayers. Be that as it may, he would have never turned his back on his parents' religion, no matter how hard she and the hallelujahs tried to convince him.

On more than one occasion, they came to his home, wearing their polyester suits and cheap cologne, and calling him brother. At first, he humored them, took the time to sit and listen, to ask questions, even. "How do you know there is a hell?" he asked. "The poor devil who goes to the other side stays there. When have you heard of a man that has gone to hell and come back to tell about it? Never." They told him that Jesus had died for his sins, had gone to hell and back, and someday, soon, he'd be returning for his people. "Jesus has been coming since I was a boy, and he hasn't arrived yet," he said, before showing them to the door. They had the audacity to make him feel damned while calling him brother. This is what the hallelujahs called each other—brothers and sisters—as if they shared a bloodline that could be traced directly back to God himself. Hypocrites. It was one thing for them to have brainwashed his wife, for them to have tried to brainwash him, even, but now for his wife and the hallelujahs to have brainwashed his kids—to have turned them against him—this was unforgivable.

The thought of standing face-to-face with her now sends the rage flaring in his veins. The bartender comes over and fills up his empty glass, eyes him as if saying, have this one on the house and then you should move along, Jose. But he's not paying attention to the bartender. He's trying to keep up with his thoughts, where, in that vast void, a new idea is dawning. It's something that stems from the same bottomless pit that drove him to the boulders behind Pascuala's house when he was seventeen and she was fourteen and kept him there, day in and day out, for three years, waiting and hoping to catch a glimpse of her face. He still remembers the moment that she stepped out of the small church in Santana, and into his life.

It was a Saturday, and he and Salvador, his younger brother, had just completed their mandatory military training and were due to perform in a parade in Santana. They were wearing their pressed uniforms and milling about with the other young men under the shade of a mesquite in the square when three young girls stepped out of the church. Though there were three, he only saw the one. Her long black hair fell loosely around her shoulders, framing her high cheekbones and her full lips.

"Que no se te caiga la baba," Salvador said, cupping both his hands under Jose's chin as if to catch the drool. "That's Pascuala, she's Manuel's younger sister." Jose knew who Manuel was. They were roughly the same age and often competed at the local rodeos. Any bull released in the horse run in front of either of them was sure to be taken down.

He watched her turn away, and then the three girls were walking down the dirt road and before he knew it he was on their heels. "Oiga, señorita," he said, trying to keep up yet look nonchalant. "Would you like to be my novia?" She pushed open a wooden gate, held it open for the other two girls to go through, and then she was gone.

"Pascuala," he repeated, later that night, and for countless nights after, while he tossed and turned in the dark. In the morning, while tilling the fields, each time the mules reached the end of a fallow, though he knew he would not see her, still, his neck craned, his head turned and he looked toward Santana. When he could not stand another day without seeing her face again, he saddled up his horse, rode to Santana, hitched it to a mesquite in the square, and waited for hours, hoping that she might once again step out of the church or happen to walk by.

After several days of riding to the square and waiting in vain, he relocated. There was a boulder behind her house, which provided him with a clear view of her courtyard, and from there he sent the rays of sunlight skipping across her front door and reaching into bedroom windows with his pocket mirror. He hoped that she might see the light and step outside, maybe even have a word with him. When this approach didn't work, he decided to write her a letter. This is something he was dreading, as he knew he had terrible penmanship—hadn't written a single word since he had been expelled from school when he was twelve years old. In the letter he wrote how he had not stopped thinking about her since the day they had met. She was his rising star and his setting sun, and if he could, he would collect all the colores in the campo and give them to her. He was willing to kill and to die for her if she so much as asked him to.

He passed the letter along to a young boy, who then handed it off to Doña Adulfa at the communal water well. Doña Adulfa was Pascuala's neighbor, and she hand delivered the letter to her. He waited for days, until finally, there was a response. He tore into the letter the minute it was in his hand, and, in it, she wrote that she would much appreciate him leaving her alone, as ever since the day he had appeared on the boulder she was practically a prisoner in her own home.

"A prisoner?" he repeated later that night at a local tavern while knocking them back, lifting his head off the bar just long enough to shove more money at the musicians and request the same two songs again. Ever since the day he had laid eyes on her, all those sappy love ballads had taken on a whole new meaning. It was as though every song ever written by a man in despair over a woman had been written just for him. While the musicians played, it occurred to him that it was she, not he, who needed to be listening to those lyrics—only then might she understand how she was tormenting him.

From miles around they heard him coming, the drums and horns echoing off the ridge as he and the musicians made their way to her house. They took their stance across the river, facing her courtyard, and from there they sent the music thundering through her front door. For months, he dragged the musicians from the rodeos, the cockfights, and the fiestas back to her house, to serenade her. Had Pascuala had a father, he would have never gotten away with his antics, but her father had been killed when she was seven years old.

Though she never stepped outside, he knew that she heard the music, and he also knew that sooner or later their paths were bound to cross again, and for that specific moment, he had committed to memory everything he wanted to say to her. Six months later, during las ferias, he and Salvador were strolling through the fairgrounds, making their way along the brightly lit cobblestone streets, when in front of the Ferris wheel they ran into Pascuala and her cousin Carmela. Standing before her sent the flood of everything he wanted to say rushing to the tip of his tongue and rendering him, momentarily, mute.

"You guys should take a ride on the Ferris wheel," said Salvador, smacking him on the back as if to dislodge something. "Come on, my treat," he said, offering an arm to Carmela, who took it eagerly.

Sitting next to Pascuala made him feel as though his entire being were vibrating on a different frequency. He stared at her delicate hands, her slim fingers resting on the metal rail, and had to resist the urge to take her hand in his. He gripped his knees and stared straight ahead as they were carried up toward the darkening sky. With each rotation, he felt time itself slipping away. It had been two and a half years since he had first laid eyes on her, and who knew when—if ever—he would be in such proximity to her. He drew a deep breath and turned to face her.

"Mire, Pascuala," he said. "I'm twenty years old. I'm ready to get married and start a family, and I would like for you to be the mother of my children."

She kept her gaze on the horizon, where the last glowing light of day was fading behind the silhouette of the mountains. He stared at her profile, traced the slender line of her nose down to her full lips, and willed them to move, to say something, to say yes, please, say yes.

"I don't plan on marrying you or anyone, for that matter," she said, and then they were descending. The ground spinning out from under them, the noise of the fair swelling up, as smoke rose from a fire pit where a whole pig rotated above the flames. "I've been contemplating what I might want to do with my life," she said, as once again they were being carried toward the sky, "and I've decided to become a nun." With a violent jerk, the Ferris wheel came to a sudden stop, leaving them suspended at the top, swaying back and forth at the tipping point.

"A nun?" He repeated later that night as he had one stiff one after another at the tavern. Pascuala a nun? It didn't make sense. There was something so barricaded about that three-letter word—nun. There was no room to negotiate, or even to argue. It wasn't like he could challenge a rival to a duel. Who would his rival be? The convent? The priest? God himself? Nun. It was the alpha and the omega, the beginning and the end.

In the following days, he started contemplating something that had never occurred to him, but the more he thought about it, the more obsessed he became with the idea, and not before long, he was making calculations—measuring the distance between town and her home in Santana. On Sundays, after misa, Pascuala, her mother, and her three sisters usually went to visit their tía Nico in town before heading back to Santana—the journey on horseback along those solitary dirt roads took about three hours. That would be the perfect place to take the women by surprise, unless Manuel was with them. If Manuel was with them, things could get complicated. So be it. If it came to blows, he was ready and willing to fight for Pascuala, to the death if need be.

He picked a date and enlisted Salvador and two of his cousins. There was a tavern two blocks away from Nico's house, and that's where he and his men were waiting when the boy he had paid to be the lookout came barreling through the swinging doors, announcing that the women were loading their groceries onto the horses. The men polished off their drinks and headed outside. Everyone knew what to do. They would track the women from a distance, and when they reached the outskirts of town, they would descend upon them, kicking up dust and disorienting them enough so that he could swoop in and claim his bride. He was feeling good, the adrenaline already surging through him, and the minute he was on his horse he dug his spurs into its ribs and pulled back on the reins with such gusto that the horse reared and sent him flying backward. He hit the ground with a thud, smacked his head on a rock, and was knocked unconscious.

The day finally came when in a fit of desperation he rode his horse out to Santana and right into her courtyard. His parents arrived close behind, already apologizing to Andrea, Pascuala's mother, from the other side of the gate, saying that the boy had been at a rodeo all day, and had gone home saying that he needed to see Pascuala, that he had to see Pascuala and, well, before they could stop him he was back on his horse and on the way. Andrea invited them in for a cup of tea, and while he sat nodding off on the couch, his parents explained to Andrea that the kids had recently taken a ride on the Ferris wheel and had talked about marriage. Andrea knew nothing about the ride on the

Ferris wheel, but she was a firm believer that marriage was not something one should rush into. She suggested they set a six-month plazo, this way her daughter would have time to think things over. His parents agreed, and when they got up to leave, they couldn't wake him. He was out cold. It was already late, Andrea gave them some spare blankets, and they spent the night in the living room. Though they woke and left before sunrise, Santana and all the nearby ranches were already abuzz with the chismes, the latest gossip—he had slept under her roof.

His parents were very punctual, and six months later they were back, asking what the girl had decided. To everyone's surprise, she had said yes. Yes, she would marry that man. They were married a month later in the main cathedral in town. She was seventeen, and she wore a proper white wedding dress and a long white lace veil. He was twenty-one, and the black shoes he wore were so finely polished that the tips were gleaming. After the ceremony, they walked across the plaza to the sprawling house with the pink limestone arches that belonged to Timoteo, Jose's grandfather. This is where the reception was held, and where they spent their first night together as husband and wife.

When they were first married, he could hardly believe that it was she—alive and in the flesh—breathing next to him. He fumbled around under the blankets, wrapped his arms tight around her small waist and buried his face in her long neck. "If you ever leave me, Pascuala, I will find you and kill you," he whispered in her ear.

"You wouldn't dare," she said, laughing at him. "Usted me lleva por dentro como la sangre en sus venas." She was right. Back then she had flowed through him like the very blood in his veins, and to kill her would be to snuff out some part of himself, but now there is only the smoldering of the flame that had once burned so bright for her.

He orders another stiff one, thinking that perhaps this was her plan all along. Get him out of the way so that she could have her blessed freedom. So that she could do as she pleased with the ministers. Take road trips with them. Stay in roadside motels with them. The last time he had seen her, they had stayed at a roadside motel in the outskirts of Monterrey. She was in town visiting her mother and he went to see her. They had sat in the kitchen and talked, and he had offered to drive her to the airport. Then, on the day she was to leave, the unexpected happened. A snowstorm blew through town, knocking out power lines, and shutting down the local airport.

The nearest airport was six hours away in Monterrey, and since he had been drinking right up until her departure, he had enlisted a chauffeur, paying a man from La Peña to drive his truck for him. They had driven out of the snowstorm and into the desert, and the whole time she was sitting next to him, she must have already been scheming, must have already known there would be no borrowed birth certificate. Had he known what her plan was then, he might have done it. How easy it would have been to pull off the road, drive into the heart of the desert, find a deep gulley, and take all her identification. Their kids would have thought their mother had gone to Mexico and disappeared.

They pulled into a roadside motel in the outskirts of Monterrey and that's where they spent their last night together as husband and wife. In the morning, he drove her to the airport and she jumped out of the truck, grabbed her suitcase, and walked away. She went through the revolving glass doors without ever looking back. It was as though she were afraid that if she hesitated, the doors of the airplane would slam shut, the engines would roar, and she'd be left behind, stranded on the wrong side of the border with him for eternity. They had been married for nearly twenty-five years, had eight kids, and she had not even bothered to say goodbye. He could have lived with the rejection from that country, and from her even, but now to be rejected by his own flesh and blood. This was unbearable. He had not only lost his firstborn—he had lost them all.

"The next time I see Pascuala," he says to no one in particular, polishing off his drink and setting the glass back down on the scuffed surface, "I'm going to put my .45 to her forehead and send her straight to her God."

The men standing closest to him chuckle, slap his back, saying cut the crazy talk, Jose. Maybe to them it's nothing but crazy talk, but for him it's something so real he can almost taste it. It is no longer something hypothetical, something festering in that deep dark pool of bitterness. It has pushed beyond the confines of his thoughts, has clawed its way to the surface—he has uttered it, and in doing so, has breathed it to life.

5 ◆ THE GRAPES OF WRATH

AS NIGHT SETTLES, the moths appear on the other side of the window, drawn by the light of the chandelier. They search the glass for an opening, a way to come inside, to move closer to the light. It's late August, the start of sophomore year, and I'm sitting at the head of the dining room table, doing my homework. I hear the toilet flushing, and then the bathroom door swings open, lighting up the corridor.

"You and your books," my mother says, making her way through the living room toward me, yawning. She looks tired. There's a certain fatigue that settled on her after my brother was killed. A fatigue that had grown deeper when about a year later, Juan, her younger brother, had also been shot and killed in Mexico, at a rodeo, something over an unsettled dispute. "Imagine if you spent all that time you spend sitting here doing something useful, like working?" she says, pulling out a chair and sitting down. "Yolanda called the other day and said they're hiring cashiers at Kmart. Maybe you should go apply. It sounds like a good job, and if they hire you full-time, who knows, maybe eventually they'll even promote you to manager," she says. "You could drop out of school, make some good money."

"I don't want to work at Kmart," I say. "I want to go to college."

"What for?" she says. "So that you can do as you please? Don't think that I don't know what goes on at those places. No. No, señorita. You are not leaving this house until you get married."

I know there is no point in arguing with her. She just doesn't get it. She was raised in Mexico, had only attended school until she was about twelve years old, had married my father when she was seventeen, and expected I would do the same. Get married, have kids, and be a housewife.

"I don't plan on getting married," I say. This is pretty much my constant refrain, whenever she says things like this, or whenever she tells me to iron Jorge's shirts, or make him breakfast, because what kind of a housewife am I going to be if I don't even know how to cook and iron?

"Your brother is the one who should be going to college. He's the man, the one that should get an education, have a career, not you," she says.

"Jorge doesn't even like school, amá. Why would he want to go to college?" I say, even though after my conversation with Ms. Flint, I had told Jorge and Yesenia that they should start paying attention in class, and whenever they didn't understand something, they should ask questions, stay after school, and get help if they had to. It wasn't too late for us.

None of our older siblings had gone to college. Rose had gotten pregnant her sophomore year and had dropped out and got married, and Sonia had eloped with her boyfriend the minute she graduated. Salvador had started working as a carpenter right out of high school, practically, and had married a nineteen-year-old girl from my mother's church and moved to Pennsylvania. Mary had dropped out of high school when she was a sophomore and had been hired at a factory, where she worked full-time to help pay the bills, while attending cosmetology school in the evenings. Chemel had been the only one who had talked about going to college and maybe becoming a lawyer. Even though he had graduated from high school at the top of his class, he too had gone straight to working in a factory to help make ends meet. He always smelled like turpentine when he came home from work. Sometimes he'd pick me up and throw me on the couch and kiss me all over my face and neck. "Gross," I yelled, laughing and trying to break free of his embrace, as his stubble scraped against my cheek and I inhaled the factory fumes coming off his hair.

"Have you heard about the rumors your father has been spreading?" my mother asks, staring out the window, looking beyond the moths that are still searching on the other side of the glass.

"What?" I ask.

"He's been making the rounds in the cantinas of Valparaíso, say-ing that I've been taking road trips with the ministers, that I must be sleeping with them, and that the next time he sees me, he's going to kill me." She nods her head and frowns as if she's already accepted her fate.

"That's crazy," I say, looking up from my homework. "Why would he want to kill you?"

"That's why, because he's crazy."

"It's probably not true," I say, and there's a part of me that doesn't believe her, that doesn't want to believe her. "Who told you that?"

"What do you mean, who told me?" she says, raising her voice, as if I just called her a liar. "Everyone has been calling—my mother, my sisters, my brother, everyone has been calling and telling me not to go back down to Mexico because your father has been saying that me and the hallelujahs have brainwashed his kids, turned them against him, and that the next time he sees me, he's going to put his .45 to my forehead and send me to my God."

"That doesn't make any sense," I say, thinking that even if she was sleeping with the ministers, that even if none of us wanted anything to do with him, what should he care? He's the one that left us, went off and started a new family. By then we had heard that the woman he was living with had had a baby girl.

"It's amazing how far the devil will go," she says, staring out beyond the moths that are still clinging to the glass, perhaps afraid to fly back into the darkness where they will be rendered temporarily blind.

A few days later, I'm sitting in the same spot and reading *The Grapes of Wrath* for my English class, and I stumble upon a word or an image that conjures a desolate scene. I can practically see my father rising from the dust and aiming his gun at my mother's fore-head, the same way he used to aim it at my forehead when I was nine years old when, after the local bars had closed, he and his buddies came stumbling into the dark house. On the other side of my bedroom door, I lay in bed, fully dressed for school the next day because I hated having to change out of my warm pajamas in the brisk morn-ing. I stared at the line of light under the door, listening to the noise coming from the living room.

"¡Otra!" I heard my father yell over the blaring music. I knew how he sat, holding his cards close and scanning the others' faces, looking for clues to the cards they held in their hands, though he never played for money. He also didn't smoke, but the scent of cigarettes soon filled my room as I watched my goldfish swimming circles in his bowl. On those nights, even if I had to go pee, I held it. I scanned my bedroom, looking for anything that might hold eight ounces. I contemplated jumping out the window and peeing outside, even, just so that I wouldn't have to step out into the living room. The record started skipping, and I knew that was my chance. One giant step and I was at the door, cracking it open. He was leaning over the consola, his back to me. I darted up the hall toward the bathroom. "Chuyita!" he yelled, and by the time I turned around, he was already stumbling toward me, his heavy hand landing on my back. "This one should have been a man," he yelled as he walked me over to his two friends. They sat on the couch, red-eyed and grinning. "She's got nerves of steel," he said, flexing his arm. His friends chuckled as they watched him reach into the back of his pants, pull out his .45, and aim it at my forehead. Then there was silence. His friends weren't laughing anymore.

"Jose, put the gun away," they said. "You've had too much to drink." I stared down the barrel of the gun without flinching. I knew he wouldn't pull the trigger. Not that night, or any of the other nights that he had tested my nerves. I knew that no matter how much he had had to drink, he must remember that I was his daughter. I shot him a smile and he exploded with pride.

"Nerves of steel," he yelled, punching his fist into the air, his two buddies laughing as if they'd been holding their breath for years. He grabbed the bottle of 1800 off the table, handed it to me, and gave me a nod. I took the heavy bottle with both hands and brought it to my lips. The sharp smell stung my nose. I held my breath, took a sip, and handed it back to him. He took a long pull, set down the bottle, and then shoved a twenty-dollar bill into the front pocket of my Jordache jeans, his eyes still gleaming.

He had bought those jeans for me, and even back then, I knew that he had bought them to spite my mother. If she could have had it her way, my sisters and I would have worn nothing but long skirts and dresses like all the girls and women at her church. What if it was she staring into the barrel of his gun—would he pull the trigger then? The book is on the table in front of me and I realize that I'm eight pages into a new chapter and have no idea what I've just read. I push it aside, open one of my notebooks, and write him a letter.

> Hi Dad,
> We've heard about the rumors you've been spreading around town. How you have been saying that you're going to kill our mother. What the hell is wrong with you? You were the one who created a mess for us, and what did you do? You ran away. You bought yourself a bulletproof vest and left, and what did you care if they had come and killed us in the middle of the night? You left us to fend for ourselves when we needed you most and now you're threatening to kill the one parent that did stick around? I wish it had been you instead of Chemel. He was more of a father than you will ever be—you fucking coward.

I sign my name, close the notebook, and go to bed, end up forgetting about the letter, as I never meant to send it. I was merely venting, putting on paper what I would have never said to his face. But that letter may have expressed something unspoken in my family, some deep sense of betrayal that we all felt, because a few weeks later, Sonia found the letter and sent it to him.

He must have been shocked when he received it, must have ripped the envelope open the minute it was in his hands. It was written in English—a language he had never bothered to learn, and so he wouldn't have understood a single word, though he must have recognized the signature: Maria Venegas. It was from one of his daughters, one of the two Marias, and perhaps a wave of joy rushed over him at the realization that one of his kids had thought of him. They may have refused to talk to him on the phone, but one of his daughters had taken the time to write him a letter. He found someone to translate it for him, and I imagine him sitting across from the translator, smiling with anticipation, watching as the person read the letter to themselves before relaying it to him, line for line, word for word—each syllable wiping the grin clear off his face.

Not long after Sonia sent the letter, one of his sisters calls us, demanding to know who wrote the letter. He had called her sobbing, saying that his own kids wished him dead.

"How dare you speak to your father like that? You have to respect him. He's your father, for Christ's sake," she says. "Whoever wrote that letter better call him and apologize."

No one ever calls him, and years later, I find out that two of my sisters had written and sent him similar letters around the same time, though Mary had added that he ought to be ashamed of himself—carrying on as if he were a bachelor while she was the one footing the bills and making sure his kids had a roof over their heads and food on the table.

It's Friday night and across the continent, high school football stadiums are lit up. The bleachers are packed with parents, teachers, and students all watching helmets collide on the open field, while stashed inside purses and coat pockets are bottles swiped from grocery store counters and parents' liquor cabinets. It's nearly halftime and across the field the stadium lights are merging into one continuous streak against the black sky. I definitely feel it now. I didn't feel it earlier, when my friend Lisa and I were sitting in her car just up the street from here, in the church's parking lot.

"Do you feel anything?" Lisa asked.

"No," I said, and she reached under her seat for the bottle of rum, which had been nearly half full when she snuck it out of her house. She emptied the rest into our 7-Eleven Big Gulp cups. The heater blew on our bare legs while we sang along to "Pictures of You" by The Cure and sucked our drinks down. Once we finished them, she had driven to the stadium, parked across the street, and now here we were, sitting in the bleachers, my blood coursing sedately in my veins.

"Do I look green?" I ask Lisa. "I feel green," I say. "Do I look green?" She glances at me and we both burst. She's laughing so hard that her mascara is running in black streams down her cheeks.

"What did you two drink?" Jeff, who's in my history class, is sitting on the bleacher in front of us. We look at him, then at each other, and again we are doubling over. I'm laughing so hard that I'm afraid I might start crying.

"Maybe we should leave," Lisa says, gasping, even though she knows I can't leave. She can leave if she wants to, but not me—I'm on probation for having missed a game. Two Fridays ago, my mother had dragged me into the city with her, to the wholesalers where she buys stock for the weekend. Afterward, I had gone to the store and helped her unpack and price everything, and I had not made it back in time for the game.

If I miss another game now, I'll be kicked off the drill team. I did the cheerleading thing for one season, and quickly realized that standing on the sidelines cheering for boys who could barely dribble across the court without being fouled was not for me. I knew that if my old "gang" could have seen me bouncing around and chanting "Be aggressive, b, e, aggressive," they would have lost all respect for me. My sophomore year, I had tried out for the drill team instead. There was no cheering involved. We needed only to show up at the home games, perform a dance routine at half time, and then we were free to leave.

Jeff is staring at us, and it feels like suddenly everyone is turning and looking in our direction, as if the entertainment is no longer out there on the field but right here in the stands. A horn blows in the distance, the players run off the field, and everyone jumps to their feet as the marching band begins to play. I stand up and sway slightly forward, manage to catch myself on Jeff's shoulder, and follow Lisa as she makes her way out of the bleachers.

"I can't go out there," she yells over the music when we make it to the grass. "I'll wait for you in the car." She turns and makes her way toward the opening in the chain-link fence. I watch her chestnut ponytail bouncing away, and I want to yell wait, please don't go, I thought we were in this together, but she's gone, and my legs are already carrying me toward the music. I join the rest of the drill team and we make our way around the track, the marching band booming behind us. The drums and horns sound like the tamborazo, like my father's music, and the sound waves are echoing in my bones and making me want to cry out like a wild cock.

The band takes their place in front of the bleachers, the drill team goes running out into the middle of the field, and I also run, not so much with them, as after them. I find my spot, stand behind the row of girls that are down on one knee. I hold my head down, and my pom-poms brush against my bare thighs while I wait for the cue. The music comes thundering across the field like a stampede of wild horses that instantly sends pom-poms punching into the air: and one and two and three and kick, and five and six and seven and punch, and one and two and turn and turn, and five and six and I'm behind. I can't remember if I should be in the front or back row, so I stay where I am and focus on the girl standing in front of me, follow her lead. I notice how the other girls are flashing a smile for the crowd, while keeping one eye narrowed on me. Their arms go up and come down in unison as they move into the kick formation, and then I'm locked in, the two girls on either side of me are practically holding me up. A row of legs fans out, opening and closing like scissors, all those eyes watching the black miniskirts parting at the pleats, revealing the white inlay underneath.

There are four blasts in the distance, and four rings of fire burst against the dark sky behind the bleachers, lighting up the faces in the stands. I almost expect to see my father sitting among them and shooting his gun into the air. The two girls on either side of me take a step forward, and leap into the air. I lose my balance, but manage to stop myself before hitting the ground. The fireworks keep going off, one after another, like gunshots—what a relief that he was gone, and gone for good.

The other girls go running off the field and I follow them, my gaze already fixed on the exit, as I take two steps to the left, then three fast ones to the right. It feels like the ground itself is shifting under my feet. I go past the line at the concession stand, catching a whiff of popcorn, and then I'm going through the opening in the chain-link fence. Once I'm on the sidewalk, I scan the cars across the street, spot Lisa, and make my way toward her.

"Maria." I hear a man's voice and my stomach plummets, because even before I turn around, I already know who it is. "Have you been drinking?" Mr. Johnson, the principal, is walking toward me.

"Nope," I say, struggling to stand up straight.

"You're not driving, are you?"

"Nope."

"Who's driving you home?"

"Lisa," I say.

"Has she been drinking?"

"Nope," I say, and he lets me go.

On Monday morning during announcements, after the football team is praised for their victory on Friday night and Julie Baldwin is congratulated for qualifying for state in cross country, there is a list of students who get called down to the office, and I'm one of them.

"Does your mother know that you drink?" Mr. Johnson asks, when I take a seat in his office.

"I don't," I say. Though I've been to bonfires and parties where other students are drinking, and I'll have a beer here and there, I've never been drunk. "That was my first time," I say, and I know by the way he's looking at me that he's thinking, sure, that's what they all say.

He explains that I'm not being kicked off the drill team, but I am being suspended from school for two weeks.

"Two weeks?" I say, suddenly feeling scared. "But I'll fall behind in my classes."

"You should have thought of that before," he says, glancing out his window. "I'll tell you what," he says and leans forward. "If you enroll in a rehab program and can bring me proof of it, I'll allow you to return to school after one week."

"Rehab?" I say, feeling like the filth of the earth. "I don't need to go to rehab."

"It's up to you," he says. "Two weeks, or one plus rehab."

I agree to go to rehab. He tells me to have my mother call him after I've spoken with her. When I leave his office, I'm already plotting, devising a plan for how I'm going to deal with this. There's no way I'm telling my mother—she doesn't know I was ever a cheerleader, or that on Friday nights, when she thinks I'm at work, I'm out there prancing around in a polyester miniskirt for all those eyes to see. I had ended up applying at Kmart, and the best thing about having a part-time job, aside from having my own spending money, is that it provides me with an alibi. I decide that I'll tell Sonia everything and have her call Mr. Johnson.

The following day, I get ready for school and leave the house at the same time I always do, but instead of driving to school, I drive the brown Chevy Nova, which Salvador gave me when he moved to Pennsylvania, to the local library. The lot is empty and I pull up next to a green Dumpster. Inside, I find a quiet spot on the second floor, in a cubicle that's next to a window. Within two days, I've already finished the reading and writing assignments for the week, and most of the extra credit. On the third day, I drive to the next town over, about thirty minutes away, to meet with a counselor. She gives me a form and a questionnaire to fill out.

Why do you drink?
How often do you drink?
Do you ever drink alone?
How many beers does it take to get you drunk?
Do you drink when you feel sad?
Is there a history of alcoholism in your family?

I fill out the form and answer all of the questions as honestly as possible. The counselor concludes that rehab would be a waste of my time, and says she'll give Mr. Johnson a call.

When I get home, later that day, my mother and Mary are sitting on the couch in the living room, waiting for me.

"How was school today?" Mary asks when I come through the front door, and I know that they know, because no one ever asks me about school.

"Fine," I say, wondering how much they actually know. Do they only know about the drinking and the suspension, or do they also know about the box I keep stashed under my bed, the one with my pom-poms, sweater, and polyester miniskirt.

"Where have you been all day?" my mother asks.

"At the library," I say.

"Cómo no," she says. "The studious young lady has been at the library all day." She looks at me as if she wants to slap me, but I know she won't because she has never laid a hand on me.

"Your school's principal called today," Mary says. "And he said that you were so drunk at the football game on Friday night, that you could barely stand up straight."

"What a liar," I say. "I only had one beer, and the only reason he knew I had been drinking is because he smelled my breath."

"You're the liar," my mother says, glaring at me. And I want to say, you're right. I am a liar. I'm a liar because you have made me one. I had tried being honest, had tried asking for permission to go to a movie or the mall with my friends on Friday evenings, but I hadn't even finished asking the question, when she was already shaking her head and saying, "No, no, señorita, no. A young lady has no business outside of her home after dark." There was no reasoning with her. I knew that if I was going to have any sort of social life, lying was the only way. I gave up asking for permission, decided I would do what I wanted when I wanted and deal with the consequences. "This is great," she says. "This is all we needed. For your father to leave so that you could pick up where he left off."

"If you think you're going to live here and do whatever you want, then you can start paying for food and rent," Mary says.

"Fine," I say, waiting for my mother to deliver her verdict.

"In Mexico, only whores drink," she says, refusing to even look at me.

Spring semester is well under way and I'm sitting at the head of the dining room table where, on school nights, I'm a permanent fixture. Though I don't have Ms. Flint for any classes, we meet after school twice a week and are making our way through the ACT prep book, one subject at a time. One week it's mock essay questions, another it's word problems. Easy to solve the word problems, simply memorize the formula and plug in the numbers: If a train leaves the station at 10:00 a.m., and is traveling at a speed of eighty miles per hour, and its destination is two thousand miles away, at what time will it reach its final destination? Speed equals distance divided by time.

I'm plugging in the numbers when I hear the music. My pen stops moving and I strain to listen a little harder. I can't tell exactly where the music is coming from, but the sound of the drums and horns is unmistakable—it's my father's music. I sit still, listening to the music as it draws near, until out of the corner of my eye I see the sheen of a black car gliding under the streetlight like an enormous fish. Its headlights are off, its tinted windows are rolled down a bit, and the music is blaring from it. Though I can't see who is behind the steering wheel, I realize that whoever it is has a clear shot of me, sitting under the light of the chandelier.

I jump up, hit the light switch, and run through the living room and down the corridor that leads to the bedrooms. Yesenia and Jorge are already in my mother's bedroom, sitting in the dark and watching as the car drives to the end of the block and stops at the intersection. It sits there for a very long time before turning left and making its way around the back of the house.

"Do you think it's Joaquín's brothers?" I ask.

"It's probably your father," my mother says.

"What should we do?" Yesenia asks.

"Are all the doors locked?" my mother asks.

Jorge and I run through the house checking the back door, the front door, the garage door, and the door that leads from the basement into our kitchen. Soon we're back in my mother's bedroom, listening as yet again the music comes thundering down the street. The car comes to a full stop at the end of the block and sits there with the music blasting for what seems like an eternity.

"Should we call the police?" I ask.

"What for?" my mother says. "What are the police going to do?" The car turns left and goes around the block a few more times before leaving.

If a southbound train pulls out of the station in the dark and is traveling at an unstoppable speed, at which point will there be a collision?

6 ◆ RUNAWAY TRAIN

HE MISJUDGES HIS SPEED, and when he hits the only curve that sits between town and La Peña, the wheels of his truck catch the gravel and it begins to roll. Within minutes, the whole town is abuzz with the latest gossip—Jose just flipped his truck at the curve. When Manuel arrives in town he hears the news and turns his truck around, thinking that perhaps he can lend his brother-in-law a hand.

He has not seen Jose since the last time Pascuala was in town, several months ago. It was a few days before she was to leave, to return to the other side, and Manuel and Pascuala were at their mother's house, sitting around the kitchen table when there was a knock at the front door. And then Jose was standing in the kitchen's doorway, saying that he wanted to have a word with his wife. By then, the whole town already knew that he had taken up with a younger woman; they had been seen strolling through the plaza and the mercado, arm in arm, like a couple of honeymooners. Manuel didn't like to meddle in the business of others, so when he saw Jose in the doorway, he pushed away from the table and stepped out of the kitchen, telling his mother that she should do the same, that whatever problems existed between Jose and Pascuala needed to stay between Jose and Pascuala.

As far as Manuel was concerned, he didn't have any issues with Jose. In fact, ever since he and Jose had become in-laws, they had always gotten along, had always lent each other a hand. When Jose and Pascuala had needed someone to take their six kids across the border, they had asked Manuel if he would do them the favor. Though

Manuel had no desire to go to the other side, he had agreed to do it. On the day of the trip a storm was raging; the muddy water ran a foot deep through the streets and no one thought the bus was going to be able to leave, but it did.

Manuel had taken the two seats at the back of the bus with the six kids, and by the time it was winding around the curves of the Sierra Madre Occidental mountain range, the youngest of the six, the four-year-old, had started complaining that she had a stomachache, and before Manuel could find a plastic bag for her, she had gotten sick and had set off a chain reaction. The bus had to pull over in the next town, and the driver made Manuel pay for the cleanup. While the bus was hosed down, Manuel purchased a sack of oranges from a nearby fruit stand, thinking the sweet citrus might be soothing for the kids. But once they were all back on the bus, he realized he had made a mistake—what he had thought was a sack of oranges turned out to be a sack of grapefruit.

Though Manuel had not planned on staying in the United States, once he made it across, Jose talked him into it, telling him that in Chicago there was so much work, they couldn't find enough men to cover all the jobs. That he could easily find work in a factory, a farm, or a restaurant, and since he had already made it across, he might as well stay and work, save up a bit of money, make the trip worthwhile. Manuel agreed to stay, and on the night after they arrived to Chicago, there was a knock at the door. It was immigration. Someone had tipped them off, saying that a truckload of Mexican men had just arrived at that house. The agents took Manuel and Jose away, held them overnight, and on the following day, they gave each a work permit and let them go. For six months they had lived under the same roof, eaten at the same table, shared the occasional cold beer on the weekends, and never once had they had an argument or even a disagreement.

Even before Manuel reaches the curve, he can see the crowd that has gathered around the truck, which is lying on its back like a giant beetle that rolled onto its shell and was unable to right itself. Manuel pulls over, and as he makes his way toward the crowd of men that are hollering over the truck and trying to pry its doors open, just above the voices of the men, on a much higher register, he hears the unmistakable whimpering, which can only be that of a woman. He thinks nothing of it, until he is squatting down and looking through the cracked windshield. Jose still has one hand on the steering wheel, his hat is lying upside down on the hood next to him, and sprawled under and around the hat are the blond-orange dyed locks of the concubine. She stares back at Manuel, wild-eyed and sobbing; a streak of blood running from her nose cuts across her forehead and disappears into her dark roots. Manuel takes one look at her, glances back at Jose, and pushes himself to his feet. To help Jose was one thing, but to help him and his concubine, well, he'd be damned. He walks away, his cowboy boots traversing the same ground he's just covered, as if by doing so he could erase his footprints, make it as though he had never been there.

Ever since that day, Jose's focus starts shifting. It's like all the fury that had been barreling toward his wife like an unstoppable train had jumped the tracks and was now speeding toward a new destination. Almost immediately after the crash, everyone starts warning Manuel, even his own mother.

"Hijo," Andrea says, "don't let your guard down with Jose. People say that he's been making the rounds at the taverns, saying that the next time he sees you, he's going to kill you."

"Ay amá, he won't do anything," Manuel says. "El que nada debe, nada teme." It's true that Manuel didn't owe anyone anything, had done nothing to provoke Jose—or anyone for that matter—and so had no reason to fear that some imbecile might show up at his door one day wanting to collect on some outstanding debt.

"El que nada debe, nada teme," Andrea says. "That's how the saying goes, but you have to be careful. They say that if you want to know the truth, just ask a child or a drunk, because they will always tell the truth. And if those are the things that Jose has been saying when he's intoxicated, it's because that is what's on his mind, and once a man begins to speak his thoughts, it's only a matter of time before his words become his actions," she says, perhaps thinking back to when Jose had been plotting to kidnap Pascuala, as he had been talking about it for some time before he actually worked up the nerve to enlist the help of his two cousins, and set up camp at the tavern near Nico's house.

"That man just knocked himself out," shouted the girl that Andrea had as her lookout, the minute his head had hit the rock.

The loading of the groceries had been a mere pretense, a lure, because Andrea had been onto him all along. She knew he was at the tavern with his men, and it was precisely because Manuel was with them that Andrea had insisted that they wait, that they spend the night at Nico's if they had to, because God forbid that man overtake them on the road and end up hurting Manuel—or worse. Since the day Jose had laid eyes on her daughter his presence upon them had been relentless, with him on the boulder, and then the endless serenades.

"That man is obsessed with your daughter, Andrea," her mother said, looking up from her knitting, when they heard the drums and horns coming from across the river for the umpteenth time, "and nothing good can come from an obsession like that."

Had Andrea's husband still been alive, he would have put Jose in his place, but he had been killed when she was thirty years old, leaving her with six kids to raise on her own. Though she probably heard the shot that took his life, she paid it no mind, as guns went off in those parts at the same frequency that cocks sang out at dawn. It wasn't until she heard the door to the courtyard swing open and heard the footsteps, which were not those of her husband, that she knew something was off.

"Bacilio, is that you?" she called out from the kitchen, where she was pouring tea for the kids. There was no answer. "Well, if it's not Bacilio, then who is it?" she said, wiping her hands on her apron as she stepped outside, and then the messenger was telling her that her husband had just been shot in front of the dry goods store. She went running, not realizing that her kids went trailing after her.

When she arrived at the store, a crowd had gathered in front of the stoop. Her husband was lying on the ground and a dark pool was spreading around his head. Andrea dropped to her knees and took him in her arms. He had been shot in the face, and though his eyes were still open, she knew he could no longer see her, nor could he see as, one by one, their kids arrived on her heels, and the way Pascuala had begun to tremble as the dark pool crept closer to her bare feet. Four men helped Andrea carry the body back to the courtyard, and there they hosed him down and changed his clothes while they waited for the coffin to arrive. In the morning, they loaded the coffin onto the carriage and took it away, buried under a mound of white flowers.

"Is mi apá really never coming back?" Juan, who was five years old, asked her every night before going to bed, and every night he got the same response, and every night he cried himself to sleep. Manuel, however, was eleven, the eldest, and he had taken his father's death with a manly resolve.

"Let's go feed our father's horse," Manuel said to Juan, on the morning the carriage took the coffin away. Ever since Andrea's husband had been killed, Manuel had been her constant companion until he married and started having kids of his own, and it's precisely on the day that Manuelito, Manuel's son, marries his sweetheart at the civil court, that the two of them are making their way down calle Atotonilco, when they run into Jose and his friend Ricardo.

"This is my brother-in-law," says Jose, throwing his arm around Manuel and introducing him to Ricardo. Though Jose has been drinking for three days straight, with barely any food or sleep, he's surprisingly coherent.

The two men shake hands, and Jose invites Manuel and his son to join them for a drink. Manuel declines, saying they have business to attend to and must be on their way. But Jose insists, telling Manuel that even though he's no longer with his sister, there's no reason why they can't still be friends. Manuel relents, agrees to join them for just one drink, but Manuelito talks his way out of it, and heads back home.

"So, Jose tells me that you're from Santana," Ricardo says once they're inside the tavern.

"Así es," Manuel says.

"I was at some horse races there a few weeks ago and lost a good bit of money," Ricardo says, removing his cowboy hat and carefully placing it on the surface of the bar. "Then, just the other day, I found out the races had been fixed."

"I wouldn't know anything about those races," Manuel says. "I wasn't there."

"But you're from Santana."

"That is correct."

"So you must know something," Ricardo says.

The bartender pours their drinks and once they've finished the first round, Jose buys another, and by the time the bartender pours them the third round, Manuel's family is already making their way along the winding cobblestone streets, past the local businesses as they close for the evening. Because even though Manuelito had started walking back home, soon enough he was running through the copper light of the setting sun until he reached the house, out of breath and shouting for his mother and sister, saying that they had just run into Jose, and he had taken his father with him, and then the three were rushing back up calle Atotonilco toward the only tavern at that end of town.

"All you men from Santana are the same," Ricardo says, polishing off his drink. "Nothing but a bunch of cowards."

"Ya," Jose says. "Let it be."

"Let it be?" Ricardo says, grinning. "You're the one who has it out for this cabrón, not me."

"I don't care who has it out for who, gentlemen," the barkeep says. "Take it outside."

The three men step outside, and when Manuel's family arrives, the argument over the horse races that may or may not have been rigged has escalated, and a small crowd has gathered. Jose's gun is in his hand, and Ricardo is holding Manuel's arms behind his back.

"Here is your man," yells Ricardo. "Suénatelo."

"Jose, put your gun away," Manuel's wife says. "You've had too much to drink."

Through bloodshot eyes, Jose stares at Manuel's face, a face that is so much like Pascuala's face—the face that had kept him nailed to the boulders behind her house for years, waiting and hoping that she would step outside so that he might catch a glimpse of her face. There's no reaching her now. Each time he calls the house and she answers, the minute she hears his voice, she slams the phone back onto the receiver.

"Suénatelo," Ricardo yells, and a unanimous gasp escapes from the crowd as Jose raises his gun and aims at Manuel's face.

"Don't do it, Jose," Manuel's daughter says as a few curtains from nearby windows are pushed aside.

"Suénatelo," Ricardo says.

"Te vas a arrepentir, Jose, te vas a arrepentir," Manuel's wife says, tears already streaming down her face.

He lowers his arm, though their voices rage on around him like an irredeemable argument. Do it. Don't do it. He has two choices now. Either he pulls the trigger or he walks away, but how do you walk away from a man you've forced to stare down the barrel of your gun? Half the town, it seems, is now standing around, waiting to see what he will do, whether or not he'll have the nerve to pull the trigger, or had it all been nothing but talk?

"Are you or are you not a man of your word?" Ricardo yells, and in a single motion Jose reaches over, removes Manuel's hat, and places it on his own head as if saying, You won't be needing this anymore. He lifts his arm, aims his gun at Manuel's face, and fires a single bullet.

"Imagine? When would Manuel have ever thought that your father would repay him the way that he did?" Tito, my grandmother, would ask me, years later. "When Manuel took you kids to the other side, he had not planned on staying, but your father talked him into it, and so he stayed and worked for a bit, and once he came back here, one day he told me, he said, 'Mamá, you should see, over there men work cleaning tables, cooking, and washing dishes. Over there men are doing for money what they would never do in their own home. It's disgusting,' he told me. Manuel believed that the best thing for a man was to work his own land, and he was right. He saved up enough money to buy a tractor, and after he came back, never again did he return to the other side, nor did he want to. When would my son have ever thought that your father would go and do what he did?

"The bullet hit Manuel right here," she said, pointing to the nook above her top lip and in between her nose and left cheek. "It broke through his front teeth and lodged itself in the back of his head, where it exploded. Had it not been for his family being there, my son probably would have bled to death right there on the street. But the thing that helped him was that his wife and daughter picked him up right away. Manuelito was there also, but the minute the gun went off he ran away, because God forbid that Jose turn the gun on him— he had already threatened him, don't think he hadn't.

"They flagged down a car and drove Manuel to the nearest hospital, two hours away. The doctor there took one look at Manuel and told his family that they should take him home, because he already knew. But how could they take him home? They had to try and so they took him to the hospital in San Luis Potosí in an ambulance. Ya ve que San Luis has some of the best doctors in the world, supposedly?

Once there they hooked him up to so many tubes and monitors, even his food had to be fed to him through a tube because he couldn't chew. My son was in so much pain. 'Mamá,' he said to me one day, 'if you were to take a hot coal and place it on my skin, it would be nothing compared to the pain that I feel.'

"For twenty days we had him in that hospital, and then one day he told me he was thirsty. He hadn't asked for anything, yet suddenly he wanted a drink of water, so I went down the hall to find a nurse, or anyone who could give me a glass of water, and when I was making my way back to his room, he walked right past me. I felt him go by in the corridor, and that's how I knew that he was gone."

7 ♦ LOVE, SWEET LOVE

DESPITE OUR INITIAL ENCOUNTER, Sophia and I end up being good friends. It's Saturday night, and we are leaving a party. We step out onto the porch when we run into a tall, dark-haired guy whom I've never seen before.

"You were in that dance show, weren't you?" he says, smiling at me.

"Yeah," I say, as the screen door slams shut behind him, leaving Sophia out on the porch. Earlier that night, there had been a dance show at the high school and Sophia and I had performed in a few of the numbers.

"You were really good," he says.

"Thanks," I say, and there is something about the way he's looking at me that is frightening and exciting all at once.

"Are you leaving?" he asks.

"Curfew," I shrug, though I have no curfew, as I don't even have permission to be out, but Sophia has to be home by midnight.

"I'm Dominick," he says, extending his hand to me. Our hands slide into each other, and the warmth of his hand in mine makes me want to stay there, in the doorway, for the rest of the night. "So?" he says, still holding my hand. "What's your name?"

"Maria," I say.

"Ah, Maria, like in *West Side Story*," he says.

"Uh-huh," I nod. Someone comes pushing through the doorway, and he takes a step closer to me. I catch a whiff of his cologne, and oh how I wish I could stop time.

"Maria!" Sophia yells. "Are you coming or not?"

"That's my ride," I say.

He moves aside, still smiling, as I slip my hand away and go out the door.

On Monday morning I walk into my first-period class, Spanish 203, and the minute I sit down, the pretty Italian girl that I've often helped with her homework turns to face me.

"My cousin Dominick really liked you," she says.

"Dominick is your cousin?" I say, my cheeks flushing at the very sound of his name.

She nods.

"After you left the party, he did not stop talking about you."

"Really?" I say, feeling like I have just struck gold, because I have not stopped thinking about him all weekend. I kept wondering where he had come from, and whether or not I'd ever run into him again.

"He's back at school now, but he'll be coming home for the summer in a few weeks," she says. "If you want, I can get you his number."

Dominick, I soon find out, had graduated from the other high school in town the year before. He and his girlfriend had been the prom king and queen, and though everyone thought they'd get married, they had broken up soon after they went off to college. I get his number and leave him a message, and when he comes home for spring break, he calls me back and invites me out for dinner. I tell him Wednesday night is good, mainly because I know my mother will be at the prayer meeting at her church until late.

On Wednesday night, he picks me up in a rusty blue hatchback and takes me to the Village Squire, one of the two fancier restaurants in town. The hostess walks us to a booth, the waitress comes over, and he orders a beer. She cards him. He pulls out his wallet and hands her an ID.

"What kind of beer would you like?" she asks, handing his ID back to him. He orders an Amstel Light, and I order an ice tea.

"It's my brother Donnie." He hands me the ID once the waitress has left, and tells me he has three older brothers and one older sister. All five of them have names that start with D: Donnie, David, Dean, and Donna.

The waitress brings our drinks. He orders a steak, and though the knot in my stomach has wrung the hunger from me, I choose the shrimp Alfredo. I've never had shrimp Alfredo before, but I like the way it sounds. The minute the waitress is gone he slides his beer across the table. We both glance over our shoulders, I take a sip, place it back, he takes a swig and slides it back to the center so that it comes to rest between us. In between sips and swigs, he asks about my family, and I tell him my parents are divorced, even though they never legally divorced, they're just separated, but I like that word—divorced. It sounds more civilized. Those who have divorced have hired attorneys and gone to court, they have stayed within the confines of the law. People who are divorced, I assume, don't threaten to kill their spouses, or their in-laws.

We had heard that my father had been making the rounds at the taverns in Valparaíso, saying that the next time he ran into my uncle, he was going to put a bullet in him—use him as bait, so that my mother would be forced to take a trip to Mexico. The rumors didn't frighten me much. They felt like news from a distant star. Like even if something were to happen, we would be too far away to be affected by it, like somehow we would be immune to it. And then we received the first phone call, and we all sat in the living room, staring at each other, at the floor, back at each other, unable to speak in full sentences. *He shot. How? In the face? Why?* It was despicable—beyond comprehension. My mother had wanted to go down right away, but her family told her not to, as my father was MIA, and what if she went down and he did something to her as well? Twenty days later, we got the second phone call, and she was on the first flight bound for Zacatecas. When she returned, she spent countless hours, entire days, even, locked away in her bedroom as the pile of dirty laundry spilled from her bed onto the floor until the rug was no longer visible. If to kill her is what he wanted, then he had succeeded on some level. As far as I'm concerned, the bullet that killed my uncle also killed my father. After that, my father was as good as dead to me.

Our food comes, and the minute the waitress sets my plate down in front of me, I realize I've made a mistake. The long strands of pasta are coiled over and around each other and oozing with a white creamy cheese sauce, a few pink shrimp scattered throughout. There's no easy way to eat it without making a mess. Dominick asks for Worcestershire sauce and another beer. I move the strands of pasta around with my fork and pluck a few shrimps out of the mess, not daring to eat a single strand of pasta in front of him.

When we leave the restaurant, it's already dark out. He tells me that David, his eldest brother, is the manager at Tavern on the Green, which is by far the fanciest place in town. It sits right on the river, and there is a small gazebo out in back where we can sit and watch the boats go by, and do I want to go grab a drink with him? Although I don't want to leave his side, I make up some school night excuse and he drives me home.

Before our next date, I go into Mary's purse, open her wallet, take her ID, and go from sixteen to twenty-five overnight. That summer, we spend countless nights drinking in the gazebo with his older brothers, and with everyone else who is home from college, as well as those who never bothered with college, the ones who stayed in town, knowing that someday they'd be taking over their father's plumbing or roofing business. They are all very impressed with my high tolerance, with how I can keep up with the guys—one for one. I tell them it's in my blood, though I don't tell them how it got there. How he who is still MIA put it there. It had been four months since he had killed my uncle, and he still hadn't resurfaced.

"Where do you think you'll be in ten years?" Dominick asks me one evening when we are sharing a pitcher of beer and cracking through peanut shells while we wait for our pizza at Verducci's.

"I don't know, you?"

"I'm not sure," he says. "Maybe I'll move out west, or maybe I'll still be here. You probably won't be in this town anymore." He wipes the peanut shells off our table and onto the floor. "You'll probably go off to college and become an elite sorority girl, and end up moving to the big city and marrying some rich guy," he says.

"What's a sorority?" I say, cracking a peanut shell between my fingers and popping the peanut in my mouth.

"You know, a sorority? Like fraternities?" he says, searching my face. "Colleges have them, they're social clubs."

"Oh," I say, though I still don't get it.

"What about me?" he says, taking my glass and filling it up. "Where do you think I'll be in ten years?"

"Who knows," I say. "I could see you still living in this town, and you'll probably be married and have a few kids by then, and maybe you'll still be doing carpentry on the side, and have a bit of a beer gut, and be balding like your dad," I say, taking a sip of my beer.

"Gee, thanks," he says, half smiling and half frowning, trying to figure out if I'm joking or not. "Is that really what you think?" he asks, and I nod, oblivious to how I've offended him.

Our pizza arrives, piping hot on a steel platter, the cheese melting around the sausage, green peppers, and mushrooms. Dominick puts a slice on a plate and hands it to me. I pick it up and the cheese oozes over the side, burning my tongue and making a mess, but I don't care anymore, I've gotten over my nerves. Once we are finished, he pays the tab, as he always does, and on the way home he pulls over in a dimly lit street and turns off the lights and the engine, and pulls me close like he always does. I really like Dominick. I like the way he puts his arms around me and kisses me, as his hands tug at my silk blouse, and un-tuck it from my denim shorts, his fingers slowly undoing each button, and then his warm hands are traveling up my back, searching, locating, and unsnapping the hinge to my padded bra. But the minute his hands start trying to unzip my shorts, I stop them mid-flight. I can practically hear my mother saying: *Una señorita que no es virgencita, no sirve para nada.* Though I don't believe that a young lady who is no longer a virgin is good for nothing, I do think that I'll wait to do that until I get married, or at least until I fall in love.

One of those nights, after going out for dinner, we pick up a movie and I suggest we watch it at my house, since Mary recently had the basement renovated and we now have a family room with a large television down there, plus, my mother is at one of her late-night prayer vigils and won't be home until well after midnight. The movie isn't even halfway through when neither of us is watching it anymore. Our lips are locked and our limbs are intertwined.

"¿Qué está haciendo ese viejo aquí?" The sound of my mother's voice practically sends me flying off the couch. I didn't hear her footsteps coming down the stairs, and I definitely didn't hear her car pulling into the driveway, and now she's standing in the doorway, demanding to know why "that man" is in the house.

"Oh, is this your mother?" Dominick asks, smiling and standing up. He goes to extend his hand to her, but seems to think better of it.

"Sácalo de aquí inmediatamente," she says, demanding that I tell him to leave at once. I refuse to kick him out, tell her that's just plain rude, and that she could at least let us finish watching our movie. But she insists that I tell him to leave, saying that this is a great example I'm setting for my younger sister. Bringing a man to the house and letting him kiss me.

"What's she saying?" Dominick asks, his smile fading.

"You have to go," I say. "I'm sorry."

"What? Why?"

"You," my mother says, pointing at him. "Out a here." She points to the door.

"Why is she so mad?" he asks.

"I don't know. I'm sorry, but you have to go," I say, making my way to the door and opening it for him. "I'll talk to you tomorrow," I say, as he walks past me.

After he leaves, my mother accuses me of being everything under the sun, the moon, and the stars.

Things between Dominick and me are never the same after that. He doesn't invite me out for dinner anymore, and eventually he stops calling altogether. I assume it's a combination of being offended by my mother and frustrated with my unzippable zipper.

8 ◆ WE CALL POLICE

THE OUTDOOR MOVIE THEATER is packed with cars and trucks, windows fogging up while hands search for buttons, snaps, and zippers—no one really paying attention to the movie, to the scene that is unfolding against the darkening sky. In the subdivision across the street, you are hanging out in Bradley's basement. His parents are out of town for the weekend, and so he's having a few people over. It's not really a party, just the usual crew—you, Sophia, the older guys you've been hanging out with for the past two years, and him—he's not a part of your group, but he's here because he's a friend of a friend.

You are sitting on top of the washing machine, breathing in the dank air while the music blares from the speakers behind you. Another shot comes your way. What is it? Number five? Six? It's number who-knows. It's number who-cares. It's Friday night. It's your final semester in high school, and come fall you'll be leaving this small town for good and there is nothing your mother or anyone can do to stop you. A few days ago, you had received a letter in the mail from the University of Illinois at Urbana–Champaign—your first choice. You had torn into the envelope the minute it was in your hands, searching the letter until you saw that one word: Congratulations. Though you had gotten the urge to go running through the house screaming: "I won, I won, I won." You didn't, because no one would have cared. Instead, you called Sophia, who had received her acceptance letter from U of I earlier that month.

"Cheers," they say, clinking your glass, and though you are seeing double and the music sounds like a loud drone, you don't want to wimp out now. You've always been able to keep up with the guys, impressing them with your naturally high tolerance. You knock the shot back and it burns as it goes down.

Through half-mast eyelids, you notice the couch at the far end of the basement, and you think that maybe you'll lie down for a bit, until Sophia is ready to go home. You push yourself off the washing machine and your legs feel heavy as they move, one foot in front of the other, and you hear someone asking if you're okay as you walk away, and you think, yes, I'm fine, I'm just going to place my cheek against that cushion there and close my eyes for a bit. An hour later, Sophia tries to wake you when she's ready to go, but she can't get you to budge.

"Leave her," Bradley tells her, and says he'll drive you home in the morning.

Sophia leaves. Everyone leaves. Except for him. Not Bradley. The other one. The one whose name you don't even know. Or maybe he did leave along with everyone else. Perhaps it hadn't even crossed his mind until he was about halfway home, and it was then that his mind went racing back to that dark basement, thinking, that girl. And perhaps it was then that he turned his car around already knowing what he wanted to do, and so he killed the lights before turning into Bradley's driveway again. Or maybe he had been calculating the whole time. Keeping tabs on your drinks while he hovered just beyond the laughter, watching you knock them back, waiting and hoping and practically salivating when he saw your body hit the couch, and so when everyone else drove away, he lingered.

By then the big screen must have been dark, and all the cars and trucks had vacated the lot, leaving nothing but trash in their wake, and perhaps he climbed into his car and lit a cigarette, not hurrying with it, waiting for Bradley to turn off the lights, and once enough time had passed, he stepped back out onto the driveway, being careful not to slam the car door, before going to the house and slowly turning the knob, hoping that it wouldn't be locked. It wasn't. No need to lock the doors in a relatively safe neighborhood, where everyone looks out for one another, where people have signs on their front windows that read: WE CALL POLICE. He entered the dark house and went down the stairs.

A few weeks later, you're late. And you're never late. Your cycle has always been very regular.

"I think I'm pregnant," you tell Sophia while driving home from the nursing home where you both work.

"That's impossible," she says. "You can't get pregnant the first time. You're probably just stressed. Wait until next month, I'm sure it will come."

She seems so positive it will come that somehow her certainty is reassuring, but still, you buy a pregnancy test. The instructions are simple enough: A dash means no, and a plus means yes. You lock the bathroom door, pull out the kit, pee on the tip, and wait. Outside, the sun is shining and the snow is slowly melting and dripping off the wooden rail on the back deck. You look at the kit, at the clear screen, and watch as the blue plus sign materializes. It's like watching a dead body float to the surface of a serene lake, and once you've seen it, you must deal with it—dispose of it before anyone finds out.

You take a deep breath, thinking, okay, I will deal with this:
One.
Step.
At.
A.
Time.
You pull out the phone book and call a few clinics in the area.

"Are you sure you want to get rid of it?"

"There are other options, you know."

"Abortion is a sin."

"Have you considered adoption?"

"Jesus loves you."

The voices on the other end start sounding like your mother, and you hang up. Jesus may love you, but He certainly can't help you now. In fact, you're starting to think that maybe this is His doing, His way of dealing with you, the same way that taking your brother was His way of dealing with your father. Maybe this is your punishment for drinking too much, for being a rebellious daughter, for taking after your father.

If there is one thing you know for certain, it's that your mother can't find out, because not only will she blame you for it, she will force you to keep it. The same way she made your sister Roselia keep hers when she was sixteen and the twenty-five-year-old guy she was dating got her pregnant. "I better not catch that son of a bitch coming around here," your father said, when he found out that his daughter had been knocked up by a hallelujah. By then, Roselia had already moved out of the house and soon she and the guy got married at your mother's church, and everyone attended the wedding except your father, and then the baby came and everything was all right—until it wasn't.

You call 411 and get numbers for clinics in the city. It's expensive—really expensive. You pick up a few extra shifts at work and start saving your money.

"Is everything okay?" Ms. Flint asks you after class one day. You were in her AP English class your junior year, and once again your senior year, and she has noticed that you are not participating in class discussions the way you used to. But how to participate when you haven't done the reading assignments, and how to read when you are having a hard time concentrating, because you can practically hear it growing, hear it ticking inside of you? There is something so sincere in her large blue eyes that you want to confide in her—tell her everything—but you feel like a fuckup, feel like you have let her down, and you press your lips tight and nod your head, but you don't dare say anything.

You walk out of her classroom and keep moving down the hallway, listening to lockers slamming on either side, and you can almost hear them whispering as you pass, because you're certain that everyone knows—certain they can all hear it ticking. And then you're walking straight out the back door and bracing yourself against the brisk spring air, the sun blurring across the student parking lot as you make your way to your car. Then it's just you and the road, and you are driving fast, driving straight out of town, though you're not exactly sure where you're going, until you are turning onto the gravel road that leads to the forest preserve on the edge of town. You drive deep into the woods, park your car in the vacant lot, climb out, and lay down on the hood. The sun feels good shining on your swollen eyelids, nothing but the sound of a few birds chirping fills the space around you. What has it been? Six weeks? Eight weeks? Your stomach has grown tight, and though your long torso conceals it, your mother has begun to give you suspicious looks.

Two weeks later, you run into Bradley at a bonfire.

"I'm so sorry," he says. "I saw him come back into the house, saw him go downstairs, I just never thought . . ."

"It's okay," you say, perhaps more to yourself than to him. Like if you keep telling yourself that it's okay, then it will be.

"If you decide to press charges, or go to the police, I'll go with you," he says.

When you're leaving the bonfire, a girl you've never met before comes up to you.

"Hey, I heard about what happened with Michael," she says. "I had something similar happen with him, and so did this other girl I know." There had been others? He had done this before? So he must have been calculating. "You should make him pay for it," she says. "If you want, I'll get you his number." She hands you a piece of paper with her name and number on it.

On Monday night you call her, because even with the extra shifts you've picked up, you still don't have enough money. She gets you his number. You call him and leave a message, but never hear back. You leave several messages, saying that you need to speak with him, but he never calls you. Maybe he's hoping that if he ignores you, you will just go away, recede back into silence. After a week of leaving messages, you find out where he lives, and one day, after school, you drive to his house.

It's a two-story blue-aluminum-siding house with an American flag waving out in front. Two white plastic ducks sit at the base of the flagpole, next to an iron bench. Yellow and red tulips line the flowerbed that runs along the base of the porch. An acorn wreath hangs on the front door. You take a deep breath and ring the bell. Almost instantly, there is the sound of footsteps approaching on the other side of the door, and your heart starts racing. Suddenly you get the urge to run away, thinking this was a terrible idea, that you should have never come here, but then the door is swinging open and there is a plump blonde woman standing there, wiping her hands on a checkered apron and smiling at you.

"Hi," you say, "is Mike here?"

"He's up in his room, sweetie," she says. "Why don't you come in?"

"No, that's okay," you say. "I'll wait here."

"Michael," she calls over her shoulder, "someone is here to see you." She glances back at you, still smiling. "Would you like anything to drink?"

"No, thank you," you say. She seems like such a nice lady, such a nice normal lady, maybe you should tell her why you're here. Let her know what type of scum she's raising under her roof.

"He'll be right down, hon," she says, turning and walking away.

She leaves the door ajar and makes her way down a long hallway that runs in between a dining room on the right and a family room with a fireplace on the left. A carpeted staircase runs up into the ceiling just beyond the fireplace. Soon she is back in the kitchen, standing behind an island, chopping vegetables. Out of the corner of your eye, you see him materialize as he comes down the stairs—white socks, scrawny legs, knee-length denim shorts, red T-shirt, and a navy-blue cap with some sports team logo on it. And then he's moving down the corridor toward you. He grabs the doorknob, steps outside, and pulls the door shut behind him.

"How did you get my address?" he asks, looking not at you, but behind you, over your shoulder, and out toward the main road where cars are whizzing by.

"From Amy Miller," you say, and he glances at you for a split second, as if trying to figure out exactly how much you know, before looking down at his socks and busying himself with rubbing a bit of dirt off one sock with the other. "I need three hundred and fifty dollars," you say.

"I don't have any money," he says, sliding his hands into his pockets as if to prove they're empty. You tell him you'll be back in a week, and either he has the money or you're going to tell his mother everything—and not just about you, but about the others as well. There's no point in threatening him with going to the police—his father works for the department.

He stares at you, hard, as if he wants to punch you in the face, but you don't flinch, you don't look away. You're certain none of those other girls he had done it to in the dark had come looking for him in plain daylight, threatening him. You climb back into your car and leave and, a week later, you're back.

"I'm sorry," he says when he hands you the money, though it's not so much an apology as it is a question, or a plea—a way of saying, we're cool now, right? You're not going to come back around here making any more threats, right?

You take the money and leave and, two days later, you're at a clinic in the city, your feet dangling over the edge of the cot, waiting for the doctor. She comes in carrying your file, sets it down on the stainless steel counter, and crosses her arms.

"It's too late," she says, and you think please don't let it be what I think it is. She explains how you've already entered your second trimester, and they can no longer perform the operation. Somehow, you had miscalculated. Time had gotten away from you, and now it was too late—too late for apologies, too late to be sorry, and too late for the life you had dreamed up for yourself—college, traveling, visiting Paris, living in New York someday—you could practically see it all receding from you. He had not only taken it—he had taken everything. Now you were just another pregnant Hispanic teenager, just another statistic.

A few days later, Sonia is taking a bubble bath and you go into the bathroom to wash up for bed.

"Are you okay?" she asks.

"Yeah," you say. "Why?"

"No reason," she says, eyeing you from the other side of the sliding glass door. "I had a dream the other day," she says, "and in it, you were all alone in the middle of a field somewhere, far away from home, and you were crying."

You sit down on the toilet and, once you get ahold of yourself, you tell her everything.

"You should talk to Mom," she says.

"Are you crazy?" you say, because you never talk to your mother about anything. There is a distance built between the two of you, a deeply rooted distrust that you can't explain. She feels it too. Sometimes she asks why you can't be more like your sisters, why you can't just open up to her. You might be living under the same roof, but it's like you don't even speak the same language.

After calling just about every clinic in the area, you find one in a suburb that is two hours away and, given the circumstances, is willing to do it, though it will cost you nearly triple. Sonia says she'll let you borrow the rest of the money and you call them back to make an appointment. The nurse explains that you have to come in the following day, as there is no time to waste. It's a two-day procedure. The first day, the doctor will insert a sponge to make you dilate, and then you'll have to return the following day. Assuming the sponge does its job, they'll be able to perform the operation. But if it doesn't work, there will be nothing they can do to help you.

"You will have to go under," the nurse says. "There could be consequences. If you hemorrhage, you could bleed to death."

Death. Was that the ultimate consequence? So be it. If you went under and never woke up, then at least it would all be over.

"Hello? Miss? Are you there?"

"Yes."

"Do you want to make an appointment?"

"Yes."

The next day you skip school and drive yourself out to the clinic. The insertion of the sponge is relatively quick and painless. The following day, Sonia drops you off on her way to work, signs you in, and leaves. A nurse takes you into a room where you slip into a light-blue gown, sit on the operating table, and wait for the doctor. The small room is filled with gleaming metal objects. Everything is sterile, cold, and sharp. The doctor comes in and instructs you to put your heels in the stirrups and slide down. You stare at the fluorescent lights above thinking, Please, God, please.

"All good," he says. He comes around one side of the bed and the nurse comes around the other. He explains the procedure and reiterates that if you were to hemorrhage, you could bleed to death, and are you sure you want to go through with this?

You nod your head.

He shoots the nurse a look and moves to the foot of the bed. You hear his stool creaking, the metal in the tray clanking. The nurse takes your hand and turns it over gently so that your palm is facing up. Even through the rubber gloves, her touch feels warm, and you don't want her to ever let go of your hand. She explains how you're going to feel a slight prick in your arm and soon you'll feel very sleepy. The minute the needle pierces your flesh you feel the instant warm flush in your veins, her voice already drifting away like a white butterfly vanishing into a dark tunnel. If you had stayed under forever, her voice would have been your farewell, same as the whisper of the river had been your brother's farewell. He had been the first to arrive and the first to go.

Two hours later the nurse's voice summons you and you come to. You're in a holding room with a few other girls who are all propped up in their individual beds. Sugar cookies and a can of ginger ale sit on a tray next to your bed. Your hands gravitate toward your stomach, moving over the starched white sheet, the blue gown. You dig your fingers into it, almost in disbelief: empty. What a relief. Your life has been given back to you.

A few weeks later, once all the anesthesia has worn off and the pain that shocked every muscle in your body the day after the procedure has subsided, something else starts growing inside of you: You want revenge. You want to make him pay—really pay. You make a few phone calls, meet a detective in the grocery store parking lot, and though she looks more like a suburban mom than a law enforcement official, you sit in the passenger seat of her blue Lincoln and answer all of her questions while she fills out a form.

"Why did you wait so long?"

"Why didn't you scream?"

"Why were you drinking?"

She concludes that too much time has passed and that even if Bradley and the other two girls testified, you don't really have a case. If you want to press charges, it will be your word against his and his lawyer will be relentless, and the newspapers will be all over it, and do you really want to put your family and yourself through that?

"Have you told your parents?" she asks. *Your parents?* You don't plan on ever telling your mother, and you have no intention of ever speaking to your father again, though he has resurfaced. You've heard he is now living in Colorado with the woman and their two kids, and that he's living under an alias and working as a dishwasher at a busy restaurant in Denver. "I think the best thing would be for you to file a police report," she says. "This way, if it happens again, he will have a record."

You file a police report and a few months later you leave for college.

Cars and minivans are parked all along the curb in front of the dorms, blinkers flashing in the late August mist. Other students rush past, carrying plastic crates, floor lamps, and pillows. I pull the last of my boxes out of my mother's grocery-store van.

"All these viejos are going to be living in the same building as you?" she asks, as we make our way to my dorm. She watches as a wave of students pours out of the building, mostly male. Not only am I living in a coed dorm, but because it sits across from the football stadium and the pool, most of the incoming athletes are in my building.

"Yeah," I say.

"That's disgusting," she says, scanning the lit dorm windows above, as if she can practically see everything unfolding there on the other side of the brick wall. All those men tossing and turning in their beds on the floor below mine, all those men stripping down in the showers and lathering up before heading out to the bars where the loose girls will be waiting.

When we reach my room, she starts unpacking one of the boxes.

"It's getting late," I say. "You should probably head back."

"Let me at least help you make your bed," she says, pulling a set of sheets from the box.

"It's okay, Mom," I say. "I can do it."

She sets the sheets down on the bed, and we head back outside. Jorge is waiting in the driver's seat and starts the van when he sees us coming.

"Drive safely," I say, climbing over the passenger seat and giving him a quick hug.

"I will," he says. "Take care."

I jump out and go to give my mother a quick hug, but she pulls me to her and holds on, and then her entire body is trembling in my arms.

"Ay, no, no, no," she wails, pressing her wet cheek against my neck, the scent of Dove soap evaporating off her warm skin.

I loosen my embrace, let my arms fall at my sides, but she hangs on, and I can feel my heart going wild, am certain that she can feel it kicking against the wall of her sternum. She's never really hugged me before, and being held by her now makes me extremely uncomfortable. The only times she had ever laid her hands on me was when I was a kid and she used to pray for me. She would rub olive oil onto her hands and then place them on my forehead, and ask God to heal the wounds in my soul. *The wounds in my soul?* This always struck me as odd, because as far as I knew, I had no wounds in my soul.

"Amá, vámonos," Jorge yells, pushing the passenger-side door open. "She didn't die, you can call her when we get home."

She pulls away, wipes her tears with the back of her hand, and steps up into the van. I reach for the seat belt and hand it to her, make sure her khaki trench isn't in the way before slamming the door shut. She rolls down her window.

"When you go to those places, you know those fiestas where everyone is drinking?" She snaps her belt in place. "Make sure you bring your own cup. There are so many diseases out there, el SIDA and who knows what else, and you just never know."

"Okay," I say. "I will."

They pull away and I watch them stop at the intersection, turn right, and then they're gone. It's raining harder and I stand at the curb for a long time, overwhelmed with a sadness that catches me off guard. Though I can't explain why, and I know it makes no sense— I suddenly feel homesick. Not for the home I just left but rather for the one I never knew.

9 ✦ THE FUGITIVE

HE HOSES BITS OF BROCCOLI and blackened tilapia off white ceramic plates. Food tickets line the counter behind him, and the glow from the burners reflects off his arm as the line cook sends shrimp sauté soaring into the air.

"I need a side of remoulade," the redheaded waitress yells as she comes through the tall stainless steel doors. They swing forward and back on the hinges and he catches a glimpse of the two officers speaking with the manager. Someone must have left without paying or used a fraudulent credit card—it happens all the time. He pulls down the coiled hose that dangles above the sink, presses the red button, and hot water rains down on silverware, plates, and coffee mugs.

"Eighty-six chocolate cake," the cook yells, pulling a ticket off the counter.

"Eighty-six chocolate cake," the redhead repeats as she goes out the doors.

He reaches into the sink and rubs pink lipstick off a mug with his thumb. Once again he pushes the red button, and turns his face away as the steam rises. He notices the manager and the two officers walking toward him.

"Armando," the manager says, "why don't you take a break? These officers would like to ask you a few questions."

He nods, wipes his hands off on his black-and-white checkered pants, and follows them, trying not to think about what they might possibly want with him. They probably just have a few more questions regarding his buddy, the weed dealer. A few weeks earlier, he had just pulled into the dealer's driveway when two police cars pulled up next to him. They had questioned him, asking what his affiliation with so-and-so was. He told them he and so-and-so were friends. That he was just stopping by to say hello, but still, they had searched his car and found the wad of cash in the glove box. He explained that he worked in a restaurant as a dishwasher during the day, and had a second job vacuuming empty office buildings at night. In fact, he had just cashed some checks. He searched his shirt pocket, pulled out a few stubs, and handed them to one of the officers.

They asked to see his driver's license, and it was only then that he felt the beads of sweat break across his forehead, uncertain if his alias would hold. He fumbled for his wallet, pulled out his driver's license, and handed it to one of the officers. The officer inspected the license, the stubs, and handed everything back to him, saying he was free to go. Had they actually counted the wad, they would have seen that the numbers were off. He climbed back into his car and pulled away, his heart racing, same as it's racing now as he walks behind the two officers, follows them out the back door and into the alley behind the restaurant. Up above, a sliver of blue sky is stranded between the tall buildings—downtown Denver. At the end of the alley, young professionals hurry past on the sidewalk, carrying briefcases, conversing, and laughing loudly as they hurry back to their offices, the lunch rush coming to an end.

"Mr. Gutiérrez, do you have any idea why we are here?" one of the officers asks him.

He shrugs, though he thinks the dealer may have put the finger on him. For the past few months, he had been selling a bit of weed on the side, to friends and acquaintances mostly, to make ends meet.

"What is your full name, sir?" the other asks.

"Armando Gutiérrez," he says.

The vague stench of something rotting in the nearby Dumpster permeates the air around them. The officers ask to see his ID. He reaches into his back pocket and hands them his driver's license. The officer turns the card over in his hand.

"Mr. Gutiérrez," he says, still inspecting the card. "We're going to need you to come down to the station, no big deal, really. We just need to ask you a few questions, we'll have you back here in no time at all."

He climbs into the backseat, goes willingly, confident that his alias will hold, but once they reach the station, they fingerprint him. Amazing that such an intricate whorl of lines and grooves, an identity he was born with, could not be so easily replaced. He doesn't see the screen light up when they run his prints, but he sees the blue tinge of light reflecting off the officer's face as he scrolls through his record. It must all be right there before him—the long trail of smashed cars and trucks he left in Illinois, the maroon Blazer he drove off the road and smashed into a mailbox, the blue Chevy he wrapped around a telephone pole, the black car he rolled twice before being stopped by a tree, and all the others. Though none of these offenses matters now. He had already done his time for being caught driving under the influence one too many times, had already spent six months in an Illinois penitentiary. Even the skipping out on bail for having used an unregistered weapon pales in the face of the real discovery—his identity. He's Jose Manuel Venegas, a fugitive. Wanted by the Mexican authorities for murder. He's arrested and held in solitary confinement.

A plate of food scrapes across the concrete as it slides through the small opening under his door. On the plate, it's the usual, a heap of something gray and mashed, some type of starch, and though he has no appetite, he forces a few spoonfuls of the tasteless muck down and slides the plate back out. This is the extent of his human contact— nothing but his thoughts to keep him company, and night after night he curls up into a ball and attempts to sleep, though his mind won't stop spinning. Who was the son of a bitch who put the finger on him? It was obviously someone who knew where he worked. He has his ideas about who it may have been, but is certain of nothing. Maybe it was the dealer, or maybe it was the woman he lives with. Each time they had an argument, she threatened to call the police. Or perhaps it was her brother: *Lay a hand on my sister again and I'm calling the police, telling them you're wanted in Mexico,* he had threatened more than once. For all he knows, it was Pascuala or even one of his own kids.

He stretches and tries not to think of the looming possibility that he may spend the rest of his living days in prison, and he can't help but think back to that hot afternoon and the relentless argument that raged around him just before he pulled the trigger. How he wishes he could return to that day and undo what he did—retrieve that one bullet. Though he had taken out other cabrones, he had never regretted a single one. As far as he was concerned, each one of those culeros got what they had coming. With the neighbor, it was kill or be killed. The pendejo at the Gato Negro had started it with him, and though he hadn't meant to kill him, he had misjudged that final blow. Real life is not like the movies. If you hit a man over the head with a full bottle of rum, it doesn't shatter into hundreds of pieces. And before these two, there had been the one in Zacatecas, the one he had lent his friend a hand with. That one had been rough, because he really had nothing against the man himself, and while they were digging his grave, the man would not shut up. He kept going on and on about his wife and kids, saying he would pay anything, do anything, he would leave the area, anything if they would please, for the love of God, just let him live. His ankles and wrists were tied with rope and it was uncomfortable to see a man squirm on the ground and beg like that.

"Shut him up," he told his friend, but the imbecile was having second thoughts, saying, maybe they should let the man go. *Let him go?* You don't drag a man out into the desert in the middle of the night, hog-tied and begging for his life, and then set him free. He threw his shovel aside, pulled out his pistol, and aimed it at his friend. "Either you take care of him, or I'll make this hole big enough for you both." His buddy walked over to the man, put two bullets in his head, and that was that.

And before those three, there had been the one—the first. Back when he and Pascuala had only been married for three years and he had gone to Mexico City to work in a meatpacking plant, where he did everything from filleting entire carcasses into separate cuts to chiseling ice off the blocks with his ice pick and packaging the meat in plastic wrap. After he had been in the city for a few months and secured a unit in the tenements, he had sent for Pascuala. On Sundays after misa they'd go visit a museum or go for a stroll through El Zócalo, he always carrying Chemel, who was two at the time, and she carrying Maria Elena, their baby girl. During the week, he rode the trolley to work while she stayed at home, cooked, cleaned, and looked after the children. In the evening, they'd go for long walks in the plaza and, for a brief moment, it seemed they could go on living this way forever and be happy.

But then there had been that one night when he never made it home. He had gone to a pulquería with a few other guys from the meatpacking plant. They had plowed through several rounds of pulque, and a few hours later, when he and his friend were waiting for the trolley, he felt it. The weight of the liquid in his bladder, pressing against the long white scar on his gut where the feds had sliced him open at a rodeo three years before. Back when he was a newlywed and feeling good, he had unloaded his gun into the blue sky as he always did. Then two feds were on him, demanding he hand over his gun, and when he refused, they wrestled him to the ground. Once the dust had settled, the feds were gone, and he was lying in a pool of blood, his intestines pushing through the long gash across his abdomen where they had sliced him open. Had it not been for his mother-in-law, and her two sisters' quick thinking, he might have bled to death, right there on the dirt. But Andrea and her sisters tied their rebozos around his waist and got him to the hospital. The doctors thought he wasn't going to survive, though after spending a month in the hospital, he had recovered, and now the scar only bothered him during times like this, when his bladder was bursting.

He looked down the street, still no sign of the streetcar, nothing but the shining rails cutting across the cobblestones. He pushed himself to his feet and wandered into the moonlit shadows of the nearby trees, and there he unzipped his pants and while his bladder emptied, he listened to the whisper of the creek below. The evening breeze kicked up a few leaves and dust, and for a brief moment he felt as though he were back out in the country. The first sparks of the approaching trolley came snapping on the wires above. He zipped his pants, turned around, and walked smack into two feds. Standing next to each other, they made a perfect ten: One was short and round, while the other was tall and slim.

"You're under arrest sir," said short and round.

"For what?" he said.

"Indecent exposure," said tall and slim.

"Indecent exposure?" He roared with laughter. There was something about the way the fed said this that made it sound as if he had been caught exposing himself to passersby. He went to push past them, mumbling something about since when had it become a crime for a man to answer nature's call, but they pounced on him, dragging him down, grappling with his flailing arms. He was aware of the ground rattling against his cheek as the trolley approached, could feel the weight of a knee against his spine and the wooden handle of the ice pick pressing into his hipbone. He struggled to break free, but the knee dug harder, and between the thrashing and the grunting, the ice pick rolled out of his pocket and onto the ground. He reached for it, grasped the smooth worn wooden handle, and, in a single motion, turned and rammed it into flesh.

Sparks rained down from the wires as the trolley came to a screeching halt. Even in the dark, he could see the frozen whites of the eyes, the fed with the ice pick in his neck staring back at him. He pushed himself to his feet, shoved past the passengers that were filtering off the streetcar, and broke into a sprint, the other fed already yelling for someone to stop that man, but no one dared, and soon he was running along the cobblestone streets, past midnight revelers and parked cars. The first blast shattered a windshield as he went by. He picked up the pace and started zigzagging as more blasts rang out, breaking car windows and mirrors, and all the while he could almost feel the bullet that would pierce his skull, sever his spine, or fracture his heel. He reached an intersection and turned right, then left on the next, and right on the one after, until he had cornered himself and was running toward a dead end. Up ahead, the bullets were already hitting against the brick wall, demolishing the brown and green jagged glass that lined its top edge. He crossed himself and in a single leap, grabbed onto the sharp edge, felt the glass slicing his hands as he pulled himself up and over. Even before his feet hit the ground on the other side of the wall, he was already running.

There is nowhere for him to run now. He sits up, draws his knees to his chest, and wraps his arms around them, his back pressing against the coolness of the cinder-block wall as once again he goes down the list of possible snitches. He dozes off and wakes to the sound of footsteps coming toward his cell. Soon the plate of muck will come scraping across the floor, he thinks, but instead there is the jingle of keys, and then the sound of metal sliding over metal as the heavy door falls open. It's dark out, and they lead him onto a bus bound for the border.

The bus is filled with other Mexican men who are being deported for one reason or another. They all wear the same bright orange jumper, their hands cuffed and resting on their laps. An armed guard boards the bus, and they pull out of Denver in the dark hours of predawn.

Sixteen hours later, they reach the border. The bus barely comes to a full stop when already it's surrounded by patrol cars. Two Mexican feds board the bus and stand guard at the front.

"Ismael Córdova," one of the feds calls out. A man stands, walks to the front of the bus, and is escorted away.

"Miguel Ramírez," the same fed reads from a list, and again a man stands and is escorted off the bus.

"Jose Venegas," the fed calls and no one moves. The fed glances at a piece of paper in his hand, and then looks at the men, scanning their faces as he makes his way down the isle, the scent of tobacco trailing in his wake.

"Jose Manuel Venegas," the fed hollers, from the back of the bus. A few men cough and handcuffs clank, but still, no one stands. Then again the boots are moving toward him and he watches them pass out of the corner of his eye. When the fed reaches the front of the bus, he turns to face the men, examines the piece of paper in his hand, and the other fed leans in and whispers something to him.

"Armando Gutiérrez," he calls out.

Slowly, Jose stands up, rising to meet that borrowed identity under which he has lived for the past four years. The other men turn to look in his direction as the fed walks toward him.

"¿Cómo te llamas?" the fed asks.

"Armando Gutiérrez," he says.

A wicked grin spreads across the fed's face, fanning his black mustache over his exposed yellow teeth. He flicks his wrist and the sheet of paper he's holding flips open. Jose follows his gaze and there, on the paper, he sees his own eyes staring back at him. In the photo, he's wearing a white cowboy hat and sporting a full beard, but there is no denying that it's the same face. Under the photo the caption reads, *Wanted for murder in Zacatecas. Considered armed and dangerous.*

"You're not Armando Gutiérrez," the fed says, still grinning. "You're Jose Manuel Venegas and you're wanted in Zacatecas for the murder of Manuel Robles."

He's dragged off the bus and escorted to a patrol car. They switch out his handcuffs for a much heavier pair. A long chain connects the cuffs around his wrists to a pair of ankle cuffs, and once he's in the backseat, they bolt the chain around his ankles to a metal rod that runs beneath him. There's no room to stretch and a fifteen-hour drive looms ahead. Two feds climb into the front seat. The last light of day is fading in the sky when they pull away from the border, and by the time they are snaking around the curves of the Sierra Madre Occidental, night has fallen.

By daybreak, they're already in the state of Zacatecas, descending into the valley of Valparaíso. It's Sunday, market day, and traffic crawls along the dusty two-lane road that leads into town. There's a new gas station on the outskirts and cars and trucks are lined up at the pumps. The sidewalks are crowded with people carrying bags from the mercado as they rush past. At El Pollo Feliz, the chickens rotate on the rotisserie in the window, juice and grease dripping, making his mouth water.

The plaza is alive with Sunday morning commotion. The patrol car pulls up in front of the steps that lead to the prison. It hasn't even come to a full stop and people are already staring, whispering behind cupped hands, and pointing. The man flipping tortillas at the taco cart ducks his head out from under the awning and looks right at him. He mouths something to the men and women who are standing around his cart, washing down taquitos with ice-cold Coca-Colas and Jarritos. A few heads turn and glance in his direction. The door swings open and all the scents and sounds from the plaza flood the car. Grease hisses on the skillet and the relentless bell of the paletero sounds out all around him, while under the shade of the gazebo, men stand with one foot propped on the shoeshine stand, eyeing him as one of the feds unlocks the cuffs around his ankles. The heavy chain rattles as it falls away from his feet.

"Vamos," the fed says.

It seems the entire plaza is watching as he steps out of the car, and a shock shoots up his spine as gravity takes him down.

"Puta madre," he mutters as his knees smack against the cobblestones, his body curling in on itself.

"Levántate," one of the feds demands, giving him a slight nudge with his boot.

He tries to push himself up, but every muscle in his body is spasmic and again he collapses onto the cobblestones—the same cobblestones where he and his cousins played at las encantadas when he was a kid. Not much has changed in the plaza since then. The cathedral still sits next to the prison, the livestock registry across the way, and the house with the pink limestone arches that once belonged to his grandfather still stands on the south end of the plaza. When his grandfather passed away, he left the house to his parents, and for all he knows, at this very moment, his parents are somewhere just on the other side of the arches. The news of his extradition has probably already reached them, traveling faster by word of mouth than in a rickety patrol car. His only hope of not living out the rest of his days in prison is the promise his mother made, all those years ago, when he was twelve years old and shot a man for the first time. *If you should ever land in prison, we've got money.*

The two feds reach down and grip him under his armpits, one on either side. They count to three, hoist him up, and drag him up the stairs, the cuffs around his ankles hitting against each limestone step all the way to the top.

10 · A FINE YOUNG BULL
(Zacatecas, Mexico, 1950s)

FIDEL HAD SPENT A SMALL FORTUNE on his bull, and had been inquiring around town since the day it went missing. It was a handsome red Angus with a solid square frame, a wide muzzle, and a scrotal circumference that practically guaranteed prized offspring for years to come.

"I think the Venegas boys have a bull similar to the one you just described up at their father's ranch," someone in town informed Fidel.

The Venegas boys may have been opportunists, but they were not thieves, and the minute they had seen Fidel's bull grazing on their property, they recognized their good fortune. If they could get the bull to breed with La Negra, one of their mother's finest and best milk-giving cows, they might end up with a fine young bull to breed with their herd well into the future. They rounded up the bull and La Negra into a stacked-stone corral that was built into the side of the ridge on one end and concealed by the eucalyptus trees that grew along the creek on the other. Had La Negra not turned out to be a bruta, their plan might have worked beautifully. Instead, for two days, they had watched as each time the bull attempted to mount La Negra, he was greeted with her long sharp horns.

"If she doesn't take him by the end of the day, we're going to have to let him go," Jose said, watching as La Negra locked horns with the bull yet again.

"Ey," Salvador said.

Salvador was a few years younger than Jose and always went

along with whatever his older brother wanted. They were sitting on the corral wall, under the shade of the eucalyptus trees. The leather satchel with the gorditas their mother had packed early that morning sat on the wall between them. Jose reached into the satchel and pulled one out, bit into it, and from the foot of the wall the two dogs eyed his hand, panting and salivating, as a thin thread of orange grease ran down the side of his arm. He and Salvador sat in silence, chewing and listening to the whisper of the waterfall behind them, watching as, again, La Negra turned and locked horns with the bull.

"Méndiga vaca," Jose said, wiping the grease from his arm on his denim overalls, though the dogs were no longer fixating on his hand. They were standing erect and eyeing the dirt trail that led up and behind the ridge, a steady rumble already building within their chests, until it erupted and they broke into a sprint and disappeared around the incline.

"You think someone is there?" Salvador said.

"Probably just a coyote," Jose said, as he reached up, grabbed a low-hanging branch, and pulled himself to his feet. He steadied the rubber soles of his leather sandals on the wall and stretched his neck up, eyes scanning the line of the ridge above.

"Maybe it's a wild boar," Salvador said, jumping off the wall and walking toward the trail. The dogs had gotten into scuffles numerous times with the boar that lived in the cave that was tucked into the boulders on the other side of the ridge.

"Nah, boar at this hour?" Jose said, still scanning the ridge, where the barking had turned to growling until the first blast put an end to it. The gunshot was so loud that it sent the bull and La Negra scampering to the other end of the corral. There was a second blast, a whimper, and then nothing but the sound of the rushing water below.

"¿Quién anda ahí?" Jose called out in an exaggeratedly deep voice. The same guttural voice he used when herding cattle or breaking horses.

There was no answer, and then he saw three dogs come around the stacked-stone wall. They stopped and sniffed at the base of the eucalyptus beneath him, and he didn't recognize a single one. He glanced at Salvador, who was standing with his arms stiff at his sides, staring wide-eyed at something behind Jose. When Jose turned around, he saw Fidel making his way around the corral, his horse concealed by the wall so that Fidel appeared to be floating.

"Quiubo," Fidel called out, as he pulled on the reins and brought his horse to a full stop. Fidel had a deep and manly voice, and at twenty-one, he was already a married man with his first child on the way.

"Buenos días," Jose said in a voice that sounded as if it had been squeezed from him. He was still clutching the branch with one hand, the gordita turning to mush in the other.

"You boys didn't happen to see a large red bull roaming around here, did you?"

"Nope," the boys answered in unison.

"Well, that's odd," Fidel said, glancing toward the creek and scratching his beard. "Because a little bird told me that you boys have a bull up here that looks an awful lot like the one I'm missing."

The boys shrugged.

Fidel dug his spurs into his horse and again he was floating along the edge of the wall, and for each step Fidel's horse took forward, Salvador took three steps back.

"Run," Jose heard Salvador whisper from behind him, but he couldn't move. His eyes were darting from Fidel to the bull, the bull to Fidel. Back and forth they went like a pendulum. "Run, you idiot." Fidel cleared the shade, cocked his head, following the line Jose had so clearly drawn with his gaze—and there standing next to the black cow was his bull.

The first blast hit the tree next to Jose and sent a shudder through him that shook the gordita clear out of his grasp. The mush soared through the air and hit the ground, where it was instantly devoured by the three dogs. The second blast severed the branch Jose was holding on to and sent him flailing, his hand still gripping the branch as his body swung forward and back, so that it looked like he was swatting at a swarm of bees. His sandals slipped off the rocks and the blue sky shifted as he fell backward.

With a single leap he turned the horizon right side up and then all four limbs were pumping as he sprinted along the river, swatting low-hanging branches while gunshots rang out behind him. He reached the waterfall and scaled down the slick face of the slate next to it. His overalls catching and tearing on thorny branches as he descended. Down he went, slipping and sliding on the moss until he landed in the mouth of the waterfall. He didn't know how to swim and was carried in the current, kicking and clawing like a drowning cat, breaking the surface now and again and taking a mouthful of air, the muffled blasts still roaring through the trees above, and then again he was under—air and water, water and air. It seemed his life had been reduced to two choices: death by water or death by gunfire. The river raged around him, but he managed to break the surface and stay afloat long enough to realize that he was drowning in a river that was barely knee deep. Coughing and cursing, he dragged himself to the muddy bank, and soon he and Salvador were running side by side along the ravine.

Even before they reached the house, they could see their mother in the courtyard, struggling to hang a soaked wool blanket on the clothesline while their father sat beneath the shade of the tin roof, leaning against the adobe wall, cracking toasted pumpkin seeds between his teeth. Jose was running barefooted, holding a sandal in each hand, Salvador limping along next to him. Their overalls were torn, mud-streaked, and soaked, their faces scraped and beet red from the sun and the chase, and before their parents could ask what had happened, they were already talking over each other.

"It was Fidel," Salvador said, bending over and gripping his knees when he reached the gate.

"He came looking for the bull," Jose said, trying to catch his breath. "And," he inhaled this word.

"He shot the dogs," Salvador said, throwing his arms up in the air.

"And then," Jose said, exhaling and pressing his right hand into his side.

"He started shooting at us," they practically shouted in unison.

"That son of a bitch shot at *you*?" their mother asked, glancing back at her husband.

They nodded their heads.

"And what did you do?" she asked.

Jose and his brother cocked their heads and looked at each other, as if this was a trick question.

"We ran away," they said, wrinkling their sunburned noses.

With a single thrust of the hand, their mother pushed the wool blanket aside and stood glaring at them.

"That culo de fuera doesn't have a sliver of land to drop dead on, and you're running away from him?" she said, taking two steps toward them. They both scurried away from the gate. "What will people think? That I'm raising a house full of cowards?" And with that final word, she sliced through the air in front of her with her right hand and held it midair, as if to make sure the boys got a good look at it, at her missing thumb—a reminder that she had lost it, not because she had run away, but because she had stayed and fought like a man on the night that two imbeciles had taken her husband by surprise. She and her husband had been at a wedding where he had exchanged words with two men, and when Belén and her husband were saddling up to leave, the two men had descended on them, shooting at her husband, and since Belén always carried a gun, she had shot back at the men and had managed to stave them off, but had gotten her thumb blown off in the shoot-out.

If there was one thing Belén could not tolerate, it was a coward. Though she stood only five feet tall, she was a fighter. She was born on the eve of the Mexican Revolution, in the spring of 1910, and had grown up in a war-torn country. When she was a child, a man had come to their corral and shot her brother, and when the man tried to escape, Belén's mother slammed the gate on his horse's face. The horse reared, the man was knocked unconscious, and before he came to, her mother had climbed the stacked-stone wall, dropped several heavy stones on his head, and crushed his skull.

"Ya, vieja," her husband said in his singsong voice, brushing pumpkin seed shells off his trousers. "That will teach them not to be messing with things that don't belong to them. I'll have a word with Fidel. Ya. Leave them alone."

"Leave them alone?" She glowered at him—he who was the biggest coward of them all, a coward for not having had the cojones to ask for her hand. Instead, he had taken her by surprise near the river. She had been scrubbing clothes near the water's edge, and by the time she heard something rustling in the bushes behind her, it was already too late. His arms reached out from the bushes, wrapped themselves around her small waist, and before she knew it, she was being dragged through the dirt and up the hill, where an abandoned adobe shack sat among the huisaches. She elbowed and cursed at the tall white man and managed to break away, break into a sprint, but at six feet two inches, his long legs easily overtook her. He hoisted her over his shoulder, held her knees tight against his chest, her rib cage grinding against his shoulder blade, bone on bone, as he carried her to the shack. "No son of mine will grow up to be a coward," she said. "Nunca." She practically spat this final word at her husband's feet before turning and disappearing into the house.

After the struggle in the shack, she had arrived back home in her torn and mud-streaked dress. A date was set, but due to the struggle she was unable to wed in a white wedding dress—the coward had taken that rite of passage from her, and for that she would forever harbor a deeply rooted rancor toward him.

"Never again do I want to hear that you are running away from anyone," she said, emerging from the house, carrying two of her husband's pistols, and handing one to each of her boys.

"Ya, vieja loca," her husband said, and she turned and silenced him with a single glance.

Jose stared at the shiny .22 caliber pistol in his hand, taken by how beautiful it was. He had never shot a pistol before, and only once had he shot anything with his father's rifle. It was a clear and windless day, and he was up at the ranch when he heard the rattling sound coming from the treetops. He thought it would pass like it always did, but instead it grew more intense and though the wind was not blowing, he felt a cool breeze on the back of his neck. When he turned around, he saw it, coiled up on the boulder behind him. He aimed the rifle at it and fired a single shot. The blast ripped the rattlesnake in half, and long after it had stopped writhing on the boulder, its tail was still going, and it was then he realized that the trees did not rattle.

"Next time someone shoots at you, let them have it," she said, looking at the boys. "Anyways, if you should ever land in jail, we've got money." And with a huff she turned and vanished into the house.

It was really Timoteo, her father-in-law, who had money. His house sat on the southern end of the plaza in town and took up an entire city block. It was a two-story, eight-bedroom house with thick adobe walls that were lined with limestone, so it kept the heat in on those cold winter nights and stayed cool on blistering summer days. Fig and pomegranate trees thrived in the courtyard, and red bougainvillea sprawled up and around the staircase. In the rear of the courtyard, heavy wooden doors led to the corrals and horse stables, which spanned three blocks deep, and in the front of the house, two pink limestone arches stood tall and proud, facing the only other

buildings in the plaza—the cathedral, the judicial building, the livestock registry, and the prison.

Had there been a bank, it probably would have sat on Timoteo's end
of the plaza, right on his property. But there was no bank in town, and
those who had money kept their gold and silver coins hidden inside
clay jugs or wooden trunks. On Sundays, when the town filled with
people coming from the nearby ranches to the mercado, Timoteo sat
in front of the two limestone arches, a trunk filled with coins next to
him, and those who were less fortunate stopped by for a chat and a
small loan—a deal that was sealed with nothing but a handshake.

It was also Timoteo who had had the foresight to purchase a family
plot in the cemetery on the hill on the outskirts of town. He owned
several properties, including the four-hundred-acre ranch with the
freshwater spring and the two waterfalls, where Fidel had surprised
the boys. And he too owned the house in the old hacienda of La Peña
where Belén and her husband lived. It was in La Peña that Belén had
given birth to eleven kids. Jose had been her sixth and most difficult
pregnancy. He'd kick at the walls of her abdomen with such force that
it sent her reeling. "This kid has the devil in him," she would say each
time she felt the force from within. Of the eleven kids, four died in
infancy, two boys and two girls, and of the seven that survived, Antonio, as the eldest, felt that defending his younger brothers' honor
was his God-given duty.

A few weeks after the chase, Jose and Antonio were riding back to
La Peña from the ranch. It was noon and they were traveling along the
river, staying close to the shade to keep the sun from biting their shoulders. Fidel was from Santana and had just set out in the opposite direction, hugging the shade along the ravine as well, and on the outskirts of
Santana, their paths collided.

"Quiubole," Antonio said, throwing his head back and staring
down the long ridge of his nose at Fidel, who was roughly his age.

"Buenos días, Antonio," Fidel said, pulling on his horse's reins and
glancing over at Jose, who was a sorry sight.

"O, o," Jose said, pulling on his horse's reins as it jerked about as if
trying to shake a fly off its back. The horse had just been broken and
wasn't used to having a rider on its spine, or the taste of metal pressing on its tongue. "O, o," Jose said as he slid around in the saddle, his
toes protruding from the stirrups, halfway out of the sandals that

had a piece of twine looped through the buckle to keep them from falling apart. He had managed to fix his sandals, but his overalls had been unsalvageable and he was now wearing an old pair of Antonio's jeans, which were two sizes too big and were held in place by a brown leather belt. The gun his mother had given him was tucked into the belt and already bothering him, pressed against the small of his back.

"I hear you're a real tough guy with those who are younger than you," Antonio said, leaning back in his saddle.

"They shouldn't have stolen my bull," Fidel said.

"Stolen?" Antonio said, trying not to laugh. "It was your bull that roamed into our property. If it wasn't such a handsome animal, I may have put a bullet in it myself, skinned it, and roasted it over an open fire. What do you think of that?"

"I don't let my cattle roam free," Fidel said, glancing over at Jose. "I think someone may have opened the gate to my corral."

"Are you calling my brother a thief?" Antonio said. "You do know what they do to cattle thieves around here, don't you?"

"Look, Antonio, I don't want to have any problems with you . . ."

"Let me tell you what the problem is, Fidel, just so there aren't any misunderstandings," Antonio said, flicking his hat up and leaning forward in his saddle. "The problem is you chasing my brothers down the river and shooting at them as if they were a couple of dogs. That's the problem."

"Oh, come on, Antonio. I was just trying to scare the scoundrels," Fidel said. "You think if I had really wanted to hit them, I wouldn't have?"

"Who knows," Antonio said. "Word around town is that you're a pretty bad shot."

"Is that so?"

"Word around town is that you couldn't hit your target if it was two feet in front of you," Antonio said, grinning.

Fidel may have been a bad shot, but he was quick on the draw, and before Antonio had the chance to fire a single bullet, two shots rang out around him. Jose's horse had never been in such proximity to gunfire and it reared with such force that it ripped the reins from Jose's grip and took off at full stride toward the mountains. One of the bullets missed, but the other hit Antonio's white mare in the forehead, cracking through her skull and piercing her eardrum, before flying out her ear and burying itself in Antonio's right arm. Antonio's gun went off only once, when it hit against a rock before disappearing into the river. Heavy with blood, his mare went down; she slumped forward and her front legs gave way as her neck craned, sending a ripple through her spine and her body crashing down, pinning Antonio's leg under her weight.

"O cabrón, o," Jose said, using that deep manly voice that still wasn't his own. He managed to regain control of the horse and by the time he turned it around, his heart was already throbbing in his ears. From afar he saw Antonio struggling next to his mare, a pool of blood spreading around them. He watched as Fidel aimed his gun at Antonio and cocked the trigger—and what should he do? There was no time to think. He tightened his grip on the reins, reached for the .22, aimed at Fidel and unloaded it, firing four shots in a row. With each blast, the space around him filled with a loud ringing sound that drowned out the beating of his heart.

Two of the bullets missed, but the other two hit their mark and left Fidel dangling from his horse.

"Did Fidel die?" I asked my father, the first time he ever told me this story. We were riding through Santana, near the same ravine where the shooting had taken place. His story was always the same—he was twelve years old, it had all started due to a misunderstanding over a bull, and his mother had handed him that first gun.

"Imagine," he would say when he got to the part where she had handed him the pistol. "My own mother."

Though the shooting had happened over the weekend and nowhere near the school, he was expelled because of it. His teacher had tried to argue on his behalf, saying that he was a bright student, and surely expulsion was not the answer. But the school's directora would not hear of it. A boy who was capable of shooting a man was capable of anything. And what if he decided to bring his gun to school? He could be a threat to the other students, and this was a risk the directora was not willing to take.

Even if he hadn't been expelled, it would have been almost impossible for him to return to school. Not only were the feds looking for him to arrest him, but Fidel's two brothers were also looking for him to get revenge. On the night of the shoot-out, the feds had arrived at La Peña, carrying their oil lanterns and asking questions. His younger sister assured them that he was not there, but still they shone their lanterns under the beds and up the chimney, and searched the courtyard, corrals, and horse stables. While the feds were looking for him in La Peña, Fidel's two brothers had stationed themselves in the plaza, and from the gazebo they had kept an eye on Timoteo's house.

From the window of one of the upstairs bedrooms, Belén had watched the brothers and their cousins trading off. Some would come and others would go, but there were always at least three of them, milling about near the gazebo, and this is why she had decided that Sunday would be the best day to make a move.

On Sunday morning, not long after the first cock had sung out, she was already putting the finishing touches on his floral-printed dress. The hem was long enough that it dragged on the floor and concealed his sandals. By eight in the morning he was already in the dress and his older sister was fussing with the bow around his waist. His mother wrapped one of her silk scarves around his head and grabbed her umbrella. When the morning service let out, the crowd flooded the plaza. He had not set foot in public since the shootout, but now out he went, arm in arm with his sister and his mother. The trio crossed the plaza, practically right under the nose of the lookouts, before disappearing around the corner. They made their way along the narrow cobblestone streets, keeping their gaze down and walking briskly until they reached the bus station.

Belén had relatives in the next town over, and that's where he stayed while his father settled with the feds, the judge, and everyone else who needed settling. Eventually, Fidel recovered, the lookouts went home, and when my father returned almost a year later, he had grown taller—already standing six feet tall—his voice was deeper, and his mother was so proud that she never lost an opportunity to brag about her son and how brave he was—how he had saved his brother's life.

Though his father had taken the pistol away and hidden it from him, he would find it and sneak it out to the corral, where he'd practice on his draw or pretend he was in a duel. He'd tuck the gun into the back of his belt and then take three steps away from the wall before turning and aiming the gun at the adobe. He never fired it, until the day he became curious about what it would feel like to be shot. How much could it possibly hurt? He squeezed his arms and legs, finally deciding on the meaty part of his thigh. He gripped his thigh muscle with one hand, pressed the barrel against it with the other, turned away, and fired a single blast. The bullet broke the skin, ripped through his flesh, and went out the other end.

"You idiot," his father said, after he had limped back to the house. "You're lucky you didn't hit the bone."

"That boy has too much free time on his hands," Timoteo said when he heard about what had happened. "And that can only lead to trouble." He suggested they send the boy off to the seminary in Guadalajara, and offered to pay for it.

My father agreed to go, so Timoteo took him to the zapatería to buy him a new pair of shoes. He had never owned a pair of closed-toe shoes; each pair he tried on made him feel as if he had stepped into a new personality. He finally settled on a pair of shiny black shoes that laced up in the front, and in the days leading up to his departure, he often pulled the shoes out of the box and tried them on. Though they were extremely uncomfortable, he liked the way they looked on his feet, liked the way they made him feel—very distinguished.

The day his father was to put him on the bus bound for Guadalajara, they knew a storm was coming long before the first clouds appeared in the sky. By midmorning, most of the turtles had already vacated the river and crawled halfway up the incline. Still, he and his father saddled up the horses and, uncomfortable as they were, he slipped into his new shoes. When they set out at noon, dark gray clouds had already blotted out most of the sky, and when they were crossing through Santana, it seemed that a war had been unleashed in the heavens. Lightning was striking down all around them, and by the time they reached San Martín, the first drops began to fall. They hitched their horses outside the corner store and stepped inside just as the full wrath of the storm broke out.

"Buenas tardes, Pedro," the shopkeeper yelled over the sound of rain pelting the tin roof, and asked where they were riding to in such torrential weather.

"I'm taking this muchacho to catch the bus to Guadalajara," said Pedro, as the muchacho hobbled over to the icebox and grabbed a bottle of Coca-Cola for himself and an ice-cold beer for his father. "He's going off to the seminary to become a priest."

"A priest?" the shopkeeper said. "That's good, Jose, that's good to dedicate your life to the church, to God," he said. "Though if this rain keeps up, you might not make it across the river. Maybe you should wait until tomorrow, Pedro."

Outside, a few men had gathered on the porch, and the brown muddy waters were already rushing along the cobblestones in front of the store's stoop.

"It's best to finish what we started," Pedro said, as two men came stumbling into the shop, shaking rain from their cowboy hats and ponchos.

"Ahora sí se vino el agua, Pedro," one of them shouted, shaking Pedro's hand.

The shopkeeper leaned over the counter, watching as my father hobbled over to his father and handed him the beer.

"What's wrong, Jose? Why are you walking around like an injured rooster?" he asked.

"It's because of my brand-new shoes," he said, pulling his trousers up so that the shopkeeper and everyone else could see the full splendor of his polished toes. The shopkeeper took one look at the shoes and started laughing.

"Well, it's no wonder they're tight, you've got them on the wrong feet." He roared.

The two men in ponchos, his father, and the others on the porch all turned and looked down at his shoes. His feet curved out and away from each other. The place erupted with laughter, and he got down on bended knee and was switching the shoes when another man came barging into the shop, announcing that the river had grown so much there was no crossing it.

His father had another beer, and then another, and once the rain subsided a few hours later, the shop cleared out and they unhitched their horses and rode back up to the ranch. The bus to Guadalajara was long gone.

11. YOU SAY JERUSALEM, I SAY PARIS

IT'S EARLY JULY, just after the summer solstice, and it seems that as soon as the sun disappears below the horizon, it's already coming back up behind the green hills of the British countryside. I've just spent the spring semester of my junior year studying abroad in Granada, Spain. Once the program ended, I stayed in Spain for a few weeks before traveling up to London with a friend and hitchhiking to Glastonbury. A truck driver picked us up and drove us most of the way, and as we flew past Stonehenge, the man told us that he had received a phone call earlier that day, a relative calling to say that his father had passed away.

"I never really knew my father," the man said. "He left when I was young." We gave him our condolences, though it seemed off, because he wasn't so much sad as conflicted—unsure of what he should be feeling. I assumed that the day I received that call, I'd have a similar reaction—not sadness, but indifference. The same indifference I had felt when, before leaving for Spain, I had heard that my father had been extradited and was now in prison in Mexico. As far as I was concerned, he deserved to rot in his prison cell.

In Glastonbury, my friend and I had met up with three long-haired and bearded guys from Chico and a girl named Abigail from Maine. We had all been living in Spain and had made plans to meet up at the Glastonbury music festival. When the festival ended, I stayed on to work, to help clean up the fairgrounds. It paid forty pounds per day and included room and board. I'd been at it for a week and had saved enough money for the last leg of my trip, for Paris.

On the day that I leave the fairgrounds, I hitch a ride into town and call home from a depot. My mother answers and tells me she's going to Jerusalem with a group from her church. Their return flight connects through Madrid, and she's going to see if she can change her return date and stay in Madrid a few extra days so that we can see each other.

"I'm not in Spain anymore," I say.

"Where are you?" she asks.

"In the south of England," I say. "I'm heading to France in two days."

"What do you want to go there for?" she says. "You don't even speak the language. What if you get lost? What if something happens to you? Why don't you come meet me in Madrid? Maybe we can even fly home together."

I try explaining that I don't want to go to Madrid because I've already been there at least three times and, besides, I'm flying back to Chicago at the end of the month. We can see each other then, but she insists that I come meet her.

"Fine," I say, wishing I had never called home. "Why don't you call the airlines and see how much it will cost to change your ticket, see if it's even worth it, and I'll call you back in a few days."

A few days later, I'm checking into a youth hostel in Paris. I spend countless hours wandering through the winding cobblestone streets, hanging out in cafés, and window-shopping at the boutiques. I sit in the park that's across the street from my hostel, writing in my journal and sketching out my design ideas—bohemian-style blouses, skirts, and dresses. I've been there for a week and am strolling along the Seine when a tall man with jet-black hair comes up to me. Though he hasn't been running, he seems to be out of breath. He's speaking rapidly and asking me something in French.

"Yo no parlo francés," I say.

"Do you speak English?" he asks.

"Yes."

"Where are you from?"

"Chicago."

"You're not an American," he says, shaking his head, digging his hands into his sides and taking a deep breath. "Where are you from?" He narrows his eyes as if to get a better look at me.

"Mexico," I say, though Mexico feels like a distant ancestor I'm no longer even related to.

"Ah, Mexico," he practically shouts. "I knew it." He holds his index finger firmly in the air. "I've never met a Mexican before, but I can tell you're not an American." He throws his shoulders back as if that's the end of that conversation. "I saw you from across the street, and I knew I had to talk to you. And don't think that I'm talking to you just because you're a woman. There are plenty of young women walking around," he says, holding his arms out and pivoting. "But there is something about you, something about the way you walk. It's, it's, it's as though you knew something." He folds his arms and looks at me as if he were expecting for me to hand over the keys to the universe. "Are you a writer?" he asks.

"No," I say. "I'm a student."

"Ah, a student," he says. "And what is it that you study?"

"Economics," I say, and tell him that my focus is international trade, though I don't bother trying to explain how someday I hope to be a fashion designer. I imagine I'll be importing fabrics from one country and exporting clothing to another, thus having a solid understanding of international trade seems like a good place to start.

"I'm a writer," he says, pulling up on his hair with a tight fist as if trying to relieve a migraine. "I've been locked up in my apartment for the last three months revising my novel. I just finished it. You're the first person I've talked to in weeks." He fumbles in his shirt pocket and pulls out his cigarettes, opens the pack, and holds it out to me. Though I don't smoke, I take one, and soon we are sitting on a bench overlooking the Seine and I'm spilling my guts to him about Mathew.

I had met Mathew my sophomore year, and we had been together ever since. Back when we had met, I was already planning on studying abroad in Spain and he talked about maybe studying in Ecuador the same semester. It was kind of perfect—we'd go off to opposite ends of the globe and come back to compare notes. But when it came down to it, he decided to go to Spain with me instead. We had been in Granada for only a few weeks when he'd started acting like my guardian, asking where I had been over the weekend, who my new group of friends were, and why I was hanging around and camping out with "the druggies." The last thing I needed after having traveled so far away from home was anyone questioning me or acting like my mother.

"I broke up with him," I say, taking a drag and choking on the smoke. "Though it was only supposed to be a temporary 'you go your way and I go mine, and we'll pick up where we left off when we get back to school' sort of break. You know what I mean?" I say.

"Uh-huh," the man says, grinning at me. I go on with my story, telling him how Mathew had left Spain the minute classes let out, but I had stayed a bit longer. He had gone backpacking around Italy with some of the other girls from our university, and after he'd been gone for two weeks, I received a seething letter from him. A letter that opened with three cutting words: You fucking cunt. He despised me, not because I had broken up with him in a crowded café in the middle of the day and had sat emotionless across the table from him as the tears streamed down his face, but because even before we had left for Spain, I had cheated on him and somehow his friend Melissa knew all about it. She had known about it the whole time we were in Spain, but had waited until they were sharing a bottle of wine in Florence to tell him everything. The thing that hurt the most about the letter was that I couldn't even defend myself against it. He was still traveling and I had no way of reaching him and telling him that Melissa had gotten the story wrong. Sure, I had kissed this particular guy, but I would have never slept with anyone else while I was still with him.

"Anyways," I say, "I've written a few poems about the whole ordeal in my journal."

"I thought you weren't a writer," he says, cocking his eyebrow and looking at me as if I've just come into focus.

"I'm not," I say. "I was just venting."

He asks if I want to read him any of it, and I tell him no, thank you, because I know that if he saw the things I write in my journal, all the things I keep locked away in my head, he'd think I was insane.

"Another time perhaps," he says, smiling and offering me another cigarette. We smoke and watch the pastel hues ripple across the surface of the river as the sun goes down behind the silhouette of the buildings.

The next day, I take the Metro to the Père Lachaise Cemetery and visit Jim Morrison's grave. I've never been to a cemetery; the only image I have of one has faded in my memory, the way plastic flowers tied to a cross and left on the side of the road fade in the sun. My cemetery sits on a hill in the outskirts of town, and though there must be numerous graves beyond its iron gates, in my version there is only the one, and I see it exactly as it was described to me—a mound of dirt marked with a simple wooden cross, though where there was one cross, there are now two, side by side.

Before leaving Spain, I had called home and Sonia told me that my grandfather had passed away. He should have died years ago, I thought. When he was first diagnosed with diabetes, he should have dropped dead right then and there. Had he died then, my father would have never talked my brother into going back to Mexico. It seemed anyone who went back to that distant, dusty land never returned.

After leaving the cemetery I pick up a phone card, and on my way back to my hostel, I find a pay phone and call home.

"Where the hell have you been?" Sonia says, when she hears my voice.

"In Paris."

"You're not even in Spain yet?" she says. "Mom has been in Madrid for like four days waiting for you."

"Why did she change her ticket? I told her I'd call her back."

"I don't know, but she's really worried about you," she says. "You better call her."

I jot down the name and number of the hotel and call right away, ask for Pascuala Venegas in room 504.

"That guest checked out this morning," the woman says.

"Are you sure? She didn't say if she was going to a different hotel or if she was leaving the city for good?" I ask, though I know it's too late—she had come and gone and we had missed each other.

On my way back to the hostel, no matter how hard I try to drown out her voice, I can practically hear her asking all the things she has always asked: *Why are you like this? Why can't you be more like your sisters? Why can't you just talk to me? Why are you so distant?*

All the questions for which I don't have answers.

When I return from abroad, I spend two weeks at home. I've been away at college for three years and no longer have a room. On the night before I leave for school, my mother insists that I stay with her.

"Madrid was horrible," she says, while we lie side by side in the dark. "I sat in a plaza scanning every face that went by, thinking that one of those faces might be you. It was just awful."

"Why did you change your ticket?" I say.

"I thought you would be there." We lie in silence for a long time. "Mateo was a good man," she says. "You shouldn't have left him. I really would have liked for you two to have gotten married." I stare into the darkness and think that maybe I should tell her what really happened. Tell her about the letter he sent me, about how each time I have called him since I got back, the minute he hears my voice, he hangs up. "Can I ask you something?" she says.

"Sure."

"Did you have sexual relations with him?"

This question catches me completely off guard. My mother and I rarely talk about anything, but we certainly never talk about sex. Perhaps what's even more shocking is her thinking that after having spent more than a year with Mathew, I may *not* have had sex with him. I can hear her breathing, can feel her waiting while I contemplate whether to tell her the truth or not.

"You shouldn't ask questions to which you might not want to know the answers," I say.

"I want to know," she says.

"I did."

She sighs.

"That makes me very sad," she says. "I really would have liked for you to still be a virgin when you got married."

12 ◆ THE WALL

ALL ALONG THE FOOT OF THE WALL, men are scattered. Some stand with the sole of their shoe pressing into the cinder block while others sit, leaning into it, the razor wire cutting into the blue sky above.

"Here," his buddy says, holding a joint out to him. They are sitting next to each other, knees bent, head back, taking refuge in the sliver of shade the afternoon sun is casting along the bottom edge of the wall.

"That stuff doesn't agree with me," he says, waving it away, saying that it either makes him sleepy or paranoid. The last time he had smoked weed, he was still living in Chicago and had stopped by to visit some friends, a young couple that lived near the bowling alley. Even before stepping onto their porch, he could already smell the weed coming through the screen door, the couple wild with laughter inside the house. They had offered him the joint, and he had taken a few drags, and later, on his way to the bowling alley, he had felt like he was suffocating in his own body. He had turned the car around and headed home to lie down for a bit, and had ended up sleeping until the next day.

"This is really good stuff, Jose," his buddy says. "It will melt your cares away."

There wasn't enough green on the planet to melt his cares away. When they first brought him back to Zacatecas, he had stood before a judge recounting the events of that day. Saying it had all started over a disagreement between Ricardo and Manuel, something about some horse races. He told the judge that he hadn't meant to shoot Manuel, that he had gone to hit him with the butt of his gun and a bullet had escaped. His testimony didn't hold up against that of the eyewitnesses, and perhaps the only part of his testimony that wasn't fabricated was his saying that he and Manuel had never had any problems, had always gotten along, and the minute his gun had gone off, he had regretted it. But it was too late for regrets, and the judge ruled that he had acted ruthlessly, and in cold blood had taken the life of his brother-in-law.

Almost immediately after he was sentenced, his parents put the house with the pink limestone arches up for sale.

"I will sell everything if I have to," his father said, after his first visit. "I don't care if I have to sell all the livestock, La Mesa, La Peña, and the ranch even. I will sell it all, but I refuse to die and leave one of my sons behind bars," he said, as if he had a choice in the matter. His diabetes had grown hungrier, perhaps aggravated by the stress of having a son in prison, and from behind the iron bars, Jose had watched the disease slowly consume his father—taking first his right leg and then the other—both amputated at mid-thigh.

The last time he had seen his father, they had pushed him in on a wheelchair, a wool blanket draped over the stumps where his legs had been. He told Jose that the house had sold. The owner of the zapatería had offered 750,000 pesos, and though it was considerably below market value, they had accepted the offer, as time was running out for all of them. Jose had been in prison for five months and there was talk of his being transferred to the much larger Zacatecas federal prison in the next town over and, if that were to happen, his fate would practically be sealed. Bribing someone in the federal system would be trickier and much more expensive than dealing with the local jurisdiction.

His parents deposited the money into an account for the attorney that was working on his case and, a month later, his father passed away. Jose had gone to speak with the comisario and asked for permission to attend his father's funeral.

"If we let you go, Jose, you're not going to try anything clever, are you?" Jose had given his word, and the comisario had agreed, because in a town where land and livestock were still bought and sold on nothing but a handshake, a man's word was only as good as the man himself.

On the day of the funeral, when the first bell rang out, Jose was already waiting for the two guards who would accompany him to the cathedral, and by the time the second bell rang out, the guards were escorting him down the limestone steps of the prison. Inside the cathedral, the air was cooler and smelled of wax and holy water. His father's coffin was sitting at the altar. The two guards waited at the entrance as he made his way toward the front, the rattle of his handcuffs mixed with a whisper here and a cough there as he walked by. The third bell rang out, the priest lifted his arms, and everyone rose. If he were going to try anything clever, this would've been when.

He took a seat in the front pew, next to his mother and sisters. After the service, he bid his father farewell and then eight men hoisted the coffin onto their shoulders and made their way out the cathedral's side door. He watched the procession as it headed toward the cemetery on the hill, on the outskirts of town, where his son was buried. The comisario had allowed him to cross the plaza and attend his father's service, but to go all the way to the cemetery was out of the question—word or no word.

A few months after his father died, they transferred him to the Zacatecas federal prison, and every day since he arrived at this place has felt like another brick in the wall. Each day solidifying against him, pushing him further from the reach of hope. He's heard that his mother's health has deteriorated so much that she can no longer fend for herself and is living with his youngest sister, who is selling off the livestock and land his father left behind at an alarming rate. If he ever does get out of this place, he'll be lucky if there is a sliver of land left for him to drop dead on.

He takes the joint, takes a long drag, though he knows no amount of weed is going to vanquish his troubles, even if Pascuala had recently sent him a letter saying that she forgave him for what he had done. That if he should ever get out of that place, she didn't want to have any problems with him. Whether or not she had forgiven him wasn't at the root of his turmoil because he knew he would never forgive himself. No amount of regret would ever make the past right again. Nothing would open the door that he himself had sealed shut with a single blast—his kids on one side of it and he on the other.

It had been ten years since he had loaded up his truck with their discarded clothing, towels from the factory where his wife worked, contraband, and a few photo albums. His baby girl, La Poderosa, had been ten years old when he left. Now she was twenty, and if by chance she were to show up on the other side of the bars during visiting hours, he probably wouldn't even recognize her. Ten years had come crashing down between them like an unstoppable avalanche. What stood between them now? Two thousand miles, these prison walls, the border itself—he would probably die inside this bedbug-infested place and never see any of his kids again.

He takes another drag and notices how, across the courtyard, heads are turning. A hand rises to scratch the welt on a biceps, eyes squint, and he gets the feeling that all these subtleties are connected—part of some grand scheme. He hands the joint back to his buddy and pushes himself to his feet, saying he's going to go lie down for a bit. When he reaches his cell, he stretches out on his cot and dozes, though there is no room for dreaming in a place like this—a place where nights are filled with thin sleep, sleep as translucent as rice paper.

13 · MAN-IN-THE-MOON MARIGOLDS

ONCE I'M BACK AT SCHOOL, I track down Mathew's number and call him several times, mainly around two in the morning, after the bars have closed. He usually tells me to fuck off and hangs up, but sometimes he'll humor me, ask how my semester is going.

"Fine," I say, and try to convince him to come over. "We don't have to do anything. It would just be nice to cuddle," I say.

"You're still hurting, aren't you?" he says.

"I already told you I was sorry," I say. "It's not like I slept with the guy."

"You're so fucked up and you don't even realize it," he says one of those nights, and hearing him say this is sort of frightening, because he knows nothing about my past—not my brother, not my uncle, nor my father—nothing. Hearing him say this makes me feel like maybe he knows something I don't know, like maybe he can see something I'll only notice once it's too late.

"Are you coming over or not?" I say, clearing my throat.

"One day you're going to wake up and realize how fucked up you are," he says.

"Fuck you," I say, because I can practically see him lying in his bed and getting off on offending me. "I'm never calling you again."

"Oh, you will."

"Mark my words," I say, "never again." I slam the phone down before he has a chance to respond, and don't ever call him. Not drunk. Not sober. Never.

A few days after that conversation, I'm at a party. I step out onto the porch and run into a friend, who happens to be talking to Melissa.

"Hey, Maria, you know Melissa, right?" he says. "Weren't you guys just in Spain together?"

"Yeah," I say, in the calmest tone I can muster, though the very sight of her face sends the blood boiling in my veins. "How was Italy?" I ask.

"Really nice," she says, half-smiling.

"So, what places did you guys end up visiting?" I ask.

"Oh, we were in Milan for like a few days, then we spent like a week in Rome, and then went to Florence, and . . . um . . ." She presses her lips tight, too tight, and her face seems to grow grotesquely larger as she goes on and on, and soon the pores on the tip of her nose are the only thing I see, because everything else has receded, and she must feel the weight of my glare because she's struggling to complete her sentences.

"Can I ask you something?" I say.

"Sure," she says, lifting her brows.

"Is your life so lame that in order to make it a bit more exciting, you have to go sticking your nose in other people's business?" I ask.

"Um, well," she scratches her neck, "Mathew is a friend of mine, and, and you shouldn't have cheated on him."

"Who the fuck are you to tell me what I should or shouldn't do?" I say, clenching my fists and taking a step toward her. She turns away and I have to contain the urge to punch her, to crack her once, hard, and drop her, but her chin is trembling so much that I sort of feel sorry for her. She seems so helpless, so pathetic, and besides, I haven't been in a fistfight since I was in sixth grade. I may not even have it in me anymore.

I push past her, go back inside, and find my friends, and by the time we leave the party, she's long gone. But after that day, whenever I happen to cross paths with her, she clears out of my way. If we are both walking down the sidewalk toward each other, the minute she sees me, she crosses the street and walks on the other side. If we're walking toward the same building in the quad, she'll go around the building and in through a different door.

The semester is well under way and I'm sitting on my bed, books and papers sprawled everywhere, when there is a knock at the door.

"Come in," I say, and Tracey, one of my thirteen roommates, pops her head in. I'm living in a four-story, fourteen-bedroom house with a full basement, ten parking spaces, and a large front deck with twelve other girls and Pablo, a foreign exchange student from Ecuador.

"Hey," she says, "I just ran into Martin McCarthy on the quad and he asked me to give you a message."

"Martin McCarthy?" I say. "Really?" Martin McCarthy had lived in the apartment below ours the year before, and though I had met him once or twice and would often run into him, we had never said much to each other beyond the initial hello. But there was something intriguing about him. He was tall, about six foot two, and even though his roommates were the T-shirt-and-baseball-cap-wearing types, he had shoulder-length blond hair that looked like he had chopped it himself. He wore vintage trousers, printed button-down shirts, black leather combat boots, and he was the lead singer of a band that was based out of Chicago. "What did he say?"

"He was all like, 'You're living with Maria, right?' And I was like, 'Yeah.' And he was like, 'Will you give her a message for me?' and I was like, 'Sure.' And he was like, 'Will you tell her that I want to have her baby.'"

"He said that?" I say, a grin spreading across my face. "That *he* wants to have *my* baby?"

"Yup," she says, "those were his words."

A few days later, I have an extra ticket to see a band that's playing at a local venue. I get Martin's number from my roommate and give him a call.

"Hey," I say when he answers. "I know you're into music and I have this extra ticket for a show, and I thought you might want to join me, but if you can't, it's no big deal, really."

He says he'd love to join me, and later that night, while sharing a pitcher of beer, he tells me he was brought up Irish Catholic and is the youngest of six, four boys and two girls. Both his maternal and paternal grandparents were Irish immigrants, and though his father was born and raised in the United States, he worked blue-collar jobs his whole life, and put all of them through college.

"We knew we had to be home and sitting at the dinner table at five p.m. sharp, every day," he says. "My job was to set out the chilled glasses of milk for everyone."

"That's so sweet," I say. Sitting down for dinner as a family was something I had always fantasized about when I was a kid. Eating dinner in our house had always been a free-for-all. Either one of my older sisters or I made dinner when we got home from school, and everyone ate as they came home from school or work, and if someone didn't like what was for dinner, they helped themselves to a bowl of cereal or a tall glass of milk and a stack of cookies. Once I had gone out of my way and had taken my mother's china from the cabinet and set the table, complete with silverware and napkins. I had made everyone wait until we could all sit down and eat together. Though they seemed confused, thrown off by the order of it all, they had waited, and when we were all sitting around the table, passing around the salad, mashed potatoes, and fried chicken, my siblings had started cracking jokes about how elegant it all was, and asked could someone please pass the butter, and why were we eating bread instead of tortillas, and why was there no salsa on the table, and why we were eating such a gringo dinner, and soon they were all roaring with laughter. Before I could finish my meal I had burst into tears, run into my bedroom, and shoved my head under my pillow.

"What about you?" he asks, pouring me another beer. "How many brothers and sisters do you have?"

"Six," I say, instantly feeling like a liar. But it's easier than saying I had seven, but now I only have six. "I have four sisters and two brothers."

"Big family." He fills his glass and holds it up. "To big families," he says. We toast, we drink. "So, do your folks still live in Somerset?" he asks.

"They're separated," I say. "My mother is still there, but my father is in Mexico."

"Whereabouts?"

"I'm not sure," I say, because I'm not about to tell him that my father is in prison. Though I had heard that his parents had sold a house they owned in order to try and bail him out. My godfather, the owner of the zapatería, had bought the house and demolished it almost immediately. Rumor had it that he had found several clay jugs filled with gold coins hidden within its thick adobe walls. There was so much money, in fact, that if he never wished to work another day in his life, he didn't have to. "We don't really keep in touch," I say.

Martin walks me home that night, kisses me goodnight on my front porch, and leaves. A few days later we go out again, and he walks me home and stays. In the morning, he asks me about the Glastonbury poster on my closet door, and I tell him about Abigail and the three guys from Chico. How we had met while living in Granada, where Abigail was staying in a cave on the other side of the Moorish wall. On Fridays after class, I'd hike up to her cave along the dirt trails behind the wall and we would all camp out for the weekend. Then, on Monday morning, I'd hike back down, just in time to make my 9:00 a.m. economics class, the scent from the campfire and a few grass blades still lingering in my hair.

The next time Martin comes over, he brings his music collection, and soon we are spending countless hours locked in my bedroom, burning through candles and listening to music. We set my five-disk changer on shuffle and one minute we're doing the tango to "Paint It Black" by the Stones, and the next minute we're improvising a dance routine to "7" by Prince. When I'm in my room, I like to pretend I'm in a New York City flat. Though I've never been to New York, my room is what I imagine a studio in New York looks like: bed in one corner, couch in the other, next to the radiator, fire escape outside the window, and the bathroom across the hall. I tell Martin that someday I want to live in New York. Since he's a musician, he thinks he might want to live in New York as well.

Halloween rolls around and before heading out for the evening, he comes over to pick me up.

"What are you supposed to be?" he asks when I come down the wide wooden staircase in a white vintage wedding dress that fits as though it were custom made for my frame.

"The bride of Frankenstein," I say. Earlier, after zipping up the dress, I had dabbed white powder on my face, frizzed my hair out, and painted a black lightning bolt from my hairline down and across my forehead with my eyeliner. I had then squirted fake blood on the side of my mouth, so that it ran over my chin and down my neck before disappearing into the low V-cut neckline of the dress.

"Doesn't she wear a black dress?" he says.

"Does she?" I say. "All right, then. I'm a bride. A dead bride. See?" I point at my forehead. "I was struck dead by lightning on my wedding day."

"There you go, that works." He offers me his arm and we head out. He's wearing a purple polyester tuxedo, a white shirt with green ruffles on the front, and a black top hat. Walking down the street, arm in arm, we must look like a bride and groom that crawled out of an abandoned trunk in a Salvation Army basement.

By the time Thanksgiving arrives, we're pretty much inseparable, and we're in my bedroom one night, listening to Pink Floyd and sending our shadows swaying along the candlelit walls. Though I've listened to *The Wall* before, I've never really paid close attention to the lyrics, which are now echoing as loud and ominous as a helicopter hovering above my bed. The song is saying something about how daddy's flown across the ocean, and I think it wasn't my daddy that flew across the ocean, but rather my brother who found the trapdoor on the river's floor and never returned. In my dreams, he has stayed forever the same age he was when he was killed—twenty-two—while I've grown up around him. We are now roughly the same age, and whenever he shows up anywhere, I'm no longer just trying to speak to him. I claw at his button-down, throw my arms around him, and hold him tight, knowing that the minute I wake up he'll be gone.

The song goes on with something about the family album, and I know that if it hadn't been for my brother, we wouldn't have any snapshots in our family albums. When we first arrived from Mexico, he found a part-time job, bought a Polaroid camera, and with it he captured so many moments in flight: my sisters and me in pigtails, standing in front of the Christmas tree, holding up a present; us sitting on my father's truck in polyester shorts and squinting in the sunlight; us standing in front of the house, my father's hands resting on my shoulders; me wearing a cone-shaped hat and standing behind a birthday cake, the candles burning and everyone waiting for the birthday girl to make a wish—if only it were that simple—make a wish and blow out the candles.

The lyrics continue, explaining how what the father left behind was nothing more than a brick in the wall, but instead of brick, I hear break, and I think that really is it, that's what that bastard left us— nothing but breaks, and I'm aware that my shadow is no longer moving, I'm standing still and am not so much hearing the music as I am feeling it. It's like a liquid that is seeping into all the deeply buried crevices where nothing else can reach. There's a familiar sentiment, a longing that I can't explain, though years from now I will find out that Roger Waters's father had been killed in a plane crash during the Second World War, when Waters was still an infant. I assume the brick in the wall must be the one that has his father's name on it—in memoriam, a substitute for what will never be replaced. It's the curse of the missing father—absent, yet ever present in his absence.

Martin seems to be tiptoeing as he comes around and stops in front of me, and it's too late because I can already feel the tickle at the bottom of my chin where the two hot streams are merging.

"Maria," he whispers, "why are you crying?"

After the holidays, I return to school with my brother's guitar. I took it down from the wall where it hung next to my mother's china cabinet for years. All but two of the strings had snapped. Martin restrings it for me, teaches me a few basic chords—the same chords my brother was teaching me when he left for Mexico. I put a nail in the wall next to my window and hang the guitar.

It's my final semester, and since I've already fulfilled most of the requirements for my major, I have a few electives. I sign up for an oil painting class and an acting class. The acting class is an introductory-level course for non–theater majors, and we spend the first week doing breathing exercises and playing icebreaker games. When the second week rolls around and we are still playing games, I pull out the course catalog and find an intermediate-level acting class taught by a Professor Stuart. The course is open to theater majors only, unless permission is granted by the instructor. I track down Professor Stuart. He's a tall, slim man with a full white beard and floppy white hair to match.

"Why don't you finish the intro class and join my class next semester?" he says.

"This is my last semester," I say.

"Well, I guess it's now or never, kid," he says. "I'll see you on Monday."

On Monday, I show up for class and am prepared to do whatever is asked of me because I don't want to let Professor Stuart down. My first assignment is a scene from Paul Zindel's *The Effect of Gamma Rays on Man-in-the-Moon Marigolds*. I'm assigned the role of Ruth and one of the other girls is assigned the role of the mother. He gives each of us a character road map that we must fill out and hand in on the day that we perform. The road map asks everything from what is your character's favorite ice-cream flavor to what is her motivation— why does she say and do the things that she does? What is it that she needs or wants from the other characters?

I pick up the play at the library and read through the whole thing once. Even though I'm not an avid reader, I love it so much that I read through it again. I complete the road map and then fill up half a notebook with my character's nuances, her likes and dislikes, right down to whether she's a cat person or a dog person and why. I decide that she's neither, since at the end of the play she kills her sister's rabbit. Why did she kill the rabbit? I come up with a handful of reasons, as a way of getting into Ruth's head, into her emotional state. I memorize my lines and meet with my scene partner twice a week to rehearse.

After three weeks, it's our turn to perform, and I'm not really nervous until I take my place in front of the class. I stumble through the first few lines, but soon I'm breathing a bit easier, taking my time to describe how I came down the stairs and saw the dying man foaming at the mouth. "Stop it, Ruth, please, stop it," the mother is yelling, and hearing how upset she's becoming only makes me want to dig even deeper, and with every step I take, the adrenaline is unleashing in my veins, making me feel like, if I wanted to, I could fly.

"Wow, you really hit the ground running, kid," Professor Stuart says, resting his arm on my shoulders when we are finished.

I feel as if I've cracked something open, like I've uncovered a secret that was hidden within me all along. If I can make a living doing this, I will never need therapy, especially if Mathew's prediction comes to pass. If I wake up one day and realize that I'm fucked up, acting might just be the thing that saves me.

14. ◆ HOUSE OF SCORPIONS

THE BOLT STRIKES against metal and the bars exhale as they slide open.

"Jose Venegas," the guard calls out. He sits up on his cot.

"You might want to bring your things," says the guard.

"Why? Where are we going?"

"You can ask your attorney that when you see him," the guard says. "He's downstairs."

He grabs the black plastic bag that hangs near the foot of his bed, his heart already racing, and then he is moving quickly and deliberately as he goes to the sink and, with a single swipe of his hand, brushes his toothpaste, toothbrush, and bar of soap into the bag—could this really be it? One of his daughters had visited him recently, and he had told her about the account his parents had set up for him, about the money they had gotten for the house with the pink limestone arches. The money had dwindled, but there was still enough there. He only needed a few thousand dollars more to complete the fee, and if she could do him the favor, loan him the money, he'd pay her back in no time at all. She had sat on the other side of the bars listening to him, but had agreed to nothing.

He lifts his cot, grabs his baseball cap, socks, extra underwear, and drops everything into the bag, then he's rolling up his wool blankets, not worrying about making them neat, not breaking his momentum, afraid that if he stops moving, the bars might slam shut for good. His cellmate sits up, blinking sleep from his eyes. The poor devil has no one fighting for him on the outside. No money. No blankets. No lawyer. No hope of ever getting out of this place.

"Bueno, amigo." He extends a hand to his cellmate. "Maybe one day I'll see you on the other side." They shake hands. He turns to leave, but stops in his tracks. "Hay se las encargo," he says, turning and handing the blankets to his cellmate.

He follows the guard down the stairwell, and even the sound of his footsteps descending the stairs has a different cadence. There's a lightness to them. He feels as if he's floating, feels like if he were to let go of the rail, he just might drift away. His attorney is standing in the front lobby, and he smiles wide when he sees him, hands him a piece of paper. He takes it and reads it fast, searching, skipping over every other word, until his eyes stop on that word that practically makes him weep—released. It's been three years since he was sentenced, but now he's holding a certified letter from the court stating that his involvement in the death of Manuel Robles was not rightfully proven, and that effective immediately, Jose Manuel Venegas is to be released. He and his attorney give each other a brisk hug before stepping outside. Even the sun on his skin feels different now that he's a free man.

He returns to La Peña, to the same place where he was born and raised. The house has been abandoned for several years, and when he arrives he finds it infested with scorpions. His father had left behind that house and several other properties. Had he been in prison any longer, perhaps his sister would have sold off all their patrimony. She had been burning through the land his father had left like a wildfire, had already sold off practically everything else, including La Mesa, and not long after he's released, he's riding back home from the ranch when he notices a man on La Mesa. He observes the man from a distance, watches him working diligently—measuring and digging. A man on his property is not in itself unsettling, but a man he's never seen before digging around on his land is. He rides up behind the man and asks what it is he thinks he's doing.

"The owner of this property hired me to install a barbed-wire fence for him," the man says, wiping a bit of sweat from his brow.

"The owner?" Jose coughs. "And who might that be?"

"El señor Márquez," the man says. Jose knows who Luis Márquez is, he owns a few businesses in town.

"Well, you can tell el señor Márquez that the rightful owner of this land has returned, and if he has a problem with that, he can feel free to come have a word with me."

He gives the man an hour to clear off the site, saying that he doesn't have any issue with him, but if he ever catches him on his property again, well, that will be as far as the man makes it.

The man never returns, as he and everyone in that town are well aware of his reputation. And it's precisely because of his reputation that six months later, while having a drink at a local joint, the waitress seems to know exactly who he is.

"You're El Cien Vacas, aren't you?" she says when she drops off his drink.

He eyes her with a mixture of suspicion and intrigue. How is it that she knows not his name, but his nickname? A nickname he's had ever since he was a boy because when he was seven years old, he had taken to bragging that he had one hundred cows up at his father's ranch.

"How do you know who I am?" he asks.

"Your reputation precedes you," she says. The last time he had been there, after he had left she'd overheard her boss saying something about how that was El Cien Vacas. How he had just spent three years in prison for killing a man, hell, he'd killed several, some on this side of the border and some on the other, word around town was that he was a dangerous man, a cold-blooded assassin. She had asked her boss if he would introduce her to this Cien Vacas next time he came in, but no introduction had been necessary. The minute he came through the door earlier, she recognized him. "Word around town is that you've made a few heads roll," she says.

"Is that so?" He's shocked by her bluntness. He glances up at her, and she does not avert her gaze. She's easily half his age and it's obvious that she's a full-blooded indigenous woman. She stands roughly five feet tall, her hair is thick and so black that it almost has a blue sheen to it. Though she has relinquished the traditional garb, has traded the brightly colored blouses and floor-length skirts that the women of her tribe wear for jeans, blouses, and cowboy boots, her features betray her. Clearly there isn't a single drop of Spanish blood in her gene pool to lighten her complexion. She is cut from the same unmistakable fabric of the Cora people—an indigenous group that still thrives in the farthest reaches of the mountains. A group that still speaks its own dialect, many refusing to learn Spanish even, viewing mestizos like himself as half-breeds—those whose veins will forever flow with the blood of the oppressor and the oppressed, both the Spaniards who invaded that land, bringing Catholicism and guilt with them, and the indigenous with whose blood and sweat the Spaniards built sprawling haciendas.

"Where are you from?" he asks.

She grew up in the sierra, she tells him, tending goats since she was practically a child.

"Goats?" Already he's making connections between the goats and his cattle, because where there are goats, there is milk, and wherever there is milk, there is moneymaking potential. He describes his four-hundred-acre ranch, complete with the freshwater spring and the two waterfalls, tells her that during the rainy season everything is vibrant, green, and beautiful. Though he doesn't mention that two hundred of those acres belong to Antonio, his older brother, but since Antonio has been living on the other side for years, and hadn't even bothered to return to Mexico for his own father's funeral, he has commandeered the entire ranch that his grandfather had left to his father.

"Do you really have a hundred cows?" she asks.

"Why don't you come out and see for yourself? We could ride out there tomorrow, if you'd like," he says, taking a swig of his beer. "Do you know how to ride a horse?"

She stifles her laughter. Tells him that not only does she know how to ride a horse, she's broken several by riding them bareback.

"Bareback, huh?" He takes another swig. "What time is your shift over?"

"At seven." She turns and glances past her boss, who is wiping down the bar, at the clock that hangs on the whitewashed wall above the dusty bottles. It's nearing three in the afternoon. "Not for another four hours."

"Can I take you out to eat?" he asks.

She smiles big, tells him to come back and pick her up at seven.

"Come back?" he says, and now it's he who is trying not to laugh as he pushes away from the table and makes his way to the bar. He tells the owner to put the drinks on his tab and that he's taking the waitress out to eat, but not to worry, he'll have her back in no time at all.

"Está bien, Jose," the owner says, giving him a nod.

"What's your name, anyway?" he asks, once they're in his truck. Her name is Rosario, and she has a five-year-old daughter named Alma. Alma's father went off to work on the other side and she never heard from him again.

At the restaurant, while watching her wash down her meal with an ice-cold beer, he propositions her. He's got a few cows that just had calves; if she can lend him a hand with the milking, she can use the milk to make cheese and they can split the profits down the middle. She doesn't say yes, one way or another, and after they finish their meal, he stops at a liquor store and picks up a bottle, and then they're flying toward La Peña.

They emerge from his house the following day and drive into town. After picking up her daughter and a few groceries, they head back to La Peña.

Two months after Rosario and Alma move in, his mother comes for a visit and she can barely contain her disgust, refusing to even taste the cheese that the indígena has made. Though Belén's own lineage was easily traceable to the Huicholes, another indigenous group that still lived in the sierra, it was a lineage she had refuted her whole life, claiming instead that she was a direct descendant of the Spaniards and that the only reason her skin was so dark was because of the garish sun. In order to prove her European ancestry to her grandchildren, she had gone as far as to remove her shoe, to show them her foot as proof of how white she actually was.

Belén is so offended with the concubine that she leaves and never returns to La Peña. It's as though she had seen the future go up in smoke before she even had a chance to protest. What if her son were to impregnate the indígena? It would be she and her bastard offspring that would inherit the house and the ranch and all that she and her husband had themselves inherited. Not long after that visit, Belén's health takes a turn for the worse and, within a month, she passes away. Perhaps she had held on just long enough to carry out her husband's final wish—to see their son set free. And who would carry out her final wish? The biggest humiliation of her life had been that due to the struggle in the shack, she had been unable to wed in a proper white dress.

"Who's the bride?" the woman at the boutique asks Jose's sister when she goes to pick up the dress.

"It's for my mother," she says. "For her funeral."

They laid her to rest in the plot above her husband's grave, and so she will remain—hovering over him in her white wedding dress for eternity. Where there were two crosses, there are now three.

His mother hasn't been in the ground a month, even, when already people are warning him.

"Jose, maybe you should leave this place," one of his neighbors tells him. "You've created too many enemies around here," he says, because already some men have been asking questions around town. *Where does Jose live? Which taverns does he frequent? What kind of car does he drive?*

"I'm not going anywhere," he says. He may have been released from prison, but he will never be free of his past, and he knows better than anyone that in a country where judges are easily bribed, people often take the law into their own hands, make their own justice. "If anyone has a debt to settle, they know where to come find me."

15 ◆ COWBOY MOUTH

THE LIGHTER FLICKS and sparks a small flame, but before the flame touches the candle's wick, it dies and the room is dark again. The sound of feet shuffling, chairs creaking, and the occasional cough fills the space. The audience is growing restless. Again, I slide my thumb over the rough surface of the nozzle repeatedly, and nothing but sparks shoot from the lighter. I grip the candle, digging my nails into the wax, unsure of what to do. We didn't rehearse for this—for what to do in case of a faulty lighter. It's opening night, there is a critic from *The Chicago Reader* in the audience, and I'm not about to let a plastic gadget ruin the show I've spent the last two months putting together.

The play is called *Cowboy Mouth*; I stumbled upon it while browsing through a compilation of Sam Shepard plays at the Harold Washington Library a few months back. After college, I moved to Chicago, and though I was working full-time at the Apparel Center, I had continued taking acting classes in the evenings. Soon, I started going on auditions, though it didn't take long to realize that most of the roles available to Latina actresses were painfully stereotypical—the main ones being the maid, the prostitute, and the drug dealer's girlfriend. And though I didn't have an accent, I was often asked to speak with one.

"What type of accent are you looking for?" I asked, as there were vast variations, depending on the character's background: Puerto Rican, Dominican, Argentinean, Cuban, Colombian, or Mexican.

"You know," they responded. "Just give us a generic Latina accent."

A generic Latina accent? What the hell would that even sound like?

I felt like I was being asked to perpetuate a stereotype with which I had never identified—the illiterate Latina. The only time I had any trace of an accent was when I got nervous; then one of two things happened: either a faint accent appeared or I started saying "like" after every other word—it was as though the white girl and the Mexican girl in me were at odds with each other, the "cheerleader" and the "gang leader" battling it out until one rose to the surface.

After reading through *Cowboy Mouth* once, I fell in love with Cavale, the female character. According to the foreword, Sam Shepard had written the play with Patti Smith by pushing a typewriter back and forth between them—he wrote the lines for Slim, the male character, and she wrote the lines for Cavale. I was drawn to Cavale: She was at once vulnerable and tough, and she was in search of her own religion—in search of a savior who would be like "a rock-and-roll Jesus with a cowboy mouth."

I called Samuel French in New York to find out the legalities behind producing one of their plays. I would need a production company, they said, so I created one—De-Jah-Vous Productions. Within two weeks, I had found a space, a director, and an actor to play Slim, and Martin, who was living a few blocks from me, had a cameo as the Lobster Man.

I try the lighter again, to no avail. The opening sequence is simple enough. Light the candle. Set it on the nightstand, and this will cue the lighting person to fade the lights up. I try one more time, and nothing but a feeble spark shoots from it and vanishes. I whip the candle clear across the stage. It soars through the darkness and hits against the brick wall with a thud and, as it rolls out of sight, the lights fade up.

We end up getting a great review. The critic writes how he was skeptical going in, as the image of Patti Smith in the role of Cavale is a hard one to shake. He writes: "Venegas puts her own urban Latina spin on the role, taking it over completely: Two minutes into the play, all thoughts of Patti Smith disappear." I read the review several times until I have committed it to memory, until it practically becomes my mantra—I love the idea of taking over something so completely that any trace of what came before disappears. It feels like an affirmation that I'm on the right path.

It's around that time that my father makes the newspapers as well. He's been out of prison just over a year when one night, while driving back to La Peña from a tavern in town, just as he slows near the only curve on the road between town and his home, his truck is lit up in a hail of bullets. The newspapers in Valparaíso the next day state that he was calmly making his way home when he was ambushed. He's quoted in the paper as saying he had no idea who would do such a thing, but that he intends to find out.

Had it not been for the woman he's living with, he probably would have bled to death in his courtyard, with no one but his dogs to keep him company. But when his body hit against the blue metal door, it awoke her. She ignored him at first, thinking, he's been drinking again, but then she heard him moan, and it was the trace of anguish in that moan that sent her rushing out of bed. She pulled the door open, and the weight of his body slumped into the house. He was covered in blood, and before she knew it, she was shouting orders at her daughter, telling her to run to Don Enrique's, say they needed help. Her daughter took off barefoot down the dirt road, running past his gray truck that was pressed up against the cinder-block wall, and within minutes she was back with Don Enrique, his truck idling outside. They wrapped him up in a wool blanket, loaded him onto the truck, and drove to the nearest hospital, two hours away.

When I hear he's been ambushed, I'm indifferent to whether he lives or dies. It's as though I've become immune to any news pertaining to him. I'm certain that it's only a matter of time before his past catches up with him, before he turns up dead, and I've decided that when that call comes, I will not shed a single tear. Yesenia obviously doesn't feel the same way, because not long after he's ambushed, she goes to visit him.

"He asked about you," she says, when she returns. To know that he had asked about me stirs a feeling of ambivalence. I'm happy to hear that he thought of me, but I'm also sad for him, since I have no intention of ever going to see him. My three older sisters had already been to see him at some point, so I was the only one of his daughters that had yet to go back. Yesenia had told him that I was acting and working as a bartender, because by then, I had quit my day job and was working in a martini lounge in Wicker Park. "He said that maybe he'll get up to Chicago sometime and that if he does, he'll go have a drink where you work."

"Yeah, right," I say, trying not to think of what a nightmare that would be. To look up from pouring a martini one day and see him standing in the doorway, like a person who's come back from the dead—my past colliding with my present, and then having to explain to the staff that the gun-wielding lunatic in the cowboy hat is my father.

Not long after he's ambushed, he's back in prison. After a night of drinking, he had been shooting his gun off in the house and a stray bullet hit the woman who is living with him.

"That poor woman," my mother says, when she tells me what happened. The authorities had arrested him and the woman herself had gone and testified on his behalf, saying that it had been an accident, that he hadn't meant to shoot her. Had the woman breathed a word of the baby she lost, the judge might have locked him away for life, but she didn't say anything and the judge ordered his release—under the condition that he would provide for the woman and her daughter until his dying day, as the bullet had left the woman bound to a wheelchair. "Imagine?" my mother says. "That could have been any one of us."

There are a handful of Latina actresses in Chicago who I keep running into at the same auditions. We share similar frustrations over the limited roles available to us, so we form our own theater troupe, meet twice a week, and begin brainstorming, writing scenes based on our personal experiences growing up in a dual culture. We perform at various theaters around the city and, within two years, we have a full-length show. We submit the script to INTAR, an off-Broadway theater company in New York City, and a few months later, we hear back. They want to workshop the play as part of their New Works Lab. We tell them fine, but if they're going to workshop our script, we want to be the actresses in it.

They agree.

On the night before I leave for New York, Martin has a going-away party for me. He makes sangria, guacamole, and beer-marinated skirt steaks on the grill—all the things I've taught him to make.

"How long are you going for?" one of his friends yells over the music.

"Just the summer," I say.

Martin puts his arm around me.

"You're never coming back," he says.

"That's not true," I say, though I've decided that if I can find a job and an affordable living situation, I'll stay longer. Especially since

Josh, one of the guys from Chico, just moved there, and Abigail is moving there within a month as well. She had gotten married two years before, and Martin and I had gone to the wedding. Then after she'd been married for about a year and a half, she called me one day to tell me that she had fallen in love. He was the owner of the gallery where she was working, and he felt the same way. Abigail filed for divorce and she and her husband split everything down the middle—he got the sailboat, which had been a wedding gift from her grandfather, and she got their savings. She had decided to take that money, go live in New York for a year, take classes at the Art Students League, and give the gallery owner space while he finalized his divorce.

"That's okay," Martin says. "I know you've always had one foot out the door." He often teases me of having the "one-foot-out-the-door syndrome." Though it's not so much having one foot out the door as an inherent attitude that I don't need anyone taking care of me. It's an inability to entrust my well-being to anyone, and years from now, when I go see a therapist, after several visits she concludes that perhaps my biggest shortcoming is that I'm self-reliant—almost to a fault.

Though I assume this self-reliance stems from my brother having left and never returned, and then my father having left without even having bothered to say goodbye, eventually it will be Tito who will point out exactly where my self-reliance stems from.

On June 1, 2001, I land at LaGuardia with nothing but a small backpack, my laptop, and my brother's guitar. Rehearsals start right away. Abigail arrives a few days before the show opens, and she and Josh come on opening night. After having a drink with the ensemble, we leave and flag down a cab. There is a party called Rubalaud back in Josh's neighborhood in Brooklyn that he wants to take us to.

"Where you go?" the cabbie asks, before we even get in. "Where you go? Where you go?"

"Williamsburg," Josh says, and the cab takes off, practically running over our feet, and leaving us standing on the curb. Cabs don't like going to Brooklyn, especially not to Williamsburg, where back in the seventies, eighties, and even the nineties, crime was so rampant that even the police didn't like going there.

A few days later, Martin is in town, and we take the L train to

Bedford Avenue in Williamsburg. It's late afternoon, and when we emerge from the subway, the first thing I notice is the sky. It's vast compared to the sky in Manhattan.

"This is it," I say to Martin, because even though I've been in New York for a few weeks, I haven't found a neighborhood where I could see myself living, certainly nowhere in Manhattan, with its nonstop traffic, crowded sidewalks, and skyscrapers. "This is my neighborhood," I say. There is something about Williamsburg that is very reminiscent of Wicker Park, my neighborhood in Chicago. Most of the buildings are brick, three- to six-floor walk-ups. There are no high-rises, no elevator men, no tourists, and hardly any traffic. A Salvation Army sits on the corner near the subway stop, and there's a Polish restaurant down the street, across from a Mexican grocery store.

By the end of the week, I've found a room for rent in the neighborhood. It's in a two-bedroom apartment that I'll be sharing with a guy named Tundae. When I had first gone to look at the apartment, I had told Tundae that I would take the room, and he chuckled, told me he had other people coming to look at the place and he'd get back to me by the end of the week. When the end of the week was nearing and I still hadn't heard from him, I started to panic. I knew this room was my shot at staying in New York. The rent was cheap—so cheap that the $2,300 I had to my name would have been enough to cover the first six months of rent.

"You seem like a nice person," he said. "But you just moved here, and you're an actress, and you don't have a job, you know what I'm sayin'? And you have that guitar, and when you play, it might be loud, and the apartment is not that big, you know what I'm sayin'? Besides, I already told this other girl that she could have the room."

"Please, Tundae, please." I swore I wouldn't play my guitar when he was home, and told him that I had so much money saved up that, if he wanted me to, I could pay the first six months up front—so paying rent would definitely not be an issue. We went back and forth a bit, until he finally relented, said the other girl was already on her way to pick up the key, but if I could get there with a deposit before she did, I could have the room.

I move in July 1, which happens to be a Sunday, and while I'm unpacking my clothes and arranging them in the closet, I hear a song that I haven't heard since I was a kid come thundering through the apartment. I go to the window, and across the street there is a Spanish-speaking Pentecostal church. Their door is wide open and the singing, clapping, and tambourine playing is spilling out onto the sidewalk. They start singing a different song, and then another, and though I haven't stepped foot in a church in years, I still know all the lyrics by heart. Whenever they introduced a new hymn at my mother's church, on the way home she would ask me to sing it, because she knew I was the one who always memorized the lyrics.

"Hallelujah," a man yells into a microphone, and his voice comes booming through the apartment.

The singing subsides, the music stops, and then the man is going on and on about how the Second Coming is upon us. How Jesus will come like a thief in the night—in the blink of an eye. Fire will once again rain from the heavens like in the days of Sodom and Gomorrah, and the Antichrist will reign on earth. I know all about the Antichrist and his reign of terror on earth after the Second Coming. When I was a kid, they had shown us a film at my mother's church that depicted what the Great Tribulation would be like. In the film, fires raged on every street corner and everyone seemed to be running for cover. A soldier grabbed a small boy and asked if he believed in Jesus, and since the boy said yes, the soldier had forced a metal rod through the boy's ears. The rod had gone in one ear and out the other, and the boy had begun to vomit instantly.

For days after, I couldn't shake the image of that boy. It had frightened me enough that every single night I prayed that Jesus would save me, my brothers and sisters, my mother, and my father—especially my father, whom we were all convinced was doomed to go to hell because he didn't believe in Jesus and he drank too much, and he called the people at my mother's church hypocrites—claimed that they were brainwashing us.

On weekday nights, while he sat in the living room watching Mexican soaps, my mother gathered us in her bedroom and read us Bible stories. There was the story of a man who had been swallowed by a giant fish and had lived inside the fish's stomach for a month before being regurgitated and had survived. Then there was the woman who had glanced back on her burning city and had thus been turned into a salt statue, and so she would remain, forever looking back on her past. And then there was Jesus—who had walked on water, turned water into wine, and had even brought a man back from the dead.

"Was Jesus Mexican or American?" we asked.

"Neither," she said. "He was a Jew."

"What's a Jew?"

My mother tried to clarify what a Jew was, told us about Israel and Egypt, about Moses and the Pharaoh, and for years I assumed these people and places no longer existed.

After each story, she'd interpret its implication—explain the importance of love and forgiveness, how if someone should strike you on the right cheek, you should turn and offer up your left. Even as my father was warning us never to run away from a fight—no matter what. My parents were polar extremes and we had grown up somewhere in between. I know that the reason why the very sight of Melissa's face had made me want to drop her was my father, and the reason why I had felt empathy for her was my mother. It was because of my father that I had never tolerated anyone sidestepping me. When I had first moved to Chicago, I had taken an "on-camera" acting class with a man named Francis Mancini. At the start of class, he had promised that we would have a reel by the end of the course—that was the deal. And though it was an on-camera acting class, there was never a camera in the classroom, and when the course ended, two weeks earlier than scheduled, no one had a reel. The other eight students were willing to let it go, but I refused—I couldn't. As far as I was concerned, he was the filth of the earth—a leech—taking advantage of struggling artists.

"That son of a bitch made us a promise, and he has to either keep it or refund our money," I said when I called each of the other students, and soon we were calling him at all hours of the day and night, and when that didn't work, we told him that we were going to put up flyers around the neighborhood with his photo on them, and the word FRAUD written above his face, so that everyone would know that he was a thief. He finally relented and made us each a reel.

I go back to unpacking and the man's voice continues to echo off the walls. He's going on and on about how now is the time to ask Jesus to come live in your heart, before it's too late, as the Second Coming is upon us. Yeah right, I think, as I hammer a nail into the wall above my bed. Jesus has been coming since I was a kid, and he hasn't arrived yet. I can't put a finger on when exactly I stopped believing in Jesus, in my mother's religion—there was no aha moment. It was more like the skepticism that my father had planted when I was a kid had sprouted and grown like a mighty weed until it had snuffed out everything else. It had been nearly fourteen years since he had left, and despite his absence, his influence thrived.

I hang my brother's guitar from the nail and leave to meet up with Josh and a few of his friends near the East River. There is a small park that sits on the water near my apartment where they often go to watch the sunset. Several post-dot-com-crash transplants from San Francisco live in the neighborhood, and Josh seems to know all of them. We sit on the large rocks that line the water's edge and watch the sun go down behind the Manhattan skyline, setting the sky ablaze behind the World Trade Center.

Money goes fast in New York—seems to evaporate right out of your pocket as you walk down the street. By the time September rolls around, I'm low on cash and getting a bit desperate. Though I've been checking Craigslist and *The Village Voice* every day and sending out résumés, I'm finding it a lot more difficult than I had expected to find a flexible part-time job that is willing to accommodate an aspiring actress. Abigail offers to get me a job at the art gallery where she works in Chelsea. She's very knowledgeable when it comes to art, and she and the gallery owner have talked about expanding his gallery when she returns to Maine, and maybe even opening one in New York. I tell Abigail that if I still haven't found a job by the end of the month, I'll take her up on her offer.

On September 11, my alarm goes off at 8:00 a.m., as it always does. I usually get up in the morning, go for a jog, and then stretch in the park on the river. I reach over, turn it off, and fall back asleep. About an hour later, it's ringing again. I go to turn it off and realize it's not my alarm but my cell. It's one of my college friends calling from Florida.

"Hey," she says, when I answer. "Are you watching the news right now?"

"No," I say, "I was still sleeping. Why?"

"Apparently two planes just crashed into the World Trade Center," she says.

"What?" I look out my window but can't see anything. I tell her I'm walking down to the river and will call her back when I get there.

Even before I reach the water, I can already see the dark cloud of smoke that's billowing against the clear blue sky. There are a handful of people in the park when I arrive: Some Hasidic men stand in a semicircle, a group of Puerto Rican boys from the neighborhood sit huddled on the rocks, a few hipsters stand around, straddling their bicycles. Everyone watches the dark gray smoke that's engulfing the upper half of both buildings as the helicopters hover near like giant dragonflies. It's surreal, like watching a movie, except that the screen is gone. I sit on the rock from where we usually watch the sunset and think they must have already evacuated the buildings, and I wonder how exactly they're going to put the flames out, imagining that they'll have to pour water down from helicopters, or something like that. I try calling my friend in Florida back, but can't get through. I try calling Martin, my sisters, my friends in Chicago, but the signal is busy, busy, busy. There's no point in trying Josh or Abigail as they're both out of town. I'm about to try my friend in Florida again when there is a collective gasp—everyone in the park seems to have inhaled in unison. I look up, and across the river, the first tower is crumbling, crashing down to earth like a giant wounded moth.

"What the fuck! What the fuck!" One of the Puerto Rican boys jumps up and starts pacing.

"This is all your fault," a man in a flannel shirt with his gray hair pulled back in a ponytail yells, and points at the Hasidic men. "It's because of you people," he says before storming off. What a rude asshole, I think as I watch him go.

"All those people. Oh my God, those poor people." A Polish woman standing next to me is muttering under her breath, tears streaming down her face, and it's only then that the magnitude of it all starts sinking in—the buildings hadn't been evacuated.

"Fuck this," a different Puerto Rican boy says as he pushes himself off the rocks and walks away, his fists pumping on either side of him, the veins in his neck bursting under the skin, the fight trapped in his bones.

A slew of text messages come through from Martin, from my sisters, from my friends, all back in Chicago: *Get out of there. We'll come get you. Leave! Come back to Chicago. Come back. Come back.*

The second building starts to crumble and I'm unable to rip my gaze from it as the sirens wail across the river, and it feels like it just might be the end of the world.

In the days that follow, I wander through the deserted streets of Manhattan and spend hours in Union Square, where flowers and candles have flooded the park. Taped on walls and streetlamps are posters of missing persons, along with descriptions of what they were wearing when they left for work that morning and who they were—a devoted wife, a sister, a fiancé, a loving father, a brother—all the missing. They had walked out the door in the morning and had never returned. I know what the missing feel like.

The one thing that begins to crystalize in the aftermath is that I'm not leaving New York—it doesn't matter that we are on high alert, that another attack seems very likely—no matter what may come next, running away is not an option. I can practically hear my father's voice: *Even if you know you're going to get your ass kicked, you stay and you fight like a man.* I feel a deep sense of solidarity with the city—like having watched the buildings crumble somehow fused my backbone to its foundation. I feel like it's my duty to stay.

"You should go see your pops," Martin tells me when he comes to visit around Halloween, because for the first time since my father left, I have started talking about him, telling stories about him and how, when we had first arrived from Mexico, he used to take us trick-or-treating to the wealthy subdivisions, despite my mother's protests, despite her claiming that Halloween was the devil's holiday. And then around Christmas, he'd take us to every church that was holding a gift drive, and as we made the rounds, the camper of his truck slowly filled up with gifts that were tagged girl: ages 2–4, boy: ages 4–6, girl: ages 7–9. When I turned nine, he had bought me a pair of Jordache jeans; when I turned ten, he had bought me a ten-speed bicycle; and when I turned eleven, he had bought me a gold chain with a gold heart pendant, which I lost the very next day. I tell Martin how my father never bothered with names, because the minute he met someone, he made up a nickname for them. How he had warned me about never running away from a fight, and it was only now that I was beginning to understand all the implications of that warning.

"Fuck him," I say, though I know that if it weren't for my father, I probably wouldn't have had the guts to pick up and move to New York in the first place. He was the swagger in my stride, the reason why I had a don't-fuck-with-me attitude, though it was also that same attitude that often got me in trouble, and could have easily gotten me killed on more than one occasion. Two summers ago, Martin and I had gone backpacking through Europe, and one night we had been hanging out in a square in London. There were some kids playing drums, and we were sitting and leaning into an iron gate near them, when a Middle Eastern–looking man had come up and started yelling at me. Until he started yelling, I hadn't realized that my head was resting on his backpack, which was hanging from the gate. I tried explaining that I hadn't seen his backpack, but the more I explained, the more he yelled, and a circle had begun to gather around us until he looked at me and scoffed. "Stupid American."

"Fuck you," I said. If there was one thing I knew I wasn't, it was a stupid American. I had seen those types, at the bistros in Paris, drinking and talking so loudly that I was embarrassed for them. I had been with those types at a national monument in Madrid, when they had broken out and started singing the American national anthem, oblivious to the glares they were getting from passersby. I may be American, and I may have done my share of stupid things, but I was not one of those stupid Americans.

"What did you say?" He took two steps toward me. We were about the same height, and he got so close to my face that I could smell his stale breath.

"Fuck." I lifted my chin and looked him in the eye. "You."

He pushed me, and before I had a chance to react, Martin had him by the throat. Later, Martin would tell me that he was watching the whole thing, thinking, she can hold her own, but the minute the man touched me, it was over.

"You're right," Martin says. "Fuck him. Don't do it for him. Do it for yourself. You need to be the bigger person, 'cause he sure isn't coming to New York anytime soon."

"I don't know, it's sort of dangerous down there," I say. There's a part of me that feels like if I were to go back to Mexico, the ground itself might open up and swallow me alive.

"I'll go with you," he says. "We can jet down for a quick trip over the holidays. Make a vacation out of it, stay in a nice hotel, rent a car, and drive out to see your pops on Christmas, just for the day. If we feel uncomfortable, we can leave whenever we want." He takes my hand. "I think it would be really good for you to go see your old man, because one day, all the anger you have toward him is going to come out and guess who's going to be on the receiving end of it?" he says, pointing at himself with his thumb.

"That's not true," I say, though I know he's right. If I don't deal with my past, in the end, Martin will be the one who bears the brunt of it.

"All's I'm saying is that he's the man who shaped you, for better or worse, and as long as he's still alive, you should go see him," he says, turning to face me. "You are such a sweet person, and the people you love, you would do anything for, give your right arm for a friend if you had to. But if anyone ever sidesteps you, as sweet as you are, you can be twice as vicious," he says. "And I know that definitely doesn't come from your mother."

Finding a job in the city post–September 11 is virtually impossible, and by the time November rolls around I've barely enough money to cover my rent when I get an e-mail from Stephanie Goldstein. Stephanie and I had worked in the Apparel Center in Chicago for a few months after college. She had just graduated from Madison and we had hit it off, but then she had moved to L.A. with her boyfriend. In the e-mail she writes that she has just relocated to New York and is running a showroom for an L.A.-based designer who has sparked a craze in Hollywood with her super low-cut jeans, and she needs someone to help her in the showroom a few days a week.

I go meet her the next day and start working the day after that, twice a week, mostly helping her with filing and making calls to buyers to set up appointments. The designer fits all the samples to her measurements, which happen to be my measurements, so whenever a buyer comes in to view the collection, I try on practically every pair of jeans for them. Business starts picking up and I'm offered full-time employment. I make them a proposition. I'll forgo certain benefits, like paid vacations and health insurance, in exchange for the flexibility to go on auditions whenever they come up—no questions asked.

They agree.

Once I have enough money saved, I have new headshots made and start sending them out to agents and managers. I hear back from a very reputable manager, and a week later I go to her office on Fifty-third and Third.

"Why New York?" she asks, puffing on a cigarette from across a glass-top coffee table. "Why not L.A?"

"I want to be a working artist, not a celebrity," I say, though I fantasize that someday I'll make it big, so big that my father will turn on the television and recognize the face on the screen. Or that he'll be driving along a desolate road in Mexico and will see my face on a billboard, and he'll elbow his buddies and say, hey, look, that's my daughter, and they'll laugh at him and say, yeah, right, you old quack. If that girl is your daughter, why doesn't she have your last name? I use an alias for my stage name. Same first name, but different last name, as if by replacing his name I might be able to sever any trace of his bloodline.

The manager signs me, and soon I'm going on auditions and getting callbacks for independent films and shows on HBO.

"I told Dad that you're coming," Sonia says when she calls me early in December. "He's excited, said to give him a call." She gives me his cell number. The last time she had gone to see him she had set one up for him.

I program the number into my cell under Dad, and whenever I scroll through the names and that three-letter word comes up, it stops me in my tracks. *Dad.* There he is, wedged between Cait and Dawn—Dad. It feels like a glitch, like a lie. No matter how many times I scroll past that three-letter word, I don't call him. It's been fourteen years since he packed up his truck and pulled out of our driveway in the dark hours of morning. Since I've waited this long to talk to him, I've decided to wait until we're standing face-to-face.

BOOK TWO

16 ◆ FAMILY PORTRAIT

MARTIN AND I ARRIVE in Zacatecas a few days before Christmas. We check into a hotel, which has a sprawling courtyard that wraps around a water fountain. Plants in large clay pots line a wrought-iron staircase and balcony. Our room is on the second floor and has exposed wooden beams, terra-cotta tiles, and a terrace that overlooks the entire city of Zacatecas. In the distance a cable car carries tourists to El Cerro de la Bufa, the highest point in town. There is a larger-than-life-size statue of Pancho Villa mounted on a horse at the top of the cerro. I've heard stories of how one of my great-uncles fought in the Mexican Revolution alongside Villa, was one of his main generals, and I still remember the sense of pride I felt when I found out that my bloodline could be traced to the front lines of a revolution.

"What did you get your pops for Christmas?" Martin asks, placing his suitcase on the bed.

"Nothing," I say. "That bastard should be happy I'm coming to see him at all."

"Okeydoke," he says, pulling out a change of clothes. "Well, I bought him a flashlight. I'll put both our names on it." The flashlight is identical to one my father used to have and was rather proud of, saying that it was the same type of flashlight the police used. It's black, made of heavy metal, and has a far-reaching adjustable beam.

Two days later, we board a bus bound for Valparaíso at noon, and by three in the afternoon it's pulling into the dusty parking lot.

Martin and I grab our backpacks and make our way through the dimly lit corridor in the bus depot. At six foot two, with shoulder-length blond hair that is cut in messy angles, he stands out among all the cowboy hats. Two doors down from the depot, there is a seafood restaurant. We step inside, find an empty booth, and slide across the orange vinyl seats. The Formica tabletop is sticky to the touch. A black plastic mortar filled with pickled jalapeños and sliced carrots and onions sits in the center of the table. The waitress comes over and we order two Coronas—the local brew.

"We made it," Martin says, holding up his beer. We toast and with the first ice-cold sip I can already feel the three-hour bus ride and my hangover melting away. The night before, we had gone to La Mina, an old silver mine in Zacatecas that had been converted to a nightclub. The DJ spun a mix of music—everything from Michael Jackson to Maná, to the occasional corrido—my father's music. When El Rey came on, the whole place started singing along and, though I knew the lyrics by heart, had memorized them during those long, sleepless nights, I did not join the massive sing-along. When the music stopped, a few men in cowboy hats standing near the bar had cried out like wild cocks and I almost expected to hear gunshots.

I take another sip. Hard to believe that by this time tomorrow, my father and I will be face-to-face. The plan is to grab a bite, check into a hotel, shower, find an Internet café, and buy a few things, especially sunblock—Martin's nose is already bright red. I notice how a woman sitting at a table in the back of the restaurant keeps glancing over at me. She whispers something to the people she's with and they all turn and stare.

"What's wrong?" Martin asks.

"Those people keep staring at me," I say, thinking that maybe we should finish our beers and leave, but then the woman is making her way over to us.

"¿Cómo te llamas?" she asks, when she reaches our table.

"Maria de Jesus," I say, stopping at my middle name, a buffer.

"Maria de Jesus que?" she asks.

"Maria de Jesus Venegas," I say.

"I knew it," she practically yells. "You're Jose's daughter, aren't you? No, no, no, I was sitting over there and kept thinking I know that face, I know that face. You probably have no idea who I am, but I never forget a face." She smiles big. "I'm your father's sister, your tía Esperanza," she says, holding her arms out to me.

"She's my aunt," I tell Martin as I slide out of the booth and give her a hug.

"Mira no más," she says, taking a step back. "You're so tall! The last time I saw you, you were about this big." She holds her hand at table level. "You must have been about three or four. How old were you when you left for the other side?"

"Four," I say.

"Four? No, you wouldn't remember me. You were too young, but that face. I never forget a face. You look just like your mother," she says. "How is she? Your mamá?"

"She's fine," I say. "She's in Chicago."

"How is everyone doing over there?" she asks, eyeing Martin.

"They're fine."

"Is this your husband?"

"No," I say. "He's my boyfriend."

She and Martin nod to each other.

"We just got into town," she says, still smiling. "We would have gone straight to your father's, but we were starving and needed to use the bathroom."

"Where do you live?" I ask.

"California. We've been in Fresnillo for a few days, but we're going out to La Peña when we finish eating." She glances back at Martin. "Have you guys been out to see your father yet?"

"We just got into town," I say. "We're going to stay in a hotel and go out to his place tomorrow."

"A hotel?" she blurts out. "What do you need a hotel for? Your father's place is right up the road," she says. "How long has it been since you've seen each other?"

"I don't know. About fourteen years?"

"So you're one of the last ones to come see him," she says. "The last time we were down here"—she pauses, looks up at the ceiling—"who was it? Sonia? Roselia?" She looks back at me. "One of them was here," she says. Over the past few years, all four of my sisters had been to see him. Sonia had been the first, had gone to see him while he was still

in prison. She had shown up on the other side of the bars during visiting hours with her two boys, and he had not recognized her. Later,
she told me that for the two hours she had been there, while her boys
played with their Power Rangers figures on the cement floor, my
father had sat across from her and cried the whole time. "Does he
know you're coming?" she asks.

"Yes," I say. "Sonia called him."

"So he's probably waiting for you." Her smile spreads ever wider.
"No, no, no, you *have* to come with us."

"No, really, it's okay," I say. "We need to shower and run some
errands. We'll take a taxi out to his place tomorrow."

"A taxi!" She starts laughing. "Why are you going to waste your
money on a taxi? We can take you there right now."

Martin and I are crammed in the backseat of the Suburban between
our backpacks and cousins that I didn't even know I had. The dust
and sweat of the bus ride is still in our hair, our pores—this is not
how I imagined my first encounter with my father. We sit in traffic,
idling past pharmacies, liquor stores, dental clinics, panaderías, car-
nicerías, and fruit stands.

"All the norteños are down here right now," my aunt says, looking back at me from the passenger seat. "That's why there's so much
traffic."

It's easy to distinguish the locals from the norteños, the rusty
trucks assembled with parts salvaged from junkyards amid the ones
that gleam in the afternoon sun and have plates from Texas, California, Colorado, Arizona, and Illinois. A local truck has a blue truck
bed that reads Toyota on the back and a gray hood with Jeep written
across the front, while the norteños drive la troca del año—the latest
model, even if it's all a façade, purchased on credit, because once the
holidays are over, the owners of those brand-new trucks will be returning to jobs busing tables, washing dishes, and mowing lawns in
order to pay off those shiny trucks. But none of that matters now. It's
the holidays, it's December, the one month out of the year that the
norteños descend upon the narrow streets of this town with their
trucks and fists full of dollar bills to spend on the músicos, at the horse

races, the cockfights, and on women. It's the one month they can live like kings. I know. This was my father's routine.

"Does any of this look familiar?" my aunt asks.

"No," I say.

"Really? Nothing?"

"Nothing," I say.

"No, what are you going to remember? You were still young when you left this place." She's right. I have no memory of this place. It's as though whatever came before that long, nauseating bus ride along the mountains had been nothing but a dream, and once I crossed over to the other side, even the memory of that dream vanished.

We clear a few speed bumps on the edge of town, and soon we're driving down a two-lane road, the wind roaring in through the open windows and whipping my hair into my face as we go flying past a lumberyard, a yonke, and dried-out cornfields. We clear a slight curve and then we're turning left onto a dirt road. Dust fills the cabin as we bounce along, driving over rocks, gullies, and a shallow river. A few cows grazing along the water's edge look up and watch as we idle past. Martin takes my hand, shoots me a smile.

On the other side of the river, there is a slight hill, and a fifteen-foot adobe wall that appears to be melting runs the length of the hill, like a fort. Two dilapidated limestone pillars stand on either side of the entrance, and a few chickens scatter as we go through. There are doorways that lead to roofless rooms built into the wall, rooms in which the afternoon sunlight is pouring in like a golden liquid, rooms that lead to arched doorways that frame the distant mountain range, rooms with trees growing from their dirt floors and nopales sprouting from their thick adobe walls—nature reclaiming its territory.

"Now, does anything look familiar?" my aunt asks as we make our way past a small church with whitewashed walls, a large bell sitting in the tower above.

"Nothing," I say. We drive by a few small houses, dogs come running out, barking as we go by, then retreat.

We pull up next to an old blue Chevy truck that looks exactly like the one my brother had driven down from Chicago when he left some seventeen years ago. I can't believe this barren, dusty place is where he spent the last two years of his life. Three dogs come running at the car, barking at us.

"Don't worry," my aunt says, pushing the door open and shooing the dogs away. "They won't bite."

She and the others make their way across the dirt road toward a small L-shaped cinder-block house with a tin roof; Martin and I follow. A pile of chopped wood sits next to two eucalyptus trees in front of the courtyard wall, and a few chickens cluck about in the shade of the trees. Clotheslines are strung across the courtyard, and jeans hang upside down and inside out next to towels. One of the towels has a pink flamingo dipping its long stick-legs into an aqua-blue pond. I recognize that towel. It's from the factory where my mother worked years ago.

His black cowboy boots and jeans are the first thing I see, the rest of him concealed behind the pink flamingo. He pushes the towel aside and makes his way toward us. He's wearing a straw hat, a plaid shirt, and walks with a bit of a limp. His right shoulder seems to hang lower than his left. It looks like it fell out of the socket and was only partially put back in place. He's thinner, seems somehow deflated. His gut is gone. I've heard he stopped drinking, maybe that's why. Either way, Sonia warned him that if he drinks while we are here, we are leaving—that is the deal.

"Look who I brought you," my aunt announces, stepping aside, as if my being here were her doing. The others move out of the way, like a curtain parting. He squints in the afternoon sun as if trying to recognize me. The skin above his eyes droops and rests on his thin eyelashes. His hazel eyes still have a tinge of green in them. He no longer has a beard, and the dimple on his chin is plainly visible—the same John Travolta dimple my brother had. He glances over at Martin, back at me, then at my aunt.

"Did you guys drive down here together?" he asks her.

"No," she says. "We were at that mariscos place. You know, the one next to the bus station? And we were just finishing our meal when I see this girl and this gringo walk in and I kept staring at her and thinking, 'I know that face, I know that face' and, look at her, isn't she Pascuala's image in the flesh?" she says. "She's darker than Pascuala, but that face. It's the same face, isn't it?"

He looks at me.

"When did you arrive?" he asks.

"A few days ago," I say. "We've been in Zacatecas."

Again he's observing Martin, who takes this as his cue to deliver the one line he rehearsed on the three-hour bus ride.

"Hola," Martin says, holding out his hand. "Me llamo es Martín."

My father shakes his hand, his gaze wandering back toward me. We eye each other, as if we were perfectly matched in a duel, uncertain of who will have the nerve to make the first move. Hard to believe that after all these years there he is—alive and in the flesh. It's like coming face-to-face with someone who's returned from the dead.

"Oh, for God's sake," my aunt blurts out. "Will you two give each other a hug?" She gives my shoulder a slight nudge. I take a step toward him. He seems shorter, like gravity has taken him down a few notches, while I've grown a few inches. I reach for him and my chest recoils as my fingertips give his shoulder blades two taps. I'm vaguely aware of his hand on my lower back.

"Where is el baño?" Martin asks to no one in particular, and my cousins start laughing.

My aunt tells him to go out in the corral. Of course—there's no bathroom. When I was a kid, I remember overhearing conversations about la luz y el agua, water and electricity, arriving at all the different ranches that sprawled from Valparaíso. La luz y el agua had arrived in San Martín, in Santana, in Las Cruces. La luz y el agua were like two long-awaited guests of honor—saints practically, one arrived streaming through pipes below and the other traveling on wires above, and sending lightbulbs shining, illuminating rooms that had only known the light of a kerosene lantern. Though they arrived in La Peña years ago, there's still no bathroom—not even an outhouse.

Martin and I take turns going out to the corral. Adjacent to it is a huge roofless room with twenty-foot adobe walls. A few wooden beams jut out into the blue sky above. I find a spot behind a green metal trough and squat down. There is a pick and shovel leaning against the far wall, and a hole in the ground that is about six feet long and three feet deep. A crow swoops and lands on one of the beams, and while watching it ruffle its feathers, it dawns on me why while camping out with Abigail and the guys from Chico in the south of Spain, there was something so familiar about going outdoors.

Once I'm finished, I climb a set of wide limestone steps at the far end of the corral. They lead to a grassy plateau, and from here, I can do a three-sixty and see where the mountains meet the sky all the way around. The sky is so vast that I feel as though I'm on a different planet.

"What's that hole in the corral for?" I ask my father when I return.

He explains that back when La Peña was an hacienda, what is now the corral used to be the church, and legend has it that there is gold buried somewhere between those four walls.

Later that night, after everyone has left, Martin and I are in the bedroom where we'll be staying. It's a large cinder-block room with high ceilings and a tin roof that rattles against the wooden beams each time the wind gusts. The wardrobe is filled with women's clothing. I assume it belongs to the woman and girl who live with my father. They're out of town visiting relatives in the sierra for the holidays.

The walls are covered with portraits of saints, including a large one of the Virgen de Guadalupe. A pink shower curtain hangs in the doorway that separates our room from the storage room and the rest of the house. At the foot of the doorway the year 1986 is etched. This must be the room my brother built. When would he have ever thought that he was building the room in which his wake would be held? No matter where I go, he always finds me. Even after I moved to Brooklyn he showed up at my front door one day. I took him by the hand and guided him around my neighborhood. We walked down to the East River and sat on the rock from where I watch the sunset. "Can you see me from the other side of the sun?" I asked, but when I turned around he was gone, had been pulled under by the turbid current.

I hoist my backpack onto the bed, next to Martin's. We pull out extra layers—long johns, wool caps, socks, and sweaters. As soon as the sun went down, the temperature dropped—desert climate. A portrait of a Spanish conquistador hangs above the bed. It's painted on red felt, and black feathers sprawl like spiders from the conqueror's wide-brimmed hat. He has a black beard and mustache and his hand is resting on his sword. On his finger there is a ring with a red stone, which resembles a ring my father used to have.

"¿Se puede?" my father calls out from the storage room.

"Ey," I say.

He comes in and stands in front of the curtain, watching us layer up.

"Make sure you shake out the blankets before going to bed," he says. "Puede que ahí anden unos alacranes." He scans the ceiling above, says that sometimes they fall off the wooden beams.

"There might be scorpions in the bed," I say to Martin, hoisting my backpack off it.

"Are you serious?" He jumps off the bed, shakes his layers out.

"So, how long are you staying?" My father asks.

"We're not sure," I say, glancing over at Martin, who is busy throwing his clothes back into his backpack. "We might leave tomorrow."

"¿Tan rápido?" he says. "So, if we're going to go out to the ranch, we would have to go tomorrow morning."

"Está bien," I say. Earlier, he had told us about his ranch that sat at the top of the distant mountain range behind his house. It has two waterfalls, a freshwater spring, and three naturally formed slate pools; it's where he keeps his cattle and the rest of his horses. He had said that if we wanted to go, we could make a day of it, pack a lunch, ride out on horses, and if Martin and I wanted to, we could take a dip in one of the pools. It sounded like an adventure, and Martin and I had decided we should go.

"But the thing is, we need to leave here by four or five in the morning. That way we can make it out there by about seven or eight, spend a bit of time, and hopefully be back here before the sun really starts biting," he says, glancing back at me, at my backpack, at Martin who is now standing next to me holding his backpack. "I also need to go to San Martín and see about borrowing a horse. I only have two here in the stable. The others are all up at the ranch," he says, crossing the room and unlocking the blue metal doors that lead out into the courtyard. "So the soonest we could go would be the day after tomorrow," he says. But not to worry, because tomorrow, after he gets the borrowed horse squared away, he can take us to some hot springs that are nearby. We can have a hot bath, get to bed early, and set out to his ranch first thing the following morning. He pulls the door open and a blast of cold air fills the room, sends the braided garlic wreath that hangs above it swaying. "Whatever you guys decide is fine, just let me know," he says, stepping out into the courtyard.

"So if we want to go out to the ranch, we might have to stay for two days," I tell Martin.

"Whatever you want to do is fine with me," he says. "Though, if we're going to stay an extra day, I need to get into town, call my parents, buy some sunblock."

"Here," my father says, coming back in with two white plastic chairs. "If you keep your things on these, they should be fine." He sets the chairs down in the middle of the room.

Martin and I place our backpacks on the chairs, and I explain to my father that if we're going to stay an extra day, then we need to go into town in the morning and run a few errands.

"You guys can take my truck," he says. "We can get up early, have some breakfast, and while you go run your errands, I'll ride over to San Martín and see about borrowing a horse."

The morning sunlight shines in through the blue metal bars of my father's bedroom window. The wool blanket on his bed pricks me through my linen skirt. I shift my weight and springs creak beneath me. Next to his bed there are a blue vinyl car seat and a small end table that is littered with toiletries—a blue plastic razor, a toothbrush, toothpaste, scissors, a bottle of brilliantine, a sardine tin filled with black hair dye, and a black plastic comb next to it. The sound of plates and silverware hitting against the slate sink filters in from the courtyard. After breakfast, Martin volunteered to wash the dishes, saying that my pops and I had a lot of catching-up to do. On the wall above my father's bed, a rifle hangs from a leather strap, which is slung over a rusty nail. A forest-green trunk sits in the far corner, and resting on top of it are his cowboy hats, each one inside a plastic cover.

A framed black-and-white photo of my father hangs above the dresser. In the photo he looks roughly twenty-seven and he's wearing a large sombrero, a white button-down shirt, tapered black pants, and a holster with a gun slung from them. He's mounted on a black horse that has a white mark on its forehead and one white foot. The photo looks like a throwback to a different era. There's a part of me that wants to ask him if I can have it, but I decide against it. Assuming that if it's the only photo of himself that he has on display, he must be quite proud of it. Next to his photo, there's one of my brother. He's standing outside in the corral next to his horse. The photo was probably taken soon after he arrived because in it he's wearing the same outfit he wore when he left Chicago: a light-blue Windbreaker, jeans, and his white leather Nike sneakers—how I wish I had hugged him goodbye.

On the same wall there is an oil painting—a family portrait of sorts. My father's face is on the upper-right-hand corner and the faces of Yesenia, Jorge, and Sonia radiate around his—immortalized in whatever top they wore to school on picture day the year before he left. I recognize the blue top Yesenia is wearing. It's actually a dress that, at one point, had belonged to me. The clatter of silverware comes from the courtyard again and I get the urge to march out there and tell Martin we are leaving—fuck the hot springs, his ranch, and his dishes—let him wash his damn dirty dishes. The green metal door that leads into the kitchen swings open and my father comes in carrying two glasses filled with water. He hands me one and sits on the vinyl car seat.

"Where did you have that painting made?" I ask, motioning toward his family portrait.

"In town," he says, turning to look at it. "There's an artist, several artists actually, and if you take them separate photos they can put them all together in a portrait for you." He glances at me. "Why? Did you want to have one made?"

"No," I say. "I was just curious."

He studies the portrait for a while.

"Yesenia really changed a lot, huh?" he says. "The first time she came down here, I didn't even recognize her." He takes a sip of water. "She smokes a lot of mota, doesn't she?"

"I don't know," I say, though Sonia told me that he had called her once, saying that he was concerned about Yesenia. That someone needed to keep an eye on her, because she had just been in town and had been seen hanging around the carnival smoking joints with the local riffraff. "La Ovejita Perdida," he had re-nicknamed her, and

I couldn't help but wonder if he realized that her being a little lost sheep might have something to do with his having left.

"And Pascuala?" he asks. "How's she doing?"

"She's fine," I say, though I really want to say *None of your business how she's doing*, as I feel he has no right to even breathe her name. "She's in Chicago."

"I heard she has a new house."

"Yeah, Salvador built it for her."

"Salvador makes good money, huh?"

"I guess. Every house he builds sells for about a million dollars," I say, though I'm sure he already knows this. Salvador has his own construction company, and in a few years he'll be building homes for the Chicago Bears, will be living next door to the punter.

"A million dollars," he says, choking on his water. "That's a good deal of money," he says, and I can't help but think how ironic that while he is down here digging for gold, on the other side of the border, most of his kids have made their own small fortunes.

A cloud of dust comes barreling through the open window as a car idles by. He stretches his neck up, looking over my head and watching the car pass as if from behind a barricade. The skin on his neck is looser and the scar where Joaquín lodged the knife under his chin is plainly visible.

"Is that the same rifle you brought down from Chicago?" I ask him.

"No, that was my father's rifle," he says, studying the rifle on the wall. "I sold the one I brought down with me; I sold most of those guns actually." He scans the floor as if contemplating something. "No, when I got here and unloaded the truck, my father took one look at everything I brought and told me I was crazy for having taken that risk."

"Whatever happened to the Puerto Rican guy you drove down here with?"

"Who knows," he says. "He spent a good amount of time down here, a few months, going to the rodeos and hanging out in San Martín and Santana. Then someone told him about the cargo and one day he showed up here." He motions to the blue metal door that leads to the courtyard. "He stood right there, asking me if it was true." He stares at the door for a long time, as if the Puerto Rican were standing there now, demanding answers. "We had a good laugh over it," he says, slapping his thigh and looking back at me. "So, how long have you lived in Washington?"

"It's not Washington," I say. "It's New York." We've already been through this, but he's confused. It's only been four months since September 11, and he keeps thinking the towers were in the nation's capital, in Washington, D.C. "I've been there for about seven months," I say.

"Aren't you scared of the terrorists?" he asks. "Maybe you should go back to Chicago." Go back to Chicago? Was he not the same man who had taught me to stare down the barrel of a loaded gun? The same man who had warned me about never running away from a fight? Another car drives by and again he stretches his neck up and watches it pass. "Did you hear about how I was ambushed?" he asks.

"Ey," I say.

"People keep telling me I should leave this place, that I've created too many enemies, but I tell them I'm not going anywhere," he says. "If anyone has a problem with me, they know where to come find me. As long as they're straight, you know, because those culeros that ambushed me went behind my back." He tells me how he had seen the blue car pulled over on the side of the road, near the slaughterhouse, and had thought nothing of it until he had seen them running back toward it. "Those cowards didn't even have the guts to approach my truck and make sure I was dead."

"Were you wearing your bulletproof vest?" I ask, thinking that he must have been. How else was it possible that he had walked away from two machine guns?

"No, I wasn't," he says, and though I don't believe him, years from now, Rosario will confirm that he wasn't. He sets his cup down on the limestone floor. "One of the bullets hit me right here." He slaps his right biceps. "That's why I don't have a lot of strength in this arm." He flexes his hand. "Two other bullets scratched my head." He tilts his head down so I can see his hairline, and there are two scars that overlap, two lines crisscrossing over each other. "Me dejaron la cruz pintada," he says, and he's right. The scar on his forehead looks like the sign of the cross.

"Did you ever find out who did it?"

"Sí, cómo no." He picks his glass up off the floor and takes a swig. "It was these two guys that someone hired, I'm not sure who, but I've got my ideas." He cocks his head and looks toward the kitchen door.

"Not that long ago, those two guys turned up dead, and the only reason why I know that is because the feds came by here, questioning me, asking where I was on such and such night. I had been out drinking with Máximo and Rogelio on that night, and so I had an alibi."

I remember his cousins Máximo and Rogelio. They had lived in Chicago for several years before returning to Mexico. Sometimes my father would hang out with them on the weekends, and once they had been drinking at Máximo's house when Máximo got it in his head that my father was flirting with his wife. They exchanged a few words, and then Máximo pulled out his gun, aimed it at my father's face from across the table, and fired a single blast. The bullet singed my father's beard before vanishing into the wall behind him. He didn't have his own gun on him, and he had pushed away from the table, grabbed his cowboy hat, and gone out the door, Máximo already apologizing profusely as he went. Then it seemed all their relatives were calling my father from Mexico and apologizing for Máximo. Even my grandfather called several times, telling my father it was a dumb and drunken thing Máximo had done, and to let it be because God forbid this spark a family feud, and then where would we all end up?

"They went and checked with Máximo, and he confirmed that we had been together on that night," he says. Each time something happens or someone turns up dead, he's sure to hear of it, because the feds always come pay him a visit. That's how he had heard about the brother of the woman he used to live with turning up dead. The brother had come down from Colorado to visit some relatives, and then they had found his body along a dirt road just outside of town. Again the feds were knocking on his door. "I told them I had nothing to do with it, but they didn't seem to believe me. They went and checked my alibi and everything, and finally left me alone." He inspects the glass in his hand. "Although if I had had the chance to get my hands on that son of a bitch, I would have strangled him myself." He knows for a fact that it was he who ratted him out, blew his cover, and had him arrested when he was living in Denver.

"How was he killed?" I ask, though I had already heard about how the man had been dragged for miles and then been run over several times so that the feds had recovered nothing but human body parts, which were strewn all along the dirt road.

"He had been run over by a car or truck," he says, taking a sip of water.

"Pobre," I say.

"Pobre pendejo," he mumbles under his breath. We hear the sound of another car approaching, and again he stretches his neck up.

"Did they ever find out who killed him?" I ask.

"Nope." He watches the car go by. "And they probably never will."

There is something about the restraint in his voice that makes me think he might not be entirely innocent.

"Where do these go?" Martin asks. He's standing in the doorway, holding the black plastic bin with the wet dishes.

We go into the kitchen and my father gives us the keys to his truck, says he's going to go saddle his horse. Once we've dried and put the dishes away, Martin and I head into town.

"Roll down your window," Martin says the minute we turn onto the road where my father was ambushed. "I want everyone to see who's driving this truck."

I roll down the tinted window, and soon we're flying around the curve and parking on the outskirts of town. We've decided that the less time we spend in his truck the better.

"You guys awake?" he calls out from the other side of the pink curtain, the lights in the storage room and the kitchen already on.

"Yeah," I say, though Martin is snoring next to me under the pile of wool blankets.

"Time to get up," he says, and I can hear him shuffling across the room in the dark before he hits the light switch.

"What time is it?" I ask, squinting in the glare.

"Just after four," he says. He's already dressed and wearing a green down vest and a camouflage winter cap with earflaps. "If we want to make it out there and back in time for you guys to catch that two p.m. bus, then we should be heading out in about a half hour or so. How'd you sleep?"

"Good," I say, sitting up and pulling my wool cap down over my ears, my breath visible in front of me.

"I left two saddlebags on the kitchen table for you guys to pack your lunch," he says, unlatching the door and pulling it open. A gust of frigid air fills the room. "You should make yourselves a café and eat something before we go, because it's a bit of a journey."

"Está bien," I say.

"I'm going to go saddle the horses," he says, stepping outside before turning and coming back in. "Make sure you don't close your eyes or you might end up falling asleep." He heads out, and I nudge Martin.

In the kitchen, Martin and I huddle around the stove, warming our hands and waiting for the water to boil. We make Nescafé instant coffee, and pack the groceries we picked up the day before—bread, an avocado, sliced ham, and a can of picked jalapeños, along with the saltshaker, a knife, a water bottle, and a few napkins.

"¿Listos?" My father is standing in the kitchen's doorway.

We polish off our coffee, grab the saddlebags, and follow him outside. It's still dark out. The dogs are in the courtyard, tongues dangling, tails wagging, and the two horses are saddled and tied to a mesquite on the other side of the dirt road. An extra saddle sits on the ground next to them. Once Martin and I are on the horses, my father hoists the extra saddle off the ground and leads the way on foot. The horses follow him and the dogs trail close behind. The moonlight creates menacing shadows as we make our way along the dirt road. Bushes look like animals lurking and cracks in the ground have the appearance of giant black snakes slithering along the terrain. We ride toward the distant mountain range, which looks like a sleeping giant under the canopy of stars. It seems impossible that the moonlit shadow moving in front of me is my father—alive and in the flesh.

"That's San Martín," he says, pointing to a few scattered lights along a nearby ridge. Once we get closer to San Martín, the scent of wood burning fills the air and cocks can be heard singing out. The horses' hooves click and clack on the narrow cobblestone paths that wind up and around adobe homes, which are tucked away behind stacked-stone corrals. We reach a whitewashed adobe house at the top of the ridge. "Wait here," my father says and disappears behind the house.

"How you holding up?" Martin asks.

"Fine," I say. Behind him, the first sliver of daylight is running along the horizon like a golden thread. "You?"

"Good," he says, smiling wide. "This is kind of amazing, huh?"

"Yeah," I say. I know that if it weren't for him, I probably wouldn't be here. We've talked about him moving to New York. I have even started looking for an apartment for us.

"A ver." My father comes around the corral with the third horse already saddled up and ready to go. "Tell Marsimino to switch to this horse," he says. "He's a lot tamer than mine."

They switch horses and we continue toward the distant mountain range at a much faster pace, and soon we are cutting through an open field, when a bird that looks like a chicken with long stick-legs goes running by, zigzagging in front of us before disappearing into the field.

"What the hell was that?" Martin calls out from behind me. His horse is clearly the runt of the three, already falling behind.

I ask my father what that bird thing was.

"Un correcaminos," he says.

A roadrunner. They really exist? All these years, I thought road-runners were imaginary, something found only in cartoons—like mermaids and unicorns.

"That was a roadrunner!" I yell back to Martin.

"A roadrunner? They really exist?" He looks in the direction where the bird went. "What are we going to see next, a pink panther?"

We both laugh and I try explaining the pink panther joke to my father, asking if he remembers those Saturday morning cartoons, the one with the roadrunner that was always being chased by a coyote and the one with the pink panther. He shrugs and says we might run into a wolf or some wild boar. Especially once we get farther up the mountain.

"There are wolves out there?" I say.

"There's a little of everything out there, even lions."

"Really? Lions?" I say, thinking it's probably too late to turn around. "There are lions out there," I yell to Martin.

"Holy shit, are you serious?"

I nod.

"And what are we supposed to do if we see one?"

"What do we do if we see a lion?" I ask my father.

"They're more like large mountain cats, rather than lions," he says, and explains how we probably won't see one, as they're not so common in these parts anymore. Though when he was a kid, they were everywhere. "If we run into anything, just remember to stay calm," he says. "If a wild animal senses fear, it's more likely to attack."

"What's he saying?" Martin calls out from behind me.

"He says that if we run into a wild animal, to just stay calm," I say.

Soon we are riding along a ravine, following a river, and the murmur of rushing water fills the space around us.

"You see those houses over there?" my father says, pointing to a ridge on the other side of the river where adobe homes are tucked among the trees and boulders. "That's Santana," he says. "That's where Pascuala is from."

I had always known my mother was from a place called Santana but had imagined it was a small town, not a handful of homes scattered along a hillside. We make our way around a steep incline, where the trail is so narrow that if my horse were to misstep a single stride to the right, we'd plunge into the valley below. There's no guardrail, no safety net—nothing.

"How often do you ride out to the ranch?" I ask my father once we've cleared the incline.

"About two or three times a week," he says. "I usually set out around four, while it's still dark, and I take my time riding out, meditating as I go." He takes the corner of his shirt and wipes dust from his eyes. "I pray and ask Diosito to look after each one of my kids. I go down the list from youngest to eldest." He counts on his fingers. "La Vicki, Jorge, usted, Sonita, Chela, Chavo y Nena," he says and tells me how, one by one, he asks God to protect each one of us, to never let us want for anything. I'm shocked to hear him say that he prays, can't help but wonder what god it is that he prays to. "It's peaceful out here, isn't it?" he says, shooting me a smile.

"Ey," I say. The sun breaks the horizon like a giant eye opening and sending its long golden lashes across the terrain, illuminating everything. It feels like the mountain itself is awakening.

It's just before 8:00 a.m. when we reach the entrance to the ranch, and Martin and I have already shed a few layers and have slathered

sunblock on our arms and faces. I've replaced my wool cap with a
straw hat, and he's replaced his with a baseball cap. My father un-
latches the long metal gate at the entrance. It yawns on the hinges as
it swings open. We follow him down an incline that leads to a shallow creek, which runs over a wide patch of gray slate. There are two
pools carved into the rock, and he tells me that my mother used to
wash our clothes in one and we used to bathe in the other. We cross
the creek and ride up the hill on the other side, where two adobe
shacks with tin roofs sit inside a stacked-stone corral.

"This is where we used to stay during the rainy season," my father
says. "This is where Chemel was born." He glances over at me. "That's
his saddle you're on." My father had bought Chemel his first saddle
and a horse when Chemel was five years old, and ever since then,
they had gone everywhere together.

A few cows have started poking their heads out from behind
boulders and nopales. Some make their way toward the corral where
the troughs are, but they stop when they see us, their heads turning
from side to side as if contemplating what to do next.

"They're hesitating because they don't recognize you," my father
says. "Why don't you two ride up along the river and round up whatever cows are in the shade near the water," he says, telling us to just
follow the dogs, as they know what to do. He's going to put some salt
in the troughs because now that we're here, the cows will be expecting it, will come looking for it, and it's not nice to confuse them.
There's a small adobe shack at the top of the ridge, and he'll meet us
up there.

"What if the cows attack us?" I ask.

"They won't," he says. "Cows are very peaceful animals."

"And the bull?"

"As long as you stay on the horse, you'll be fine," he says.

Martin and I follow the dogs along the ravine, where clusters of
cows are sitting in the shade and lazily swatting flies off their rumps
with their tails. They eye us as if trying to decide whether to take us
seriously or not. The dogs run up, barking at them, and the cows push
their cumbersome weight off the ground. They come to stand and
slowly start making their way toward the troughs.

When we reach the adobe shack at the top of the hill, my father is already there, his horse standing next to a tree that is split in half and tinged with black soot. He's holding a pair of binoculars to his eyes and scanning the canyon below.

"Take a look down there and tell me if you see anything moving around," he says, handing me the binoculars, and that's when I see the gun, black and heavy in his other hand. I have not been in such proximity to a gun since he lived with us, and the very sight of it makes me flinch. I can practically hear my mother's voice: "Why are you going to go see that viejo?" she had said when I told her about the trip Martín and I were planning. "What if he does something to you, or to Martín?"

I scan the canyon below as fast as I can, keeping one eye on his gun.

"Nope," I say. "Nothing."

"I thought I saw something down there." He slides his gun into the back of his belt and I'm glad to see it gone. I hand the binoculars back to him. "On a clear day, you can see all the way to Jalisco with these," he says. Jalisco is the next state over, where Mary lives with her husband and kids.

"What happened to that tree?" I ask.

"It was hit by lightning," he says, turning to look at the tree, and explaining that Salvador, his brother, had just ridden up here when a storm broke out. He got off his horse, tied it to the tree, went into the shack, and he probably hadn't even cleared the doorway when lightning struck the tree and killed his horse. "Had it hit a few seconds sooner, it probably would have killed Salvador too," he says.

"How was he killed?" I ask, because I knew that his brother Salvador had been killed when he was twenty-two years old, that it had happened right around the time my brother Salvador was born, hence the name.

"Him and another guy liked the same muchacha," he says as he starts making his way back down the incline and we follow. "So they already had it out for each other, and then one day they got into it, and ever since that day, Salvador started saying that the next time he ran into that fulano de tal, they were going to kill each other. Then about a month later, they were both at a rodeo up in Las Ajuntas, and sure enough, the minute their eyes locked, they pulled out their guns and shot each other."

"And they both died?" I ask.

"Ey," he says. My mother once told me that after Salvador was killed, my father often woke in the middle of the night, pushed the blankets aside, and stumbled out into the courtyard where he wailed out loud until dawn.

When we reach the corral with the two houses and the salt troughs, a sea of horns is visible above the stacked stones.

"There are a lot of cows missing," he says after doing a head count. After his father died, his younger sister and her husband had moved all the cattle to their ranch, and when he was released from prison, he had gone over to their place one day and said he was there to pick up his father's cattle. His sister wasn't there, and her husband had tried to put up a fight, but had thought better of it.

"How did you know which cows were your father's?" I ask.

"They were branded with his fierro," he says. "There were only about twenty or twenty-five left, they had already sold most of them off. I brought them back here and bought a nice bull, and little by little I started replenishing the herd." He speculates that he now has about a hundred cows, and I can't help but think that he is living up to his nickname—El Cien Vacas, a nickname he's practically had his whole life. Though I'm not certain of how he ended up with such an odd nickname. "When I first came back here, everyone thought that it was only a matter of time before I drove everything into the ground, but God has helped me to thrive. Everything I do, all of this, it's all for you guys, for my kids," he says, glancing over at me, and I sort of feel sorry for him, because deep down he must know that we don't need any of this. He points out the different cows he's given to each one of my sisters, along with whatever offspring they've had, and then he points to a calico-colored cow with long, gray horns and says that one is for me.

"Thanks," I say, and can't help but wonder what he would do if I decided to take my cow back to Brooklyn with me.

Martin and I find a spot under the shade of a tree and pull the food from the leather satchels, make three torta sandwiches, and offer the first one to my father. We chew in silence, and it's so quiet that when a hawk flies by overhead we can hear the steady beat of its wings flapping.

"If you guys want to make the two p.m. bus, we should be heading back soon," my father says when he finishes his sandwich.

"What time is it now?" I ask.

"It's probably around nine-thirty," he says, glancing up as if measuring the distance between the sun and the horizon. "If we leave here by ten, we should be getting back to La Peña around one."

We clean up and he takes us on a hike along the creek, says he wants to show us the waterfall and the freshwater spring. The waterfall is nothing but a sheet of water streaming down the gray slate and trickling into a small pool below.

"You should come back in the summer, during the rainy season," he says, kneeling next to the pool. "That's when everything is green and beautiful and the waterfall is full." He scoops some water into his cupped hands and drinks it.

"You drink that water?" I say. "Isn't that dangerous?"

"Dangerous?" he says, leaning back on his heels and looking up at me, at the water bottle in my hand. "This water is probably cleaner than the water in that bottle," he says. "This is the same water you used to drink when you were a kid." The sunlight is reflecting off the surface of the pool and sending ripples of light shimmering across his face. "You guys should try it," he says.

"You want to try the water?" I ask Martin.

"No, thanks," he says.

I hand him the water bottle, kneel down, and reach into the pool. The water feels delicious—ice-cold. I scoop some into my cupped hands, lower my head, and lick.

"It's good," I say, and again my father is eyeing me as if he were trying to recognize me.

The ride back is much faster and hotter, and by the time we get home it's nearly 1:00 p.m. My father unsaddles the horses, and while he takes them back to the corral for watering, we carry the saddles into the storage room. Ropes, harnesses, and horseshoes hang from nails on the cinder-block walls. A large bag of dog food sits on the limestone floor next to a sack filled with corn kernels and one filled with pinto beans. There are six steel trunks stacked on top of each other and leaning against the wall. A small wooden saddle sits on the floor in front of the trunks and two wooden cheese presses sit next to the saddle. It takes all our energy to hoist the horse saddles onto the cheese presses, like my father told us to do.

"I'm beat," Martin says, collapsing onto the bed.

"Me too," I say, crashing next to him. We stare at the wooden beams above; the tin roof snaps under the heat of the afternoon sun. If a scorpion were to fall from the rafters now, we probably wouldn't even have the energy to try to dodge it.

"You know what would be great right now?" Martin says. "An ice-cold beer."

"I'm starving," I say.

"Me too," he says, inhaling and letting out a long exhale. "If I closed my eyes, I'd fall asleep," he says.

"I can't feel my legs," I say.

The dogs are in the courtyard drinking water from the rubber tire. The water was frozen over when we left this morning—but is completely thawed out now. I hear the sound of his spurs scraping across the courtyard.

"Listos?" He is standing in the doorway and holding a coiled rope. "If you guys want to make that two p.m. bus, we've got to get going."

"There's no way in hell I'm getting on a bus," Martin tells me.

"Is there a place that sells cold beer around here?" I ask my father.

"Only in town," he says, inspecting the rope in his hand. "If you guys want to wait and catch the bus tomorrow morning, we can drive into town and grab a bite. There's a rotisserie that sells whole roasted chickens, they're delicious, really nice and juicy. We can get one to go, pick up a six-pack, and eat back here. But it's really up to you guys. Whatever you want to do is fine with me." He scans the wall behind our heads, pretending not to notice that we're spent, and it dawns on me that he knew it all along—knew there was no way we were going to be on that bus.

We want to make the 10:00 a.m. bus, so we get up early the next day and pack our bags. Martin and I are in the kitchen boiling water for Nescafé when my father comes in carrying four brown eggs and places them in the basket on the table with the rest of the eggs. When we lived in the Chicago suburbs, he had found a farm that would sell him eggs. He always claimed that eggs from a farm were better than the store-bought ones, though back then, I was too young to care or understand what the difference was.

"Can I take that small wooden saddle that's in the storage room?" I ask.

"I still use that one sometimes," he says. "But if you want, after you guys eat breakfast, we can go down to the other house. There are two wooden saddles out there that I don't use anymore."

"What other house?" I say.

"The one we used to live in before we left for the other side," he says.

After breakfast, we follow him down the slight hill on the other side of the dirt road. The scent of wood burning fills the air, and there is something so familiar about that scent, though I can't place it.

"What's that smell?" I ask my father. "The wood burning, what type of wood is that?"

"Encino. It's the same type of wood Pascuala used to cook with when we lived here," he says.

"She cooked with firewood? Where?"

"In the kitchen, in the wood-burning oven," he says, and it dawns on me why, when I was sitting in front of a fire in the south of Spain, the scent of the wood burning had conjured my mother so vividly that the space around me became infused with her presence. I waited for the feeling to pass, but it lingered like a prolonged déjà vu. Like a faded memory insisting I remember it.

"Is that your daughter, Jose?" His neighbor calls out when we are crossing in front of her courtyard. She's an elderly woman wearing a wide-brimmed straw hat, an apron, a long skirt, and dark wool socks pulled up to her knees. Smoke is billowing from the chimney behind her and her Chihuahua is barking next to her.

"Ey," my father says.

"A ver," she says, drying her hands on her apron and making her way to the gate. "Which one is she?" she asks, squinting at me. Deep grooves are carved into her sunburned face.

"Maria de Jesus," my father says.

"Maria de Jesus," she says, smiling at me. She has no teeth, only two yellow ones on the bottom that make her look like she has an overbite. "So you're one of the younger ones," she says, glancing over at Martin. "Is this your husband?"

"No," I say. "He's my boyfriend."

"How long are you staying?" she asks.

"We're leaving today," I say.

"So soon?" she says. "Didn't you just arrive a few days ago?"

"Ey," I say.

"That's too bad, pero bueno, at least you came to see your father," she says. "I've known your father since he was a boy, no, lies, I've known him since before he was even born. His parents used to live in that house." She points to the small adobe house next door to hers. "I remember when his mother was pregnant with him. He used to kick her so hard that she would say he must have the devil in him." She looks back at my father. "Right, Jose, that's what your mother used to say?"

"Ey," he says. His mother was a petite dark-skinned woman who had come to visit us in the Chicago suburbs when I was about six years old. She insisted that I sleep with her, which always frightened me because my mother had told us that she was a bruja—had been practicing Santería her whole life. A few times she had fallen off the bed in the middle of the night, and then she would wake the whole house screaming for my father, saying that the brujas had come and carried her off the bed.

"That's the house where your father was born, and you probably were too, right, Jose? Wasn't this muchacha one of the ones who was born in that house?"

"Ey, that's where her umbilical cord is buried," he says, looking toward the house, which has a small front yard that has been overtaken by tall weeds and is surrounded by a stacked-stone corral. He excuses himself, saying that we'd best be going or we might miss our bus.

We make our way to the gate and he untwines the rusty metal hanger that holds the wooden gate to a post. We follow him through the tall weeds, and he pulls out a skeleton key and turns it in the keyhole to a heavy green wooden door, and gives it a slight push. The door swings open, sending a layer of dust rising from the limestone floor before hitting against the adobe wall. Inside the air is cooler and thick strands of dust-covered spider webs hang from the wooden beams above. Portraits of saints and outdated calendars hang from the whitewashed adobe walls. A metal bed frame is pushed up against the far wall. There's no mattress, only the exposed rusty springs.

Wooden crates filled with old horse harnesses, saddlebags, and farming tools are piled up in the corner. Next to the crates are two identical wooden saddles.

"Who slept in this room?" I ask.

"We all did," he says. "Pascuala and I slept there." He points to the metal frame. "And over here," he says, motioning toward the crates, "there were two beds. Chavo and Chemel slept in one, and all you girls shared the other. This is the room where you were born," he says.

I stare at the frame and can't help but think that I may have been born on that very bed. I feel as though I've traveled not back to Mexico, but back in time. Like I've opened a time capsule and have stepped into a place where time has stood still for centuries. Years from now, my mother will tell me that on the morning I was born, my father had just returned from taking the cattle to the river and she was already in labor. He went down the road to get the midwife, was gone a mere fifteen minutes, and by the time they returned, it was already too late. Her water had broken and I had come out riding on the tail end of that wave. Hard to believe this dark and dusty room is where I drew my first breath.

"This is the room where I was born," I tell Martin, who is standing behind me, observing the portraits on the walls.

"Amazing," he says, taking the room in. "Man, you are so lucky that your parents left this place when they did." He puts his arm around me. "Can you imagine if you had been raised here?"

He's right. By simply having crossed the border, I had leaped ahead generations.

When we arrive at the depot, people are already boarding. We pull our backpacks out from the back of my father's truck and throw them under the bus next to plastic crates tied with rope, boxes bound with twine, and vinyl bags sealed shut with duct tape. I sling the blue duffel bag that has the wooden saddle in it over my shoulder and we get in line.

"You should put that with the luggage so you don't have to carry it the whole way," my father says.

"That's okay," I say. "I don't want it to break."

A man has parked his fruit cart in front of the depot; cups filled with sliced coconut, mango, papaya, and watermelon line the front of his cart. He squeezes a fresh lime onto one, sprinkles it with chili powder, and hands it to a woman. They both seem oblivious to the flies and bees swarming around them.

"Do you want a fruit cup for the ride?" my father asks.

"No, thank you," I say, as the line moves forward. I'm aware of how everyone is stealing glances at Martin.

"Um, cómo se dice, 'it was nice meeting you'?" Martin asks.

"Gusto en conocerlo," I say.

Martin turns to face my father and repeats this line. They shake hands, my father gives him a nod, and Martin boards the bus.

"Ándele pues, mija," my father says as the last few passengers squeeze past us and onto the bus. "You know that whenever you want to come back, my home is your home." He suggests I take his address and phone number. I grab a notebook and a pen out of my straw bag and jot down the address for La Peña. It's the same address where I used to send my brother's letters. The same address where Sonia had sent my father the letter I never meant to send—years from now, Alma will tell me that when they had first moved in with him, after having one too many drinks, sometimes he would start crying and saying that his own daughter had sent him a letter saying she wished he was dead.

"I'll write to you," I say, though I know I won't.

"I'll be waiting for your letter." A faint smile flashes across his face. His eyes glaze over, his chin starts quivering, and he presses his lips tight, forcing the tears to recede. "We should try and keep in touch while we still can," he says, "while we're still alive."

We give each other a quick one-handed hug, and our faces brush past one another. His cheek is at once warm and smooth, yet rough with stubble. I give him a nod and board the bus, take the seat next to Martin, place the duffel bag on my lap, and I'm already having a hard time drawing an easy breath. His sudden display of emotion caught me off guard. I thought we would shake hands, go our separate ways, and that would be the end of it. But the sight of his chin quivering shattered something inside of me.

The bus pulls out of the depot and I lean over Martin to look out the window. My father is still standing in the gravel lot, holding a red handkerchief. We catch each other's eye, and I wave at him. He waves back. The bus pulls away and he's left standing in a cloud of dust. I start fumbling around in my straw bag for my sunglasses and put them on, because no matter how hard I try, I can't force my tears to recede.

Martin hands me a wad of toilet paper, takes my hand, and the minute we clear the last speed bump on the edge of town, the bus gets a flat tire.

17 ◆ THE MUSEUM

FIVE YEARS LATER, I return to visit him. I fly to Chicago, and from there I drive down to Valparaíso with Roselia and my mother. By then, my mother is spending most of her time in Valparaíso with my grandmother. We stop off in Real de Catorce on the way, an old silver mining town that Martin and I had talked about visiting, though we had never gotten around to it. After I'd been in New York for a year, I had found us a one-bedroom apartment, and for yet another year I had waited for him. But something always seemed to come up with his band—they were recording another album or doing one more tour. I finally called him and told him I had booked a flight to Chicago for the weekend and needed to speak with him.

"About what?" he asked.

"It's nothing," I said. "Really, I just need to speak with you in person. That's all." I could have said, "It's been two fucking years." I could have said, "My feelings have changed." I could have said any number of things, but back then I was unable to articulate something I could barely admit to myself.

The next day, while I was gathering my things at work and getting ready to go home, he came through the glass doors of the showroom and walked right up to my desk.

"Don't do this," he said before I had a chance to say anything. But it was already done. Two years was not such a long time, though it was long enough.

That same summer I received a phone call from one of Abigail's friends. After spending a year in New York, Abigail had returned to Maine to find that the gallery owner still hadn't finalized his divorce. He was having second thoughts, had started pushing her away. The last time I had talked to Abigail, she had been sitting on the edge of her bed, and though she could see the sun was shining, she could not muster the energy to go outside.

"I feel numb, I feel numb, I just feel so numb," she kept saying, aware of how wrong it was: that her sister had just had a baby, that she was now an aunt, and that she didn't care—she didn't feel anything at all.

I had suggested she consider going off the meds. That perhaps they were impeding her ability to feel. Besides, she wasn't so much depressed as she was heartbroken, and if that coward was having second thoughts, so be it. Eventually, she'd find someone who would truly appreciate her. But she didn't want anyone else, she only wanted the man she had been building her life around for the past two years. She called me a few days later and was in better spirits, said she had gone to see a psychiatrist who had lowered her dosage. Then, about two weeks after that, I got the call.

"Oh, Maria, I don't know how to say this," her friend said. "But Abigail is dead."

Dead. There was that awful word from which there was no return—dead. It was her mother who had found her. Abigail was facedown on her living room floor, her arms folded above her head as if she had become overwhelmed with fatigue and had decided to lie down for a nap, right there on the cool floorboards. Her face and body were bruised, and a single thread of blood had escaped from her nose. An autopsy revealed that she had been seizing for hours before suffering a brain aneurysm.

Years later, her mother would tell me that there was a history of seizures in her family, from her husband's side. And the meds Abigail was on were known to cause seizures, especially during that critical window of increasing or decreasing doses, though perhaps Abigail had been unaware of this family history, given her fractured relationship with her father. He had left with his lover when Abigail was still in high school, and though she would often call and make plans with him—to go see a movie or go out for dinner—time and time again he had blown her off, had left her waiting. Her fractured relationship with her father was something I'd been unaware of, as neither of us ever talked about our fathers.

Losing Abigail not only forced me to question what I was doing with my life, it also made me rethink my relationship with my own father. For years, he had been my best-kept secret, and though I never talked about him or the past, my writing had started gravitating toward him. Though I was working full-time, I had continued taking acting and writing classes in the evenings. Acting may have been the craft through which I had accessed my emotions, but writing was the tool through which I had begun to reckon with the source of those emotions.

After writing a short story about how my father had shot the neighbor, the instructor suggested I apply to an MFA program. I applied to Iowa, Hunter, and Columbia. By then I was working as an account executive at Juicy Couture and had a high salary, a clothing allowance, a 401K, health insurance, an assistant, and my own office on the sixteenth floor of the Empire State Building. I was accepted to all three programs, resigned from my post, and practically hightailed it back to Mexico.

It's early May when we arrive in Valparaíso, and after Roselia leaves, I spend two weeks in town with my mother and Tito. On the day before I leave for La Peña, we go visit a small museum in town. A room in the back of the museum has the remains of a prehistoric mammal. They sit inside a glass case, along with a card that explains how an elderly man from a nearby ranch had uncovered the bones while digging near the river and donated them to the museum.

Tito and I stroll through the main room, where there is an array of antiques—a phonograph, a typewriter, men's shaving gadgets, and reading glasses. A cobalt-blue wooden trunk sits near the doorway, and on top of it are several irons, ranging from three to eight pounds. On the far wall are several framed photographs with a sign written above them that reads HACIENDAS DE VALPARAÍSO.

"That is the entrance to La Peña," Tito says, leaning in for a closer look at one of the frames. It's a black-and-white photo of the pillars that stand at the entrance to La Peña. "La Paña. That's what you used to call it because you couldn't pronounce it," she says, adjusting her headscarf. "You probably don't remember, but after your parents left, not a day went by without you asking about them. Every single day you asked me to take you back to La Peña, and every day I explained to you that your parents were no longer there, but I don't know, I guess you were just too young to understand. The others were older, they understood what was happening, but not you, and it got to the point where you would ask anyone who came by the house if they had seen your mami, papi, and Jorgito. If we went to the mercado, la plaza, la panadería—you were asking people if they had seen them. They gave you a dulce de leche, a chicle, anything to get your mind off them, because everyone knew that your parents had gone to the other side.

"The day came when they had been gone for three months and still, first thing in the morning, you were asking me to take you to La Peña, and, well, what was I to do? I took you back there, to that house where you were born, so you could see for yourself, and once you saw that they weren't there, never again did you ask about them—nunca. After that day, you stopped talking altogether. You were so smart, you already knew how to say everything, but for about two weeks you didn't utter a single word. Not to me, or anyone," she says, still examining the photo, and I'm aware of a vague pain in my arm where my nails are digging so hard that they might be drawing blood. "Those pillars probably aren't even there anymore, huh? They've probably crumbled by now," she says, glancing back at me.

"No," I say, staring at the photo, which wants to blur behind the glass, but I refuse to let it. "They're still there."

She looks back at the photo and carries on, as if she were speaking to it instead of me.

"When your parents finally sent for you, you didn't want to go. It had been two years, and by then you were so attached to me that you didn't want to leave. But imagine if I had kept you here? One day, you would have grown up and resented me for it. On the day that you left, we took you kids to your grandparents' house. You know, the one that used to sit in the plaza, the one your grandparents sold after everything happened with Manuel? You probably don't remember, but that's where you left from, and Manuel went with you. He hadn't planned on staying on the other side, but your father talked him into it. He stayed and worked for a bit, and when he came back here, never again did he return to the other side, nor did he want to.

"Manuel believed that the best thing for a man was to work his own land, and he was right. I think the reason why this country is so behind is because all of its men have abandoned their fields to go work on the other side—and for what? Because, really, it's a miserable wage what they are paid, and you tell me if that isn't true, but what is one to do? In the past it used to be easier to earn a living. When you were kids, we had cornfields and peach orchards, but ever since they passed that free-trade agreement with the north, they've made it more difficult for us. It used to be that if you went to the mercado, anything local was always more affordable, but now the produce they bring from the other side is cheaper, and how are we supposed to compete with that? Everyone has abandoned their fields, and no one bothers with saving their seeds anymore. Only God knows where we will end up.

"I remember the day that bus pulled out of town, I turned to Lupe and said, 'When will we ever see those kids again?' But here we are, right?" She smiles at me. "That's good that you've come back to see us, that you're going back to La Peña to spend time with your father, because whether we like it or not, in this life we only have the one. Your father went and did what he did with Manuel, and for that I can't say I wish him any harm, but I can't say I wish him any good either. Each one of us will have to settle our debts with God. Only He knows why your father is still here."

"What are you guys looking at?" my mother asks, coming from the room where the animal's remains are kept.

"It's the entrance to La Peña," Tito says. "I was just telling Chuyita how she used to call it La Paña." She walks away, goes strolling along the wall, looking at the other photos. My mother comes over and has a look.

"Ah, cierto," she says, leaning in. I stare at her profile and feel as though I'm seeing her for the first time. *Why are you like this? Why are you so distant? Why can't you just talk to me? Why, why, why—* She must have known why all along. Only once had she tried talking to me about when they had left us in Mexico. I had already graduated from college, was living in Chicago, and she and Jorge had driven into the city to run errands. Then, on their way home, a blizzard had paralyzed traffic on the expressway. When they called from my mother's cell, they happened to be near the exit that led straight to my apartment. They came over and ended up spending the night. Jorge stayed on the sofa and my mother and I shared my bed.

"Where did you get that portrait in your living room from?" she asked when we were lying in the dark.

"At the secondhand store," I said. The portrait was an oil painting of a small girl, four or five years old. She wore a green scarf around her chestnut hair, and a single tear had escaped from her large brown eyes and was running down her rosy cheek. I had purchased the portrait at the Salvation Army. It was on display in the window, and when I had spotted it from across the street, it had stopped me in my tracks. The next thing I knew, I was at the counter, forking over forty dollars for the painting.

"Does it remind you of anything?" she asked.

"No," I said, thinking it an odd question. What was it supposed to remind me of?

"It doesn't remind you of when we left you in Mexico?" she asked. "You don't remember if after we left you felt scared, or sad?"

"I don't think so," I said. "I don't remember."

The wind outside roared and the plastic on my window ballooned with air. We lay in the faint white glow of the moon and snow, and then I heard her sniffling. I reached over to my nightstand, pulled a few tissues from the box, and handed them to her.

"I should have never left you," she said, and it was then that I realized she was crying. "I wish someone had told me, 'Don't leave this little girl. Take her with you. She's too young. If you leave her, you will never find each other again.' But I had no one to turn to for advice, and your father was of no help. He could have carried you. I was carrying Jorge, and he could have carried you."

"Amá, it's okay," I said. "You did what you had to do."

"I should have never left you," she said, turning to face me. "Can you ever forgive me?"

"Amá, it's okay, really." I tried to explain that it was something that happened all the time, had been happening for centuries to immigrants and refugees around the world—parents and kids were separated for a year, or two, or ten—it was no big deal. So I thought, because back then I was unaware of what we had lost when we crossed the border.

"Look," my mother says, turning and making her way to the blue wooden trunk near the entrance. "They call these antiques. These aren't antiques." She picks up one of the irons. "When we lived in La Peña, I used to iron your clothes with these. I had about six or seven of them. When you go see your father, ask him to let you into that house where we used to live." She places the iron back down on the trunk. "I bet those irons are still there."

18 ♦ DUST DEVILS

ALL ALONG THE ABANDONED FIELDS, they are already forming. It's as if men who fell on that very spot years ago now inhale the wind, rise up under its spell, and go spinning, kicking up dust, grass blades, and twigs—dust devils. One comes twirling over the field, crashes into the stacked-stone corral that surrounds the house where I was born, and sends the tin roof rattling above.

Across the dirt road, the green hammock I strung up when I first arrived three months ago is blowing around in the wind and getting entangled in the branches of the mesquite. I had come prepared to stay awhile, had brought a hammock, my laptop, my stovetop espresso maker, a stack of books, a guitar, and my running shoes. Every morning, I wake before the sun has cleared the distant mountain range, and while my father and Rosario milk the cows in the corral, I grab my iPod and go on a long jog along the dirt roads, my father's dogs panting and running by my side. Another gust comes flying over the wall, and I turn away from it.

I reach into my cargo pants and pull out the peyote button that I've kept stored in the refrigerator since the day I arrived. I wrapped it in a paper towel, stashed it in a brown paper bag, and then slid it under a pile of hard tortillas inside the vegetable drawer, hoping that neither my father, Rosario, or Alma would find it. When we stopped in Real de Catorce on the way down, Roselia had gone off into the desert the following day and picked two buttons, one for her and one for me. She had eaten hers right away, but I had held on to mine. Though I'd had several opportunities to try peyote while traveling around Europe, especially in Amsterdam, I had always known that if I was ever going to try it, I wanted it to be here, in Mexico, the place of its origin. Since I'll be leaving in a few days, it's now or never. I put the first wedge in my mouth and chew the thick, slightly bitter pulp. My sister had sort of coached me on what to expect, explaining that it was stronger than weed, but not quite as strong as mushrooms, and that I should take it on an empty stomach. She also told me that I must take it with a purpose—put an intention out in the universe—like making a wish.

If only I could go back in time and rescue myself from the silence that gripped me on the day my grandmother brought me back to this place. If I hadn't uttered a word to anyone for two weeks, then where had I gone? I must have been regrouping, because if it was possible for your parents to vanish, then anything in this world was possible. During those two weeks, I imagine I was assembling a shield, something that would protect me from ever being hurt again—my own bullet-proof vest. And what was the point of going through life constantly guarded against love? Martin was right. I had gone to New York and never returned. If I could ask the universe for one thing, I'd want to be released. Surrender my shield—leave it here on the very stoop where it first gripped me. Before leaving Tito's house, I had asked my mother what it was like when we were reunited in Chicago.

"Don't you remember?" she said. "I wasn't there when you arrived. I was at work, at the hotel where I cleaned rooms, and when I got home, Maria Elena had already given you all a bath and changed your clothes. Everyone ran to hug me, but not you," she said. "You stood off to the side, looking around, and you seemed so lost. It was like you had no idea where you were standing anymore."

I put another wedge in my mouth, and a gust comes over the wall and sends the weeds in the front yard swaying. Hard to believe that my umbilical cord is buried somewhere beneath them. I feel that if I were to drop to my knees and start digging, uprooting weeds and clawing through the dirt, I would unearth my umbilical cord—guided to it by some deep intuition.

"What are you doing out here?" my father calls from the other side of the gate.

"Nothing," I say, wrapping my hands around what's left of the button and sitting up straight.

"I'm going to bring the cattle down to the river for water," he says. "Do you want to come with me?"

"Sure," I say, though I had planned on spending most of the day on the hammock, closer to home in case the peyote made me feel sick, or worse.

He tells me to go get a satchel ready, while he saddles the donkey. I finish the rest of the button and make my way back to the house, walk past the mesquite where El Relámpago is tied. El Relámpago is the horse my father is breaking, and he's kicking at the ground with his front hoof, seems frustrated to be saddled up yet going nowhere. El Relámpago was born at the ranch, and ever since he was a colt he had roamed free around the four hundred acres with his mother, until recently when my father had brought him down to the corral to break him.

In the mornings, before saddling him up, he runs El Relámpago in circles, a few laps to the left, and then a few to the right. El Relámpago goes bucking and kicking up a dust cloud around my father, sometimes rising onto his hind legs, trying to break free of the harness and rope around his head before crashing back down like a lightning bolt—a relámpago. After he tires the horse, he saddles him up and ties him to the mesquite in front of the house for a few hours so that he will get used to having a saddle on his back.

I grab a leather satchel from the storage room, go into the kitchen, and shove an orange, a water bottle, and two ice-cold cans of Modelo into it. I rationalize that if the peyote gets to be too intense, an ice-cold beer or two might help blunt its effects. In the bedroom, which I'm now sharing with Rosario and Alma, I rub sunblock on my arms and face, throw on a long-sleeved white cotton tee, grab my straw hat, and head back outside.

My father takes the satchel and slings it over the neck of the wooden donkey saddle, which is identical to the one he gave me on my first visit. He holds the donkey still, as he always does, while I step into the stirrup and kick my leg over the saddle. He hands me the reins, and once he's on El Colorado, his other horse, we make our way around the back of the house and up the dirt trail that leads to La Mesa, the dogs trailing close behind. La Mesa is where he keeps the bulk of his herd during the dry season, and though the property no longer belongs to him legally, as long as he's alive, it will continue to be his land all the same.

We ride alongside the deserted cornfields, where nothing but a few dry cornstalks are reaching toward the blue sky, as if praying for a single drop of rain. The sun bites our shoulders, and the wind gusts and sends a dust devil twirling across the field; it collides with an abandoned tractor and explodes into a thousand particles. One at a time, they continue to materialize and go barreling across the expanse, as if taking turns, like men at a rodeo. My father rides a few strides ahead of me and doesn't seem to notice or care about the mini twisters. Then I notice one is coming right at us and watch it, thinking it will change its course. Instead, it seems to be gaining momentum, its funnel growing higher and wider as it approaches.

"Apá!" I yell, but he doesn't hear me over the roaring wind. "Apá!" I yell again, as it draws near. It looks like it might have enough force to send us both flying over the distant mountain range.

"¿Quiubo?" He stops and turns his head sideways, shoulder bracing against the wind.

"Mire." I point in the direction of the approaching twister, and the minute he sees it, his hand flies to his hat.

"¡Cuidado con la gorra!" he hollers back, and I grab my hat just as it crashes into us—a single blast of dust, like someone has slammed a door on the side of the mountain. The gust whips my hair and the pink linen scarf I keep tied around my hat into my face. The scarf is my own safety net—from a distance, anyone can see that the person riding with him is a woman. Even if he has enemies out there, they tend to leave women and children out of it.

When we reach La Mesa, the dogs are the first to enter, crouching under the barbed-wire fence that surrounds the property, like they always do.

While rounding up the cattle, my father waves me over to a patch that is overgrown with weeds. He points up at the sky where three vultures are circling.

"Do you know what they're doing?" he asks. I shrug, and he motions at the tall weeds, where two calves are curled up next to each other and sleeping. A cow stands watch over them, while the other cow is napping nearby. He tells me that the cows take turns resting and watching over their young so the predators won't get them. Just two weeks ago, the coyotes had killed a calf. He didn't seem surprised, said the cow was always leaving her calf behind, was more concerned with keeping up with the herd rather than staying near her young.

We round up the last of the cattle and soon we are trailing behind the herd as it makes its way toward the river. Their hooves kick up the loose dust in the field, sending it rising like brown smoke. The cows with calves stay in the back of the herd. My father had explained that they do this to keep their young from being trampled. We are about halfway across the field when my left knee starts hurting. I pull my foot from the stirrup and stretch my leg—an old childhood injury coming back to haunt me.

When I was nine years old, we were on a family outing in the park, and while my mother and aunt flipped tortillas and skirt steaks on the grill, my father and the other men hung out in the parking lot, drinking beer and blasting ranchero music from his truck. I was playing soccer with the other kids, and a boy who was easily twice my size and I went running for the ball at the same time. He collided into my leg, pinning my foot under his weight as we both went crashing down. I felt things twisting, even thought I heard something crack as my knee was wrung out and the sky shifted. Through the tall grass blades, I saw my mother running toward me, her brown, floral-printed dress flowing in the breeze.

"It's broken," I yelled. "I heard something snap."

She helped me to my feet, helped me limp to the picnic table, and handed me an ice-cold can of beer, told me to hold it to my knee, which was already swelling.

"What happened to you?" my father asked when he came down from the parking lot. I explained what had happened. "Does it hurt?" he asked, reaching into the cooler, grabbing a beer, and cracking it open. I nodded. "Well, if the pain doesn't go away," he said, looking at the can in my hand, "drink that beer and you'll soon forget about it." He turned and made his way back to his music.

The next day, my knee was about five different shades of purple and had swelled to the size of a softball. When my father came home from work and I was hobbling around the house like an injured bird, he had driven me to see an old man that he knew—a curandero. The old man had sat me down on a wooden chair in his kitchen and, after squeezing and prodding my knee with his long fingers, he had determined that nothing was broken, that it was only my nerves and tendons that were twisted over and under each other. He grabbed the bottle of Crisco off the fridge, rubbed some on his hands, and then reached for my knee. His hands were warm, almost soothing, until he started digging, kneading, and rubbing with so much force that it felt as if my knee were caught inside a meat grinder. My father stood on the front porch, on the other side of the screen door, turning away from my cries, and then he was in the kitchen offering me a Blow Pop.

My knee fully recovered after that, and had never given me problems until after I moved to New York. I had an MRI taken, and when the orthopedic surgeon looked at the results, he asked if I had suffered a knee injury when I was a child. He explained that I had a bit of extra bone mass on the side of my knee, and often if a bone sustains a fracture or a break, it will go into trauma and generate more bone mass in an attempt to heal itself.

Though my knee rarely gives me trouble, it has been flaring up since I've been here, perhaps stressed by my morning jogs and the long horseback rides. Each time we've ridden out to the ranch and back, it has throbbed on the way home. I reach down and start massaging it. The donkey comes to a sudden stop, draws a deep breath, and lets out a long cry. His belly starts pulsing as he inhales and exhales rapidly, singing out, and I feel as though he's drawing his breath from my lungs, like we've merged and become one. He seems excited; I wouldn't be surprised if he started prancing sideways.

"What's he doing?" I call out to my father over the roaring wind.

"He's happy because this is his land," he yells over his shoulder. I assume he's referring to Mexico, but then he points across the river to San Martín, says that's where he bought the donkey. He turns and notices my leg, dangling next to the stirrup. "How's your knee holding up?"

"It's fine," I say.

"You should keep your foot in the stirrup," he says. "That donkey can be sneaky. The minute you let your guard down, he'll have you sitting on a cactus."

I slide my foot back into the stirrup, tighten my grip on the reins, and we continue toward the river. Soon the front of the herd has reached the ravine and the cattle start making their way around the boulders and tall weeds that line the water's edge. We ride into the shade of a mesquite and watch them pass, until the tail end of the herd has disappeared around the weeds.

"Did you see your cow?" he asks, and I tell him no, though even if I had, I wouldn't be able to pick it out of the herd. When I first arrived, he told me that my cow had had a calf a few years back. Then both the calf and the cow had more offspring and I now had four cows.

"You want a beer?" I ask.

He holds up a finger and waves it back and forth.

"Not now, but maybe on the way back," he says, and then he's sitting straight up on his horse, stretching his neck up, and scanning the ridge on the other side of the river. "Did you hear that?" he asks, tightening his grip on the reins.

"Hear what?" I ask, watching as he reaches into the back of his jeans and pulls out his gun. The very sight of it still makes me uneasy.

"Wait here," he says, and rides off, the back of his shirt billowing in the wind until he has vanished around the ravine.

What is it that he heard? Was it a person or an animal that sent him full stride down the river? What should I do if I hear gunshots? Would I be better off staying on the donkey and cutting back across the field, or should I take off on foot along the river? More places to take cover along the river. I get off the donkey, and the minute my feet touch the ground I'm aware of the peyote, coursing thick and slow in my veins. I had noticed a faint trace of it earlier, when I felt as though the donkey were drawing air from my lungs, but now, standing on the ground, I feel about fifty feet tall, am convinced that if I took two giant steps to the north I'd clear the distant mountain range in no time at all. I'm almost certain that if I were to reach out, I could run my hand along the spine of the horizon. It's as if every particle in my being has expanded beyond the confines of my flesh and blood and has merged with my surroundings—I feel at once connected to the soil, the wind, and the sky.

Another gust comes whipping down from the mountains, skims a layer of dust off the plain, and whips it into the cornfields below, where I assume the dust-devil rodeo is still raging at full gallop. A cloud passes by like a white sheet drifting across the blue sky. It eclipses the sun and sends a shadow gliding over the terrain. More clouds continue to float overhead, and as each of their shadows traverses the field, I can practically feel time itself moving. With each passing shadow, I get the feeling that another day has slipped away. How many years are in a day? Is the span of a lifetime measured from the moment the sun rises until it sets? What were fourteen years in the face of eternity, anyway? Nothing but a handful of days.

Again the wind comes gusting and sends a blanket of dust flying into the cornfields below, and I get the feeling that my father is down there, has gone off to dance among the dust devils. What if he doesn't come back?

A rustling comes from the weeds behind me and when I turn around, a cow is standing there and staring at the donkey and me. More cows are making their way around the boulders and weeds, and once they see us, they too come to a halt, until the entire herd is at a standstill, staring at me, as if awaiting instructions. There is no way I can take the herd back across the field by myself. I scan the ravine in the direction my father went, but there is no sign of him. What if he doesn't come back?

The bull pushes his way to the front of the herd and stops, as if demanding to know why the cows are not moving. He's a wide and heavyset Angus bull, with thick blunt horns. What if he charges at me? I do a quick inventory of what I'm wearing: orange KangaROOS sneakers, brown cargo pants, white cotton tee, straw hat, pink scarf—good, no red. Slowly, I bend my knees and start collecting all the rocks within arm's reach. I fill my cargo pockets, secure one in each hand, and stand up. It feels like a face-off—the bull and his herd versus the donkey and me.

"¡Vaca!" I hear my father grunt from the other side of the river, and the herd jerks forward as if whipped by a giant lasso. They start moving across the field. "Vámonos," he says, and once he's standing in front of me, it's as if he was never gone.

"Where did you go?" I ask, dropping the rocks in my hands and emptying my pockets before getting back on the donkey.

"I thought I heard something," he says. We ride behind the cattle and dust rises from their hooves, engulfing us like a thick fog, and I feel as though we could get lost in this dusty terrain forever, this place where the streets still have no names. "Were you throwing rocks at the cows?" he asks, once we're halfway across the field.

"I was afraid the bull might charge," I say.

"No, ese huevón," he says. "He's too lazy to do anything. It's the cows with the calves you need to look out for. They can be a bit unpredictable, especially if you get too close to their cría, but other than that, cows are very peaceful animals. You shouldn't throw rocks at them. It's important to treat animals with love."

A tapestry of flies lifts off the ground with a single buzz as I let the weight of my body fall into the hammock. El Relámpago is still tied to the tree in front of the house, still kicking at the ground. The blue metal shutters in my father's bedroom window are closed. When we got back from La Mesa, after we'd unsaddled the horse and the donkey, he said he was going to lie down for a nap. Across the way, Doña Consuelo is watering her plants. Her husband is sitting in his wheelchair under the shade of the tin roof, his oxygen tank next to him. When I first arrived, Doña Consuelo had waved me over and asked if I had come to stay with my father for good. I told her no, and she said it was nice that I had come to see my father all the same, that when he was first released from prison, he used to spend hours, entire days even, sitting under the mesquite in front of his house, drinking, listening to his music, and crying. "And do you know why he was crying?" she asked. "He was crying for you, for his kids. He was convinced he was going to die all alone down here, far away from his family, like a dog—those were his words."

The sun shines through the branches of the mesquite and sends dispersed patches of sunlight gliding over me as I sway back and forth. Up above, there are three blackbirds circling like sharks against the blue sky.

"Ay," Alma cries out, and her laughter fills the air. She's sitting at the top of the limestone steps at the far end of the corral. Her long, jet-black hair conceals her face as she concentrates on strumming the guitar, practicing the three basic chords I taught her. When I first arrived and heard her call my father "papi" it had caught me off guard, and I had thought how ironic that he left us in Chicago, and the other two in Denver, and here he is, raising a child that isn't even his own, and raising her as if she were a boy. He had taught her how to saddle up and ride a horse, how to lasso a cow, and how to drive stick shift. The three of us had gone to the mercado a few days earlier, Alma was sauntering back to the truck, and he yelled out the window, "Camina con ganas, chingado." Once she climbed back into the truck, he was still yelling at her, saying that she best pick up the pace—start walking like she meant it, or the world was going to bulldoze right over her. "Ay," she cries out, and again the air is infused with her laughter.

An elderly man is making his way across the dirt road in front of the church. He presses on his cane, lifts his right shoulder, thrusts his weight forward, and as he slumps back down onto his cane, his kneecaps seem to bend backward. The wind skims a layer of dust off the road and sends it flying past his feet. It no longer has the same force, no longer strong enough to make the devils rise up under its spell. A long strand of yellow plastic flowers left over from El Día Tres de Mayo celebration dangles from the church's tower. The strand is blowing around in the dying wind, gently knocking against the church's tall wooden doors, and I'm overcome with the urge to go knock on my father's bedroom door, to wake him up and talk to him.

Up above, beyond the branches of the mesquite, the three black-birds are still circling, and I feel as if it's me they are watching, but then I notice the dead baby chicken. Its body is caught in the branches and its wing has flapped open. When we returned from La Mesa, Alma and Rosario were in the courtyard hanging laundry and lis-tening to music from an old silver boom box. I was in the kitchen getting a drink of water, when a gust had come flying through the window. It was so strong that it felt like the entire house trembled. It whipped my hair into my face before barreling into the storage room and onward to the bedroom, where it opened Alma's notebooks and sent her love poems flying into the air. Then, just as quickly as it came, it was gone, and I heard Rosario screaming something about how the wind had taken her baby away. When I stepped back out into the courtyard, Alma was holding the black chick in her hand. Its neck was drooping over her finger and small drops of blood were escaping from its beak and exploding on the cement below like black raindrops.

"That broom was the assassin," Alma yelled excitedly, pointing at the green broom, which was lying lifeless on the ground. The gust had flung the broom over the clotheslines, from one end of the courtyard to the other, and it had crashed down on the chick, snapping its neck instantly. Rosario told Alma to go dispose of the dead chick, and Alma had walked across the dirt road and flung it into the field, but its body had obviously been intercepted by the branches of the mesquite. The three blackbirds are still circling above, and once again there's the relentless urge to go wake my father, to talk to him, while I still can, while he's still alive.

Chickens scatter as I trudge across the dirt road. The air inside the house is much cooler, and until my eyes adjust, everything goes momentarily dark. Rosario is in the bedroom, knitting and watching an afternoon soap. I go straight to the kitchen, to the fridge, crack a Modelo open, and take a swig, thinking it might help calm the emotions that are flaring up. His bedroom door is closed, and I stare at it for a long time, contemplating whether I should wake him or not. There are three bullet holes in the door. I squat down and run my finger over them. They are covered with something that feels like clay. How is it possible that he had escaped so many bullets? It seemed he'd been dodging them his whole life. One bullet is what it had taken for all the others—his brother, my brother, both my mother's brothers, and her father—how had he managed to escape so many? Who was watching over him and why?

He had once told Sonia that when he was a kid, human skeletons were strewn all along the mountainside—remains from the Mexican Revolution. He used to play with the bones, had even taken to giving them makeshift burials, and while covering a skeleton with dirt and twigs one day, a soldier had appeared before him and thanked him. My father had asked the soldier if he would protect him, if he would be his guardian. The soldier agreed, then walked right into him and vanished. Perhaps it was the spirit of that revolutionary man who had been watching over him, or maybe shooting himself in the leg when he was a teenager had been the equivalent of giving himself the antidote.

I polish off the beer and knock on his door. It's loud, metallic, and though I want to turn and run away, I wait, listening, my heart racing. There's no response. Good, I think. I tried. Perhaps now the voice will leave me alone. I go to the fridge, grab another beer, and head for the outdoors.

"¿Quiubo?" he calls out.

"¿Apá?" I stop in my tracks.

"¿Ey?"

"Are you still sleeping?"

No response.

"I want to talk to you," I say.

There's a long silence.

"Give me five minutes," he calls out, his voice heavy with sleep.

I grab an extra beer out of the fridge and wait, hear him shuffling around in his room, hear the squeak of the metal shutters, and then the white line of light appears beneath his door.

"Adelante," he says.

I push the door open, and he's sitting on his bed, in a pool of afternoon sunlight. He blinks sleep from his eyes, his bare feet resting on top of his black plastic sandals.

"Want one?" I say, taking a seat next to him and holding out the extra beer.

"No, gracias," he says.

I take a gulp and stare at our shadows stretching across the floor, not sure where to begin, not even sure of what I want to say, though I can feel him looking at me—waiting.

"You know that country in Europe where marijuana is legal?" I say, glancing over at him.

He frowns.

"Well, there is a country in Europe where mota is legal," I say, "and several years ago, when I was backpacking around Europe with some friends, I went there, and in a shop they sold peyote buttons in small clay pots, and my friends wanted to try it, but I refused because I always felt like if I was ever going to try peyote, I wanted it to be here, you know, in Mexico. And do you remember this morning when I was sitting on the stoop of the other house?"

"Uh-huh," he says, narrowing his gaze on me, as if he's trying to figure out where I'm going with all of this. And maybe I don't even know where I'm going with all this, but I do my best at explaining that I had just eaten some peyote, and what my intent had been, because Tito had recently told me about the day that she had brought me back here, and how after that day I had never asked about them again. Then, when the broom snapped the chick's neck, it had felt like it was me, like it was a reenactment of that day, because when I realized they weren't here, it must have been the equivalent of having my neck snapped.

"It's like I died here," I say, and try explaining that whatever person I was on my way to becoming, was forever altered in that moment, so that the girl who arrived at that stoop, and the one who left, were no longer the same. "Or maybe I wasn't the one that died, but you and mi amá were, because when I realized you guys weren't here, I must have thought you were gone forever, must have mourned you as if you were dead. You know what I mean?" I say, glancing over at him.

"Well, yes," he says, clearing his throat. "I guess you were too young to understand what was happening, so you must have thought something had happened to us."

"Right," I say, "but maybe having lost you at such a young age turned out to be a blessing in disguise. Maybe it was that initial experience that helped me to bear the brunt of all that came after. Like when you left Chicago, it didn't really faze me because I had already lost you once," I say. "But not Yesenia and Jorge. When you left, it probably affected them more than anyone, because they had never been apart from you."

His hands are gripping his knees and he contemplates the ground for a long time before glancing over at the extra beer.

"A ver esa cerveza," he says, and I hand him the can. He cracks it open, takes a gulp, and stares at the far wall, seems to be pondering something, and perhaps he's thinking about the time he called home and no one wanted to talk to him, or maybe he's thinking about the day that he pulled out of the driveway in the dark hours of morning, not knowing it would be years before he would see any of his kids again.

"When you left, if you knew you weren't going to come back, why didn't you say goodbye?" I ask, turning to face him.

He studies the label on the can in his hand, as if the answer to my question might be written there in the fine print.

"I was planning on going back," he says. "But then someone told me that the police were looking for me. That there was a warrant out for my arrest, and that I'd be best off staying away."

"But by then, you were already living with that other woman, weren't you?"

"That too," he says, craning his neck and scratching his chin. "I think that if Pascuala hadn't converted to that religion, we may have made it. Ever since she became a hallelujah, we started having problems," he says, though he probably knows that their troubles began the day he laid eyes on her. My mother always claimed that she didn't want to marry him, but if she hadn't, he would have taken her by force, had already tried once. She maintained that she never loved him, a sentiment that grew louder after he left, and no matter what either of them alleges, I'll never know the details of whatever conversations transpired behind their bedroom door. "Then everything happened with Manuel and after that, I knew there was no going back." He takes another swig. "My poor brother-in-law, we even got along, you know?" he says not to me but to our shadows. "Pero, bueno," he says, slapping his knee. "It's best not to dwell on the past too much, it will only bring us down." He polishes off his beer. "So," he turns and looks at me, "you were on your airplane all day, huh?"

"Ey," I say.

"What's it like?" he asks, though I'm pretty sure he knows what it's like. A few years back, Yesenia had brought him some peyote that she had picked herself, and she had explained to him that it was medicinal, that perhaps it could help him make peace with his past.

I tell him it's intense, but mellow. How it skews the perception of time and distance—makes an hour feel eternal, and a lifetime fleeting.

19 ◆ BLUE DRESS

ON THE DAY that I leave, I sit at the top of the limestone steps in the corral and watch my father run El Relámpago in circles. El Relámpago goes bucking, kicking up a ring of dust around my father. Sometimes he rears, rises up on his hind legs, jerking his head from left to right, trying to free himself from the harness before crashing back down to the ground. El Lobo runs up to the horse, barking at him. El Relámpago lowers his head to the ground and charges at the dog, and when he's close enough, he bucks, attempting to kick El Lobo with his hind legs.

"Lobo, cabrón," my father yells, and the dog goes away.

After my father saddles up the horse and ties him to the mesquite in front of the house, he drives me into town and drops me off two blocks away from Tito's house. I'll be spending the next week with my mother and Tito before flying back to New York. Since I arrived, I've gone back and forth between Tito's and La Peña, between my mother and father. The last time he dropped me off at Tito's, my mother opened the door and hugged me. "This is the house where we lost each other," she said. "Maybe this is where we'll find each other again."

I set my stuff down on the sidewalk and climb back into his truck, reach over and give him a hug and a kiss on his cheek, and I catch a whiff of alcohol coming from his breath. I know he's been drinking again, I've smelled a trace of it here and there. Rosario told me he keeps bottles stashed everywhere—in his bedroom, the kitchen, the courtyard, his truck, and even the corral.

"I'll be back as soon as classes let out in December," I say. "For the holidays."

"Ándele pues, mija." He says that he'll be here waiting for me, that as long as he's alive, his home is my home.

Two days later, my mother, Tito, and I are at Mary's house, in Jalisco, three hours away. It's just before midnight and we are getting ready for bed when the phone rings. It's Rosario calling to say that my father has had an accident. He'd been drinking since the day I left, and had come home earlier that day, saddled up El Relámpago just after sunset, and set out for his ranch. Somewhere along the way he unloaded his gun into the sky. The horse had never been in such proximity to gunfire and reared, fell backward, and crushed him against the rocks near the river. If it hadn't been for a man who happened to be riding on a nearby ridge, he might have lain near the river until morning. The man offered him a hand, but my father told him not to move him, because he could tell that he was in pretty bad shape. He told the man to go to La Peña, ask for Rosario, and she would know what to do.

"He's all broken," Rosario says, though she doesn't elaborate when we ask, broken how? After the man arrived, Rosario had called an ambulance and they had picked up my father and driven him to the nearest hospital in Fresnillo, two hours away.

Mary and I drive to the hospital and the road stretches endlessly before us. The fields on either side of it are pitch-black, and I stare into the darkness and try not to think about what we will find when we reach the hospital, try not to think about all the different ways in which he may be "broken." We drive in silence and the whir of the tires on the asphalt fills the cabin. There's something almost hypnotic about the fluid rhythm, and before I know it, each breath I draw has fallen in sync with the cadence, has turned into a chant: *Please don't die, please don't die, not yet, please don't die.* I had just begun to get to know him and was not prepared to lose him again.

"Your father is lucky to be alive," the doctor says when we arrive at the hospital at 2:00 a.m. He informs us that my father has eight fractured ribs. One of his lungs has completely collapsed, and the other is only about 30 percent functional. They have inserted a plastic tube through either side of his rib cage to help drain the fluids that have accumulated in his lungs. The tubes are slowly filtering blood and dark fluids into two large glass jars that sit on the floor on either side of his bed, like external glass lungs.

"Apá," I say, leaning over his bed. His eyes are bloodshot and weary, and his lips are chapped and laced with dry blood. I catch a whiff of alcohol coming off his breath, strong and sour. "How do you feel?" I ask.

"Bien," he says, attempting to smile, though it looks like it pains him. He glances from my sister to me to her, and asks who else came. We tell him it's just us, and that Rosario and Alma are napping in the lobby. He asks for a drink of water, but the doctor says that until they can determine if his intestines are functioning properly, he can't eat or drink anything, it's too dangerous. After the doctor leaves, again he asks me for a drink of water—practically begs for it. I pull my water bottle from my bag, find a clean paper towel, soak it, and squeeze a few drops onto his parched tongue.

In the morning, after nodding off by his bedside all night, we call the rest of our siblings in Chicago. Sonia arrives the following day, and my mother picks her up and drives her to the hospital.

"Why didn't you call me?" my father asks Sonia. "I could have gone and picked you up at the airport."

"Oh, yeah," she says. "And what would you have done with those jars?"

"These?" He looks at the tubes jutting from his chest and a sullen expression overshadows his face, as if he's just realizing that the tubes are attached to him. He says that he could have pulled his truck right up next to the bed, loaded the jars in the back, and then driven to the airport.

I shoot Sonia a look. After the first night, it was clear that something was wrong—really wrong. One of the first storms of the rainy season had raged all through the night, and he had not slept a wink. He was convinced the rain was pouring down the walls inside the hospital, kept asking me how they were going to get all that water out. Lightning flashed through the ward and then he was clawing at the sheets, convinced he was slipping into a dark tunnel at the foot of his bed. When I asked the doctor why my father was hallucinating, he cited a number of reasons. It could be the strong painkiller he was on, or the lack of oxygen to his brain since he was breathing with less than half a lung. Also, the elderly had a harder time recovering from these things, he said.

"He's not that old," I said, and the doctor motioned to the head of my father's bed. There among the gleaming knobs, switches, and valves was a piece of paper that read:

Jose Venegas
65

Sixty-five. That number looked like a misprint, like a mistake. Until I saw that number in writing, I had continued to think of him as forever forty-five—the same age he was when he left Chicago. My father might be sixty-five, but he was far from elderly. One of the first things he had asked the doctor was how long before he could ride his horse again, saying something about how the rainy season had just begun, and he needed to move his cattle from La Mesa to his ranch before the fields started sprouting. The doctor had chuckled and told him not to worry so much about his cattle or getting back on his horse. He needed to focus on getting better first, on getting out of this place, where half the men were here thanks to their horses.

Jorge arrives the following day, and the day after that comes Roselia—this is how my mother gets roped into the situation, gets caught up chauffeuring us around.

"Who brought you?" my father asks Roselia.

"Mi amá," she says.

"Your mother is here?" he asks, his face lighting up a bit, though he looks beyond fatigued. He hasn't slept at all since he arrived three nights before. "Is she going to come see me?"

"What do you think?" says Roselia.

He shrugs, sort of looks like a child that has just been scolded.

"Do you want her to come see you?" I ask.

"If she wants to," he says, swatting at a green smudge on his sheet. Earlier, they had fed him his first meal—mashed greens, and peaches in thick syrup. Though he had a hard time bringing the plastic spoon to his mouth, he had insisted on doing it himself and ended up spilling half of it on the sheet.

"I'll ask her for you," I say.

He nods and swats at the smudge again, keeps thinking it's a spider. I grab my bag and head out to the parking lot. Though the sun is shining, a gentle rain is falling, and the scent of wet earth fills the air. It has stormed every night he's been here, and every night he has been wide awake and watching the lightning flash through the ward. One minute he's aware that he's in the hospital, and the next he thinks he's out on his ranch. The tunnel at the foot of his bed has not stopped spinning, and the day before, they rolled a new patient in and he had watched unflinchingly as the two male nurses hoisted the man onto the bed next to his.

"Why did you bring that dead man in here?" he hollered at them. I shushed him, told him the man wasn't dead, as one of the nurses pulled shut the thick rubber curtain between their beds.

Later that night, while lightning flashed outside, he had been in a panic. Staring wide-eyed at the curtain and saying that the dead man was standing right there, next to his bed, and holding his hand out to him.

"Apá, there is nothing here," I said, going to the side of his bed and running my hand along the curtain. "See?" Eventually, he calmed down, though he didn't take his gaze from the curtain for the rest of the night.

"How's your father doing?" my mother asks when I climb into her Jeep. She's been shuttling us between the hospital and her sister's house, where we have been eating, showering, and sleeping.

"Not good," I say, explaining how one minute he seems coherent, understands where he is, but the next minute his mind is gone and he thinks he's out on his ranch, herding his cattle—even swears he can hear the tamborazo blaring all around him. "He's convinced that the man in the bed next to his is dead," I say.

"Maybe he hit his head when he fell," she says, pulling out of the parking lot. "There are a lot of rocks near that river where they found him."

I had already asked the doctor if they had checked his head, but he said that if the doctor who was on duty when my father arrived hadn't ordered a CT scan, then it wasn't necessary. When I asked if they could give him a sedative to help him sleep, the doctor explained my father's situation as a catch-22. Since he hadn't slept at all, there was a chance he could go into cardiac arrest, but he also had a very faint heartbeat, and a sedative might stop his heart altogether. Even though it didn't make sense, I had sat next to his bed, trying to accept this dilemma, thinking that maybe this was the way his life was going to end. Not with a bullet but with his heart. And what if he did die? Would it be so bad? My cousins still lived in and around town, and I'm sure they'd be relieved to know that the man who killed their father was gone. Tito and my mother would probably breathe a bit easier, as well. Recently, he had taken to driving circles around their house, blaring music from his truck, playing a ballad that he used to serenade my mother with before they married.

"He asked about you," I say to my mother when we pull up in front of my aunt's house. "He asked if you were going to go see him."

"You should have never told him I was here," she says.

"He figured it out," I say.

"I don't know what to do," she says, gripping the steering wheel and staring straight ahead. I can see the conflict on her face. If he dies, she might regret not having seen him, but what if she opens that door and then he survives?

"I think if it's going to make you feel better, then you should go see him. Don't do it for him, do it for yourself," I say, using the same reasoning Martin had used on me.

"It's not like I can remove that blood from your veins." She glances over at me, and it's as if she can see his blood and her blood forever interlaced and swimming in my veins.

The following day, she drives me back to the hospital, and Sonia and Jorge say that my father had kept the entire wing up all night. One minute he was yelling something about how the dead man was standing at the foot of his bed and the next minute he was trying to get up and leave. He demanded to know who had taken his boots and put him in that blue dress. The jars scraped along on the floor, as they struggled to hold him down. They had asked for a sedative, and received the same catch-22 response.

"Apá, how do you feel?" I ask, and he says he's fine, though he looks beyond exhausted, seems to have aged twenty years since he arrived. The oxygen tube has slipped out of his nose and is resting on his chest, and his blue gown is stained and draped loosely around his exposed shoulders. He seems so helpless. I adjust his nightgown, place the tube back in his nose, and turn the oxygen knob up a few notches.

"Inhale," I say, thinking maybe a boost of oxygen to the brain will help clear the tunnel through which his mind keeps slipping. He takes a deep breath. None of this makes sense. What are we supposed to do? Sit by his bedside and wait until his heart stops beating?

"Again," I say, and he inhales with less gusto. I can't help but feel partially responsible for his condition, like perhaps he had risked his life, put himself in the hospital, just to keep me around a little longer. He must have known the horse would rear if it heard gunshots. Perhaps this was his backward way of showing his love for me.

"Again," I say, and he inhales, and swats at the green smudge on his sheet, still thinking it's a spider. What if he dies? Will I be able to live with knowing that I watched him slip away and did nothing to help him? I go to the foot of his bed, pick up his chart, and start jotting down all his stats: blood pressure, meds, heart rate. Martin has a friend in Chicago who is a doctor, and I think I'll send him an e-mail. Get a second opinion.

"Hola, mija," he says. I look up and he's looking at someone behind me, and just seeing the way his face is lit up, I know that it must be my mother. He smiles wide and stares at her in awe, as if the ceiling has opened up and a ray of sunlight is shining down just for him. This is probably not the way he imagined a reunion with my mother. With him lying in bed, stripped of his cowboy boots, and wearing a blue dress.

"Your kids asked me to come pray for you," she says, holding her purse against her chest like a shield. "Do you want me to pray for you?"

"That might be a good idea," he says, still staring at her in disbelief.

She takes two steps toward his bed and tells him to close his eyes and repeat after her. His whole face puckers up as he squeezes his lids tight, seems to be using all his might to keep them shut.

"Dear God," she says, closing her eyes and bowing her head.

"Dear God," he repeats.

I stand at the foot of his bed, watching as his eyes snap open and he gazes at her, repeating every word that is rolling off her tongue as if he were afraid to let a single syllable slip from her lips onto the floor. I glance back and forth between them, and can't believe that here, standing in the same room, in such proximity, breathing the same stale air, are my parents—reunited after twenty years.

"I come to ask your forgiveness," she says.

"I come to ask your forgiveness," he repeats.

"Please, forgive me for all the pain I've caused onto others," she says.

"Please, forgive me," he says. His smile waned, and he looks as though he wants to reach out and take her in his arms.

"For all the pain I've caused onto others," she repeats.

"Forgive me, Pascuala," he says, and she opens her eyes and glares at him. "Forgive me for having left you with the burden, with all the kids," he says, "and for having ended your brother's life. Please, forgive me." They stare at each other, and for a split second I think it actually might start pouring rain inside the hospital. "Ever since I left you, my life has been unstable, I've done nothing but roll around, and . . ."

"I have already forgiven you," she says, thrusting her chin up. "Now, let's ask God to forgive you." She closes her eyes, continues with the prayer, and though he repeats everything she utters, he does not take his gaze off her.

"Amen," she says, and opens her eyes.

"Amen," he says, once again smiling wide.

"Take care of yourself, Jose," she says, and turns to leave.

"Wait," Sonia practically shouts, jumping away from the wall where she and Jorge have been standing semiparalyzed—as shocked as I am to be seeing our parents standing face-to-face after all these years. "I want a picture," she says, already clawing around in her purse. She pulls out her camera, hands it to me, and runs to the head of the bed, waving my mother over. My mother goes and leans in on the other side, and I snap the only photo of our makeshift family reunion. They say a photograph is worth a thousand words, but no camera could have captured the magnitude of that moment.

Again my mother goes to leave, and this time it's my father who calls after her.

"Can I have a hug?" he says.

She stops, places her purse at the foot of his bed, pivots, takes two swift strides toward him, gives him two quick taps on his shoulders with her fingertips, and a kiss on the cheek. She turns and grabs her purse, and though his arms are still rising to meet her embrace, she's already gone.

Later that day, I send Martin an e-mail detailing my father's condition, and ask if he can please forward it to his friend, Eric, the doctor. Eric responds almost immediately. *Does Maria's father drink? Is it possible he is going through alcohol withdrawal? Is he having trouble sleeping? Does he feel he's slipping off the bed? Is there a tunnel? Spiders? If so, have her call me ASAP.*

"The painkiller your father is on is not enough to make anyone hallucinate," he says when I call him. "It's aspirin, basically." He tells me that my father is having classic alcohol withdrawal symptoms, and that he needs a sedative immediately. "If they don't give him a sedative, he will have a heart attack. I'm surprised he hasn't already. I honestly don't understand how your father is still alive."

After getting off the phone with Eric, I go straight to the hospital and practically demand they give my father a sedative. The doctor tries to explain his catch-22 theory yet again, and I stop short of telling him to fuck off—how was it possible that they didn't know my father was going through alcohol withdrawal, while a doctor thousands of miles away had diagnosed him based on an e-mail? Perhaps to them, if he were to have a heart attack, he'd be one less "elderly" person on social security or one less drunk on the street. Maybe to them, he was just another patient, but to me, he was my father—the one and only.

The head of the hospital comes down to have a word with us, saying they will give my father a sedative, but if he never wakes up, they won't be to blame—we will. Is this really what it had come to? Whether my father lives or dies, somehow being our responsibility?

"Fine," I say, knowing that if my father never wakes up, at least I can live with knowing that when he was unable to fend for himself, I had not turned my back on him.

Once they give him the sedative, he sleeps for thirty-six hours straight, waking only now and then to ask for a drink of water. When he wakes, the tunnel and the spiders are gone, and so too is the man who had been in the bed next to his. The man had died in the middle of the night. Had gone quietly, without making a fuss—he, too, had fluid in his lungs.

Three days later, my father is released from the hospital, and Yesenia and I drive him back to La Peña. It's been raining so much that the face of the land itself has been transformed. On either side of the road, the fields that had been parched and dusty now stretch all the way to the horizon shimmering with different shades of green.

When classes let out in mid-December, I pack my bags, a stack of books, running shoes, and a month's supply of espresso. On the night before I leave for Mexico, I throw a going-away party, an apple-pie party. I make the pie from scratch, using Abigail's recipe, and while it's in the oven, a bottle of tequila makes its way around the room. This has been my routine for the past two years. The minute classes let out for summer or the holidays, I'm throwing a going-away party and hopping on the first flight back to Mexico.

"So, where in Mexico are you going?" Matt yells, over the music. "Are you going to the beach?"

"I'm going to see my father," I say.

"Nice," he says. "You're going to go spend the holidays with your parents?"

"Not exactly," I say, making my way to the kitchen to check on the pie. Though my parents had had that moment, their brief reconciliation two years earlier, and my father had not stopped talking about my mother, how she had been to see him, and who knows, maybe once he got out of that place, they could work things out. But deep down he must have known that the past would forever run like a deep, dark vein between them.

"Almost ready," I yell over the music as I pull the pie from the oven and cheers erupt from the living room, where everyone is dancing to a mix of hip-hop and disco.

When I had returned to New York after that trip, I suddenly felt like an outsider in my own neighborhood. Williamsburg had undergone massive construction that summer, and new buildings, complete with doormen and elevators, had sprung up on every other street corner, it seemed. I was walking home from class one day and had come to a full stop at an intersection. Where there had never even been a stop sign, now there was a traffic light. Before there had been no need for stop signs or traffic lights, as there was hardly any traffic, but now the line of cars waiting at the light stretched all the way down the street like a metallic snake. And dispersed among the cars was the one thing that had been as uncommon in Williamsburg as tourists— yellow cabs. It was disorienting.

I set the pie to cool on the counter, next to the cheese and charcuterie boards, and grab two pints of vanilla ice cream from the freezer. For the past two years, the gentrification had continued at such a rapid pace that each time I went to Mexico and came back, another slew of buildings had gone up, another wave of foreigners had moved in, and another handful of friends who could no longer afford the rising rents had moved away, including Josh. He had moved to Bushwick, and within a few years would be returning to California. I felt more and more like an outsider as I watched the neighborhood I had fallen in love with practically vanish from underneath me.

Another bottle of tequila makes its way around the room and I take a swig, knowing that I'm going to feel it on the plane in the morning.

20. SHOOTING GUNS LIKE SHOOTING STARS

SCATTERED STARS BEGIN TO APPEAR, one by one, like eyes glistening against the cobalt sky. The sliver of moon doesn't illuminate enough of the darkness, out there beyond the courtyard, on the dirt road where the dogs have fused into a ball of claws and teeth tearing through the night. Out there where dust is already clinging to fresh blood. One dog breaks from the pack and runs toward the church that sits under the single light post in La Peña. A cloud of dust rises toward the light as the pack pounces on the one that broke from them, the one that tried to get away. A log collapses in the fire, red sparks soar into the cool air, mingle with the growling, and then vanish.

"Should we do something?" I ask my father.

"About what?" he asks, leaning back in his white plastic chair, his legs extended in front of him and crossed one over the other so that the soles of his cowboy boots are almost in the fire.

"The dogs," I say. "Won't they kill each other?"

"Nah, they'll work it out," he says, taking a swig of the rum and Coke in his nicked tin cup.

The battle continues to rage in front of the small church, while in the distance, along the dark ridge, lights from other ranches are coming into focus. Out there where a pair of eyes could be watching the glow of the fire dance across our faces. Normally, we don't stay outside past dark. Once the chickens have tucked themselves into the branches of the eucalyptus trees and the sun has gone down, we go inside, lock the doors, and stay put until morning. I hook my index finger in the rubber band holding my ponytail and slide it off, let my hair fall freely around my shoulders.

"Why are they fighting like that?" I ask. My father is now down on one knee, rearranging the logs in the fire. "Maybe it's a sign," I say.

"Yeah, maybe," he says. "Maybe La Huesona is on the loose, desperate to take a few more souls before the year ends." He rolls a thick log into the fire. "Only a few hours left," he grunts as he centers it in the burning pile.

Maybe he's right. Animals are always the first to know. When I had been here for the holidays last year, the dogs had howled all through the night, and then in the morning, we found out that the ninety-two-year-old woman who lived across from the church had died at dawn. My father and I had gone to the service, and afterward we followed the procession, the truck with the coffin and the one with the musicians guiding the way to the cemetery. As we idled along, the drums and horns seemed to be pounding in my chest.

"With the music, you kind of get the urge to cry, huh?" my father said, staring out his window.

"Ey," I said. When I had first gone to the cemetery on the hill I had stood at the foot of my brother's grave, staring at his name carved into the stone, and had hardened against it, had refused to shed a single tear. "Did you guys have music at Chemel's funeral?" I asked my father, and he said there were so many people at Chemel's funeral that by the time the truck with the musicians reached the plaza in town, cars were still pulling out of La Peña. We drove along in the procession and I could feel him staring at my profile, and then I was fumbling around for my sunglasses, as if they might be able to dam up the tears that had been years in coming.

"This log should last us all night, or at least until the New Year," he says, taking his seat. "Encino. Great wood. I chopped it myself. It doesn't burn down as fast as the others." He glances at me and follows my gaze out to the rumbling that is now moving around the back of the house.

"I think one of those dogs is in heat," he says. "That's why they're all worked up." I lean back into my chair and take a sip from my rum and Coke. The dry heat from the fire feels good on my bare arms. "You see those three stars?" he asks, pointing at the Big Dipper. I look past the clothesline and electrical wires that hang above. "When we were kids," he says, "we used to call those Los Reyes Magos."

"Over there," I say, "they call those the . . ." The word eludes me. It's like this sometimes. I can't find the right word in Spanish and hesitate. "It's, um, it's like the small pot or pan," I say. "Or like the big spoon. See how the three stars are in a row? How they seem to form a handle?"

"Uh-huh," he says, and though his face is still turned toward the sky, he's giving me a sideways glance, a one-eyed squint.

The sky is filled with stars, thousands of them sitting around the moon, waiting for the New Year to arrive. A small piece of raw meat clings to the clothesline above. A few days ago, a cow broke an ankle and had to be put down. My father had salted the meat that didn't fit in the freezer and hung it on the clothesline to be dried by the sun. Raw meat hung like laundry in the courtyard for two days. He reaches up, plucks the piece off the clothesline, and throws it into the fire.

"I made that rope when I was in prison," he says, pointing at the clothesline. It's a yellow rope that's tied to an extension chord that is then tied to the water-well post. "That one and the pink one I tied to your saddle this morning," he says.

"They teach you how to make rope in jail?" I ask.

"They teach you how to do lots of things," he says. "If you pay attention, you come out knowing more than when you went in. I gave those ropes to my father, when he came to visit me to tell me they had sold the house in the plaza and deposited the money in an account for the lawyer that was working on my case."

The dogs have worked their way around the corral and are now barreling down the dirt road toward us, the snarling louder and louder as they approach.

"Maybe we should go inside," I say.

"Nah. If we go inside, we'll fall asleep," he says, perhaps thinking back to last year when I had picked up a bottle of red wine and made us a filet mignon and mashed potato dinner, and by the time midnight arrived we were both passed out. "It's nicer here, by the fire. We can have a few drinks, a bit of a plática, and after the New Year arrives, we'll go inside and iron our ears out." He looks at my bare arms, my ripped jeans. "You want to borrow a jacket?"

"No, I'm fine," I say, taking a gulp from my cup.

"Do you really want to go inside?" he asks.

"Maybe," I say.

"Well then, we should put out the fire," he says.

We sit in silence for a while. I stare out past the dirt road, past the house where both he and I were born, and can't help but feel like we are being watched. I sit up and face him.

"What if someone shoots us?" I ask.

His whole body turns toward me.

"No, no, mijita," he shakes his head. "¿Qué pasó? Don't think like that." He reaches into the fire, grabs one of the logs, and flips it. "No one is going to come bother us here, not at this hour, not just any pendejo would come near here," he says. "Besides, it's the holidays, everyone is too busy celebrating."

Everyone is busy celebrating—celebrating and drinking; drinking and celebrating—all day long men have been knocking them back at the rodeos, the cockfights, the horse races—the sun beating on their eyelids, vision blurring, old conflicts rising to the surface. It's during the holidays that tragedies seem to happen around these parts. It was on Christmas Eve, twenty-two years ago, that my brother was shot, fell facedown in the river, and drowned. My mother had recently taken me to Las Cruces and I had stood near the river's edge, watching the frigid water rushing over the smooth stones. His sweetheart's house still sat on the boulder across the way, but she was long gone, married and living on the other side. For years I had blamed my father. Had blamed him for convincing my brother to come back here, for keeping him just a little longer, just until the holidays, but how could he have foreseen what was coming?

"Do you know what ever happened to the guy that killed Chemel?" I ask.

"Ouh, a ese méndigo cojo, yo mismo me lo chingué," he says, staring into the flames. "After I came back down here, I went looking for him in the prison but was informed that he had been transferred to the federal prison in Zacatecas, so I drove there, and they told me that he had been sent to a mental institution in Guadalajara. I took the overnight bus to Guadalajara, only to find that he had been released, but I kept the word on the street and waited, knowing that sooner or later that son of a bitch would have to turn up," he says, taking a swig. "Then I heard he was living near the border, in Mexicali, working as a paletero. There was a tavern he frequented, and I was told that if I were to show up at said tavern on any given weekday between such and such hours, he would be there. I recruited two others, and we drove up there. We found the tavern and sure enough, there was that méndigo, sitting at the bar and having a beer as if nothing had ever happened."

"And you recognized him?" I ask.

"Sí, cómo no, méndigo cojo," he says. "One of the men I was with went up to him and put his arm around his shoulders. "Hola, amigo," he said. "Do you remember me?" The méndigo shook his head, saying no, he did not. "You might not remember me," the man said, leaning in a bit closer, "but I'll bet you remember Chemel Venegas, don't you?" he said, pressing the barrel of his gun into the méndigo's ribs, right through his coat pocket. It must have been at that moment that the son of a bitch realized his past had caught up to him." He polishes off his drink and tells me that the cojo didn't even bother putting up a fight. He went quietly.

This isn't the first time he's told me this story. Over the past few years he's told me the same story, and each time the story is exactly the same—almost verbatim, and there's something about its exactitude that makes it seem a bit too polished, like he's recounting a story, not as he witnessed it, but as it was related to him. And what does it matter whether he killed that cojo, or had someone do it for him— nothing will ever bring my brother back, nor erase the nightmares that have haunted me for years.

"No, está cabrón, mijita," he says. "If anyone ever took one of my kids like that again, in such a cowardly way, or hurt one of you, even, I'd go after them, and I don't care who tried standing in my way— brother, father, sister, mother—I don't care who, they'd get trampled all the same." The other two brothers had skipped town when he returned, and years later he heard that they had both died, car accidents or something like that. After he was released from prison and came back here, he had kept an eye on their father. "That's all you really have to do," he says. "Just watch their moves, know what doors they're going in through, and which ones they're coming out of, and then when they least expect it." He shrugs. "That man eventually died of a heart attack," he says. "Who knows, maybe he knew I was watching him and he got so scared that he croaked."

He's back on one knee, adjusting the logs in the fire, and I can't help but wonder what he would do if I happened to show up here one day with the dog of dogs that found me passed out in the basement. A ride out to the ranch—beyond the reach of any antidote, and fifty scorpions in his pants ought to do it. I polish off my drink, and stand up.

"Is there any more left?" he asks, grinning at me, a glint of the fire in his eyes.

"Yeah," I say, taking his cup. "I'll go make us two more."

The minute I step away from the fire, the cold air grips me. Night has fallen and so has the temperature. I make my way to the kitchen and hit the light switch. The single lightbulb covered with a layer of grease and dust dangles from the black cord that's slung over the wooden beam. The fried chicken Rosario and I made earlier sits in a large, green plastic bowl on the table with a cheesecloth draped over it. Grease is already seeping through the fabric. Since the day I arrived, two weeks ago, he kept mentioning how he had a taste for that fried chicken from the other side, how he hadn't had it in years, how he used to eat at the fried chicken place all the time, and how even the side dishes weren't bad. I went into town, downloaded the KFC recipe off the Internet, bought two chickens, two bottles of Crisco, a few potatoes, and some greens: fried chicken with two sides.

I grab the bottle of rum from behind the white, rusty metal cabinet where I stashed it earlier and mix two more drinks. This was the deal we made when he arrived slurring and glassy-eyed, pulling his red truck right into the courtyard as Rosario and I were finishing frying the chicken. She had gone to bed, and I agreed to have a few drinks with him, celebrate the New Year, as long as he gave me the bottle, let me be in charge, monitor how much more he drank, make sure he didn't have too much, black out, forget where he was—who he was with.

I hear his truck door slam shut and expect to hear a corrido come blaring through the house, but the music never comes. I mix our drinks, making mine a double, his a lot weaker, and head back outside. He is sitting in front of the fire, right where I left him, as if he had never moved. I hand him his drink and sit down; he takes a sip.

"Uouh, this doesn't taste like anything," he says, taking another swig. "It tastes like pura Coca-Cola." He eyes me. "Did you put anything in here?"

"Yeah," I say.

"No parece." He grins and glances at my cup. "A ver," he says. "Let me try yours."

I hand him my cup and he takes a gulp.

"A jijo!" he coughs. "Did you put the rest of the bottle in here?"

"There wasn't much left." He takes another swig. "Are you sure you don't have another bottle stashed somewhere?" I ask.

"No, that was it," he says. "And the only reason I had that bottle is because I ran into a buddy of mine in town and he gave it to me, wanted me to go with him to the cantina, but I told him one of my daughters was in town, and that we were going to spend the New Year together."

I take both cups. Empty my drink into his, then pour it all into mine, back and fourth I go, mixing the two together, then hand his cup back to him. El Lobo comes up and nudges my elbow. I pet his head, run my fingers down his neck; it's wet, sticky. I set my drink down and run both my hands down his neck, then hold them to the fire. They're covered in blood.

"Se lo chingaron," he says, looking at the blood. He walks over to his truck, which is parked right behind us, comes back with a flashlight, gets down on one knee, and aims the beam at Lobo's neck. I hold Lobo's head still—there's a deep gash about two inches long on his neck, oozing thick blood. "They ripped his tumor off," he says, pointing at the spot. "Right there he used to have a bump and now it's gone," he says, being careful not to touch it, not to get blood on his hands. "That's good." He stands up. "Now I won't have to cut it off."

I press my finger gently against the gash. Lobo yelps.

"He's bleeding a lot," I say. "Shouldn't we take him to a dog doctor or something?"

"He'll be fine," he says, grimacing at the blood. "You should wash your hands." He points the light toward the gray slate sink.

I walk over to the sink, grab the pink bar of Zote soap from under it, and adjust the hose between my knees, bend into the ice-cold stream of water while he holds the light over me.

"This is the flashlight you gave me for Christmas last year," he says.

It's a long, black metal flashlight with adjustable beams—identical to the one Martin had given him on our first visit. He had told me how he really liked that flashlight because it had such powerful beams, but he had lost it. He and his buddy were driving home from a fiesta in the next town over, and since he had had too much to drink, he let his friend drive his truck, and though he kept telling him to take it nice and slow, because it was best to arrive late rather than never, still his friend had gone off the road, and as the truck began to roll, the flashlight had been thrown from it.

I place the soap back under the sink and am still hunched over when we hear the first gunshots. Only a few scattered blasts in the distance, then they seem to get louder and closer like an approaching hailstorm, and soon they're all around us. My father drops the flashlight into the back of his truck, goes into the house, and comes back out with two loaded guns, hands me the bigger one, a .357 Magnum.

"Truénela," he says.

The light from the fire is reflecting off the long silver barrel and the mother-of-pearl grip. I turn it over in my hands, taken by how beautiful it is.

"I don't know," I say. "I've never shot a gun before."

"It doesn't matter," he says, a huge smile spreading across his face. "Just point it straight up and shoot it."

I look at the gun. Hesitate. If I shoot it, I feel as if I will have crossed some line, a transgression—a .357 Magnum took my brother's life.

All around us guns are going off. He points his at the sky and unloads it, shooting fast, one right after another, the way he used to do in the Chicago suburbs when we were kids.

"See," he says, his eyes dancing with excitement. "Just point it up and shoot it."

"Bueno," I say. "No puedo pensar en qué otro lugar sería mejor, um, estaría más bueno como para truenar . . ." What I'm trying to say is that if I was ever going to shoot a gun, I can't think of a better time or place, but again my Spanish is failing me and I'm slurring my words and now he's looking at me like maybe he's regretting having handed me a loaded gun.

"Truénela," he says, his smile fading.

I turn around and point the gun straight up, hold it over my head with both hands. I look toward the small church in the distance, press gently on the trigger, and am surprised by how hard it is. It's as if the force of gravity has reversed its course and is pushing back up against my finger. I press down harder. The pressure releases, fire shoots from my fingertips, and sparks rain down from the electrical wires above as a high-pitched ringing sound fills the air. I hear my father yelling something, but I can't hear what he's saying. It's as if I've slipped into a water well, my ears slowly filling with water and muffling the sounds around me. The only thing I hear with utter clarity inside this space I have cracked open is the loud ringing. Its steady pitch sounds like an om.

"Do you hear that?" I yell to my father over my shoulder, as instinctively my hands move to cover my ears, and for a split second I forget I'm still holding the gun.

"¿Qué?" His voice is so faint that it sounds like he's yelling at me from the other side of a thick wall.

"That ringing sound," I yell back to him. "Do you hear that?" I turn around and he's ducking behind his truck.

"Cuidado con la pistola," he says, looking at my swaying hand, the gun pointing slightly in his direction. "Empty it out," he says. "Point it straight up and shoot it. Fast. One right after another, it sounds prettier that way."

I turn around and hold the gun up with both hands, point it at a slight angle away from me. There is nothing but the stars and the sliver of moon above, and though there is no music playing, I swear I hear the tamborazo coming down the mountainside, the drums and horns thundering all around me. I aim at the moon, convinced I can put a hole in it. Fire shoots from my hands as four bullets follow each other into the night sky, and with each blast, I feel the adrenaline unleashing in my veins. I look at the revolver and am overwhelmed with the urge to shoot it again. *It sounds prettier that way.* Amazing that all those blasts that robbed me of hours of sleep were like music to his ears. It all makes sense—his music, his guns, his drinking— they all go hand in hand.

I give the gun back to him, and he passes me a heavy, blue, square-shaped glass bottle.

"I thought you didn't have another bottle," I say.

"I just found that one in my truck," he says.

Even before the bottle touches my lips, I smell the sharpness of tequila. I take a sip and hand the bottle back to him.

"Are those the same guns you brought down from Chicago?"

"No," he says. "I sold most of those."

"What about your bulletproof vest?" I ask. "Do you still have it?"

"Ouh, who knows what happened to that vest." He takes a long pull. "I think I sold it, or maybe I gave it away, I don't remember."

He hands me the bottle and I lean into his truck, prop my foot up on the tire.

"How did you know Joaquín wanted to kill you?" I ask.

"I just did," he says. "There was something about him, he was a little too friendly." He turns the revolver over in his hands. "That night he had thrown his arm around me and patted my back, acting like we were best buddies," he says, "but I knew he was checking to see if I had my gun. We were playing cards and I said I was running home to use the bathroom, and I did. I used the bathroom and then I grabbed my .45." I take another sip and hand him the bottle. "Then when I went back outside, he proposed a toast, a brindis, and with one hand he held up his beer and with the other he buried a kitchen knife in my neck." He forces down a gulp. "But the bullet turned on that son of a bitch."

"Did you ever find out who hired him?" I ask, because this is something I've wondered about over the years.

"Quién sabe," he shrugs, though years from now Rosario will tell me that he had told her it was the guys who had killed my brother because they knew it was only a matter of time before he returned to Mexico looking for them.

"You know, when everything happened with Joaquín, the papers the next day reported that it was due to an argument over who would drink the last beer," I say.

"¿A poco?" he asks, chuckling a bit. "That's what the papers said?"

"Ey," I say. "You didn't know that?"

"No," he says, laughing a little harder, and I guess it makes sense that he wouldn't know, as he was in intensive care for two weeks afterward, the doctor telling us that my father was lucky to be alive, how the blade had missed his jugular by a hair. "Imagine that? Killing a man over a goddamn beer," he says, and he's laughing so hard that it makes me start laughing, and soon we're both leaning against his truck, howling with laughter.

In the distance, three fireworks race into the sky, their tails trailing behind like comets, like shooting stars that crash-landed in the mountains years ago, and are now returning to their home in the universe.

On the day that I leave, he drops me off at the bus station like he always does.

"How are you going to get that back without breaking it?" he asks, looking at the clay water jug in my arms.

"I'm going to carry it on my lap," I say. I had found the jug inside the house where I was born a few days before. Each time I've come down, I've gone inside that house and dug around, and I've always emerged covered in dust and carrying something that I want to take back to New York: rusty skeleton keys, white tin bowls, my grandfather's branding rod, leather satchels, sheep shears, rake heads, kerosene lamps, and six of my mother's irons. Back in New York, my apartment seems to be turning into a mini museum, slowly filling up with relics I've salvaged from my past. The last time I was here, he gave me an old machete he no longer used. It came in a leather sheath, and the machete had a desert landscape etched on one side of it and an inscription on the other. "I'll be back in the summer," I say, giving him a hug and a kiss on the cheek.

"Ándele, pues, mija," he says. "I'll be here waiting for you."

21 ◆ QUELITES

IT'S MID-JULY, the start of the rainy season, when I arrive in town early on Sunday morning. I take a cab to Tito's house and my mother is walking out the door to go to the mercado, so I join her. We pull into the dusty gravel lot and make our way along the narrow passageways between the booths. There is everything from fresh produce and homemade cheese to hand-carved wooden bowls and used clothing.

"Why are you buying so many groceries?" my mother says, watching as I stock up on fruits and vegetables. "We've got plenty of food at home."

"I'm bringing it to La Peña," I say.

"Don't they have any food out there?" she asks.

"I just want to bring the things I like to eat," I say.

"When are you planning on going?" she asks, though she knows the main reason for my being here is to spend time with my father, who is recovering from yet another horse-riding accident. Three weeks ago, El Relámpago had left him lying on the rocks near the river again, with four fractured ribs and a dislocated hip. He had been lying out there in the rain all night, and right around dawn, two men had spotted his horse, still saddled up and grazing in a field with a herd of free-roaming horses. They set out, riding along the river, until they located him. A crust of mud had dried all around him, hypothermia had settled on his bones, his breathing was shallow, and his skin so pale that not long after the men found him, once again the rumors that he was dead were running rampant through town.

"I don't know, probably tomorrow or the day after," I say.

"¿Tan rápido?" She tells me that she was going to go to Chicago, but then she waited because she knew I was coming. "If you're going to go and stay with your father, then I'm going to leave tomorrow also," she says. It's always like this, always a struggle over who I'm going to spend more time with, though she knows that when I come to Mexico, spending time with my father is my priority. I can see her in Chicago, or if she ever wanted to, she could come visit me in New York. I've been there for eight years, and she has never been out. "Why don't you stay with me for a week and then go to La Peña?" she says when we are loading the groceries into her Jeep.

"A whole week?" I say. "He just had an accident. He's already been waiting for me since Wednesday."

"Well, that's why he has that vieja there, isn't it? So she can help him." By "that vieja" she means Rosario, who sometimes is there and other times isn't—has left him for the umpteenth time. Alma had left for good the year before, had eloped with her boyfriend. "I'm the one who should have left," my mother says. "Then maybe now you'd come looking for me instead of that viejo." We climb into her Jeep, and soon we are idling along in the Sunday bumper-to-bumper traffic. "Your father never cared about anyone but himself," she says. "He never loved you guys."

"That's not true," I say. This is something she's been telling us since the day he left—"your father never loved you guys." And for years I let her say it, absorbing those words, until I believed them. He never loved me, and I'm okay with that, I don't need his love anyway—so I thought. But now I've seen the way his chin quivers each time he drops me off at the bus station, each time we say goodbye, and perhaps we're both hyperaware that any one of those farewells could be our last. I know that he loves me and I refuse to let her, or anyone, take that away from me. "Whatever happened between the two of you, happened," I say. "But he loves me. I know he loves me."

We sit in silence in the line of traffic, exhaust and dust coming in through the open windows. If she could have had it her way, I would have never come back to see my father—none of us would have. Even Salvador had been down to see him recently, and when he was here, my mother had complained that she had hardly seen him, as he had spent most of his time shuttling the concubine to and from the hospital in the next town over. He had taken her to have an operation so that she might walk again, which was possible, since her spinal cord was not damaged and she still had feeling in her legs. Though the operation had gone well, she had not healed properly and was still in a wheelchair.

We are crawling past the livestock supply store when I see his red truck go barreling along the shoulder, driving against the flow of traffic on the other side of the road before cutting across the parking lot and sending a cloud of dust rising in his wake.

"There he goes," I practically shout. "Follow him."

"I'm not following that viejo," she says, keeping her gaze straight ahead. We go back and forth, me telling her to pull over and she refusing to do so, until I start gathering my grocery bags, and when she sees that I'm about to jump out of the Jeep, she pulls over.

"You better hurry up, or I'm going to leave," she says.

I zigzag around cars and trucks and make my way across the parking lot, gravel crunching under my flip-flops as I go. I watch him step out of his truck and then stand there, holding on to the door as if he were catching his breath. He's reaching for something on the seat when I come up behind him.

"Quiubo, Don Jose," I say in an exaggeratedly deep voice. He turns around and when he sees me, a big smile spreads across his face.

"¿Cuándo llego?" he asks, throwing his shoulders back and attempting to stand tall, though he's still holding on to the door.

"Apenas," I say, setting the bags down on the gravel and giving him a hug and a kiss on the cheek. He pats the middle of my back with his free hand.

"How's your hip?" I ask.

"It's coming along," he says. "I was wondering what happened to you. I just called Sonia this morning, but she didn't know anything."

I tell him how I had flown into Mexico City and had spent a few days visiting with a friend of mine, a journalist who lives in New York but spends his summers in Mexico City. How I had missed the overnight bus the day before, and so had had to wait an extra day, and had gotten into town just in time to come to the mercado with my mother.

"Your mother is here?" he says, stretching his neck up and scanning the cars behind me.

"Yeah, she's down there near the river," I say, and pick up the groceries, tell him that he might as well take them with him, and that I'll be out tomorrow.

"Oh, why tomorrow?"

"Mi amá says she's leaving for Chicago, so I'm going to spend the day with her." I place the bags inside his truck, on the floor in front of the passenger seat, and notice the cane next to the gearshift.

"Is that your cane?" I ask.

"They gave it to me when I left the hospital, but I don't like to use it," he says. "If my body grows accustomed to it, my hip might not heal properly."

"Maybe you should get rid of that horse," I say, pointing out how this is the second time El Relámpago has nearly killed him, and how is it that the saying goes? Three's a charm?

"A la tercera es la vencida," he says.

"That's right," I say. "Well, I better go before mi amá leaves me." I give him a quick hug and ask if I can borrow his cell phone, because I may be receiving a call on it. Before leaving New York, I had submitted a short story to a British literary journal that had expressed interest. Since I knew I was going to be in Mexico, and more or less off the grid, I had e-mailed the editor my father's cell number in case they needed to reach me.

He hands me his cell phone and I run back across the parking lot. Once I've crossed the road, I turn around and see him making his way to the supply store. His hands are clutched in fists on either side of him and he's moving slowly. With each step he takes, he looks as though he is apologizing to the gravel for treading upon it.

His cane is nowhere in sight.

A few days later, my father and I are kneeling shoulder-deep in the weeds that are sprouting like a green wildfire inside the horse run. A yellow plastic bowl sits between us.

"Is this a quelite?" I ask, holding up a weed I've just yanked from the ground. There are several plants that are very similar to quelites and he had told me to be careful, as some of those plants are poisonous.

"Those leaves are too round," he says, taking one from the bowl and handing it to me. "You see how the leaves on this one are more jagged?"

I inspect it. "And notice how it has a slightly red hue underneath and around the edges? That's how you can tell it apart from the others."

I'd never heard of quelites, but when my mother and I were at the mercado, I almost bought a bunch. The woman selling them had explained that they were a type of wild green, similar to spinach, but even more nutritious. "Don't waste your money," my mother said. "Those grow all over the place in La Peña. When you get out there, ask your father to show you." They really were everywhere, sprouting along the side of the house, around the stable and the corral, and all along the edge of the dirt road that runs up to the mesa. I cut a few more, throw them in the bowl, and notice a woman who is carrying a basket enter from the other end of the horse run.

"Buenas tardes," she says, giving me a nod as she walks past. My father tilts his hat, looks up, and when she sees him, she stops in her tracks.

"Jose? Jose Manuel, is that you?" She clutches her basket. "I thought you were dead."

"Dead?" he says. "Where did you hear that?"

"In town," she says. "Everyone was saying that your horse crushed you, left you lying by the river."

"People are saying that because that's what they would like, to see me dead. But as you can see, here we are, alive and kicking."

"Ay, Jose, that's not true," she says, trying not to laugh.

"If it were up to the townspeople, I would have been dead years ago," he says. "But the good thing is that it's not up to them, but to God. The day He decides your number is up, a fly could land on your shoulder, kick you, and that would be the end of that corrido."

She laughs and glances back at me.

"Is this your daughter?" she asks.

"Ey, she's visiting from the other side."

"That's good that you come spend time with your father," she says. "How do you like it here?"

"I love it," I say, though I don't trust my Spanish enough to try and explain why. To say how the sky here feels immense compared to New York, or how I love getting dirt under my fingernails because it makes me feel closer to home. Or that I love spending time with my father, how each day I spend with him feels stolen, like maybe he's tricked destiny, keeps cheating death, just so that we can have a bit more time together. I've begun to think that maybe he is indestructible— that he just might outlive us all.

"How long are you staying?" she asks.

"I'm not sure. Maybe five or six months," I say, though I'm leaving in four weeks, but I think it best not to let anyone know what my plans are. When classes were winding down in May, I'd heard about a jailbreak at the Zacatecas Federal Prison. In the dark hours of pre-dawn, a convoy of SUVs had pulled into the prison's parking lot, and within five minutes had driven away, taking fifty-three inmates with them—all of whom were believed to be members of the most ruthless drug cartel in Mexico. I hadn't thought much of the jailbreak at the time, and though nothing in town seems out of the ordinary, stories of people being picked up by SUVs and vanishing are already surfacing everywhere. Even my mother had warned me to be careful before leaving for Chicago.

"Five or six months?" she says, "that's a good amount of time." Her eyes come to rest on the bowl. "You guys are picking quelites, huh?"

"Ey," my father says. "When this muchacha got here a few days ago, she said she wanted to pick quelites, so I brought her out here. ¿Cómo ve?"

"Está bien," she says. "You just have to be careful. Some of these plants are poisonous."

"Yeah, that would be rough," he says. "Imagine? To spend the morning picking quelites, just to go and kick the bucket by the end of the day."

She starts laughing, hugs her basket to her chest, and says she must be on her way.

"That woman is a widow," my father says the minute she's out of sight. He tells me that she's from Tejones, the small neighboring ranch that sits on the other side of the river, and when she was first married, one of her daughters fell into the water well. "She was small, must have been about two or three years old," he says, glancing over his shoulder as if to make sure the woman is gone. "Then her husband jumped in to save the daughter, and he drowned too."

"They both *drowned*?" I practically shout, because I was expecting the story to have a happy ending, not suddenly take a turn for the worse.

"Ey," he says. "They went together."

"What an idiot," I say. "Why didn't he use a rope or something to anchor himself?"

"Who knows? I guess in the moment, he panicked, wasn't thinking clearly."

I throw another bunch into the bowl and he reaches in and pulls out a weed, shoots me a look.

"That's kind of funny, that that woman thought you were dead, huh?"

"Ey," he says. "People ask me all the time if I have a pact with the devil. They say, no Jose, you've escaped death so many times, how do you do it? You must have a pact with the Other One. But I tell them, it's just Diosito that watches over me." He throws another bunch into the bowl. "That's probably good enough," he says.

I squat down next to him and he reaches up and places one hand on my shoulder. I grab onto his elbow and help him to his feet. He grunts as he pushes himself up. I pick up the bowl and we make our way back to the house, walking slowly, his hand holding on to my shoulder for support.

"When El Relámpago left me by the river, my leg was turned so far out that it looked like it wasn't even attached to me anymore," he says, taking a moment to catch his breath. "I knew I was hurt, knew I shouldn't move, but I dragged myself away from the water because I also knew that if the rain continued, it was only a matter of time before the river grew and gave me a free ride to the other side."

22 ✦ EL CIEN VACAS

HE SITS IN HIS TRUCK, music blaring, eyes fixed on the horizon where gray clouds are burning like embers against the darkening sky. Earlier, we had gone to a mechanic's to pick up a minivan my father was having fixed. The mechanic had just returned from Oaxaca, from visiting his wife's family, and had offered us a cup of mescal that his father-in-law had made. It was super smooth and I had stopped at one cup because I could already feel it warming my veins, but my father had had a few more. "You have to be careful with this stuff, Jose," the mechanic had said when we were leaving. "It has a way of sneaking up on you."

Is that what happened? The mescal had snuck up on him? I had driven the minivan back home, following him on the main road, and he had stopped and picked up a six-pack before driving out of town. We hadn't even reached the curve when he had already slowed to a crawl. This is probably the reason why he had survived so many crashes. Whenever he was drinking and driving, he drove so slowly that he might as well have been pushing his truck home. When we pulled up in front of the house, he had killed the engine, but the music was still blaring and he refused to get out of his truck. Rosario had taken one look at him and had gone inside, as if saying, he's your problem now.

"Apá," I call to him, but the music swallows my voice before it even reaches him. He's looking straight ahead to where the donkey is tied to the mesquite where he left it in the morning. Though the donkey has gotten itself entangled in its own rope, I can tell my father is not looking at him but beyond him. He seems lost in his thoughts, in his music. *Does he even remember that I'm here?* I reach over him and grab what's left of the six-pack off the seat, and notice the empties scattered on the floor of the truck. He doesn't budge. I pull the keys from the ignition, and the minute the music stops, his head jerks up, as if he had just fallen asleep behind the wheel and has suddenly come to. His bloodshot eyes slide in their sockets, shift toward me, and refocus.

"Why did you turn off the music?" he mumbles.

"Because. It's getting late. Come on. Let's go put the donkey in the corral. He's all tangled up down there."

"How did he get down there?"

"You put him there. This morning. Don't you remember?"

He shrugs, reaches for the ignition, and realizes he's still holding a beer in his hand. He polishes off what's left and throws the can on the floor. It clanks against the other empties, and he starts feeling around on the seat next to him.

"What happened to my beer?" he asks.

"I put it away," I say, though I can feel the weight of it dangling from my index finger.

"Go bring me my beer," he says.

"Apá," I say. "If you don't stop drinking, I'm going to leave."

He glances at me and looks like he's about to say something, but his face puckers up and he turns away. I had left once before due to his drinking. He had gone into town in the afternoon to run errands, and then at about 2:00 a.m., I had awoken to the sound of the drums and horns approaching from a distance. It was like listening to the fury of some long-ago nightmare drawing near. I should have never come back to this place, I thought then, as every molecule in my body stood at attention, listening as he pulled up in front of the house, knowing that it was only a matter of time before the first blast, and I'd wished with all my might that I could vanish. But there was no escaping. The only way out was through the courtyard, and what if I happened to step outside as he fired the first bullet? I might not be as lucky as him.

I had lain in bed staring into the darkness as one after another, his corridos came booming into the bedroom—the same corridos that had kept me up for hours when I was a child. I still knew them all by heart. The stories of men rigging railroad tracks and hijacking trains; men driving cargo across the border, only to discover that someone had put the finger on them; men who had faced the firing squad without ever betraying their dignity; men who had surrendered their life for the love of a woman; men who had fought in the revolution and died defending their country; men who had saddled their horses and set out with the first light of morning, riding full stride across the desert, not stopping to rest until they reached the border; men who took the gamble, took the law into their own hands—some won, some lost, and others lost it all.

After sitting in his truck for about half an hour, he peeled back out and left, his music fading in the distance as he went. When he still wasn't back in the morning, I packed a small bag, thinking I'll be damned if I'm going to wait around here for him to show up and turn my day into a living hell. I set out on foot, crossed the river, and waited for the 9:00 a.m. bus on the main road. I stood under the shade of the mesquite, trying to shake the sting of his betrayal. It was the only rule, the unspoken rule—if he got drunk, I would leave. But then again, we had shared a few drinks here and there, so maybe the rule had been tarnished. Perhaps the exact spot where the line was drawn had begun to blur. I had taken his cell phone with me and had gone to Tito's house, and for the next two days he was calling from Rosario's phone morning, noon, and night. I had ignored his phone calls, then on the third day, he had Rosario send me a text: *Chuyita, where are you? Your father says he is sorry. He's not going to drink anymore. And where are you so he can go and pick you up.* I let one more day pass before calling him back.

He's staring at the steering wheel now and tears are streaming down his face.

"Apá, let's go inside so that you can eat something," I say. Food— this was my mother's trick. She knew that if she could get him to eat something, he would lose his appetite for alcohol and pass out soon enough.

"Orita, orita, orita," he mumbles. He reaches for the keys and realizes they're no longer in the ignition. "Let me listen to one more song," he says.

"And then you promise you'll come inside and eat?"

He nods. I hand him the keys and go around the back of his truck, squat down, and stash the six-pack inside El Negro's house before making my way across the dirt road, toward the donkey. Doña Consuelo is outside watering her plants.

"Your father has been drinking again, hasn't he?" she says when I'm crossing in front of her gate.

"Ey," I say.

"I heard the music and that's how I knew. What are you going to do? Are you going to leave again?" I'm surprised she knows I had left before, though it seems everyone knows everything about everybody around here.

"No, it's getting late, I'll probably just stay here," I say, though I don't tell her that I feel somewhat responsible for this. That I should have knocked that cup out of his hand the minute he finished the first mescal. His tolerance is obviously not what it used to be. When he was younger he could go for two or three days without stopping.

"The last time you left, I saw your father. He was moping around, and I said, what's the matter, Jose? Your daughter left because you were drinking, didn't she? And I told him that he ought to be ashamed of himself. I did. I told him just like that. I said, shame on you, Jose. Whenever your kids come to visit, even if you get the urge to drink, you have to resist it. You have to respect your kids. You've already put them through enough. That's what I told him, don't think I didn't," she says. "He sort of just listened to me, but he didn't say anything. Your father might be what he is, and has done what he has done, pero eso sí, he has never disrespected me. On the contrary, after he was released from prison and came back here, he told me that as long as he was alive, no one was going to come bother us, and it's true. Just take a look around at all these abandoned homes, and all of their owners living on the other side, and do you think anyone is going to come try to break in? Nunca. And it's because of your father, because he's there, and everyone knows what he's capable of."

The music comes thundering across the dirt road and she glances toward his truck.

"Well, there he is," she says. "But you know why your father is like that? It's because of his parents, because they never reined him in, never gave him a good word of advice. On the contrary. I'm going to tell you a story, and this is something I saw with my own eyes and heard with my own ears. Don't think it's a story that someone else told me, it's something I witnessed myself," she says. "Ya ve que your father's parents used to live in this house?" She motions to the house next door to hers. "Well, when they were still living here, one day your father came running home from school and he was crying. He must have been about seven or eight because he wasn't much taller than this gate. I saw him go flying by, and his mother was outside chopping onions on a butcher block, and he went running up to her, threw his arms around her legs, and buried his face in her skirt. 'What's wrong?' she said, prying him off her. 'Why are you crying?' She demanded to know, and the poor thing, he was crying so hard he could barely catch his breath, but he managed to tell her that some older boys had been pushing him around. I think that was around the time when they had started calling him El Cien Vacas, because he had taken to bragging that he had one hundred cows up at his father's ranch. Well, believe me when I tell you that she grabbed the knife she had been chopping the onions with and handed it to him. 'Pues ve, y chíngatelos,' she said. Those were her words. 'Pues ve, y chíngatelos.' Imagine, your own mother handing you a knife and telling you to go mess someone up? Well, that is exactly what she did, and the boy just stood there gasping and staring at the knife in his hand, and well, there he is now." She looks toward his truck, from which the music is still blaring. "How much longer are you staying?" she asks.

"I'm not sure. Maybe another four or five months," I say, though I'm leaving by the end of the week. I could probably just tell her the truth, but I think it best to be cautious, figure that if anyone is getting any clever ideas about kidnapping me, if the word gets out that I'll be here for several months, they might be more inclined to take their time about it. Rosario had recently told me about the Hernández brothers, how among the three of them, they owned half the businesses in the next town over. Their father disappeared and then they received a phone call. They were given an amount and a deadline. When the money failed to arrive by the given date, they received a package—inside was their father's finger. They scrambled, sent the money, and imagine, to be out half a million dollars and for what? They never saw their father again. "How were we supposed to know he was diabetic?" was the only apology they got from the kidnappers.

My mother had also told me about the son of a señora she knew. He had just arrived from the other side driving a brand-new truck, and the SUVs stopped him in the outskirts of town. They took his truck away and then drove him out into the middle of the desert, where they stripped him of everything and beat him within an inch of his life. They had left him for the vultures, but a few days later he resurfaced in town, wearing nothing but his bruised kneecaps and his shattered pride. He was one of the lucky ones.

A different señora's son had also disappeared, and when she failed to come up with the money, the kidnappers called and told her that if she ever wanted to see her son again, she could go fish him out of the reservoir. She wanted to give him a proper burial, so she hired a professional diver to retrieve his body. The diver returned wide-eyed, empty-handed, and speaking in incomplete sentences, saying he didn't know which one to bring back. "There are so many bodies down there," he told her.

I tell Doña Consuelo that I'd best be going, as it's getting dark and I still need to bring the donkey to the corral and give him water.

Even before I reach the donkey I can see that all four of his legs are entangled in the rope. He's jerking about and I approach him slowly and run my hand down his neck.

"O, o," I say in a deep voice, the way I've heard my father talk to the horses. I untie the rope from the mesquite and pull it down, over, and through the thorny brambles. "O, o," I say, as I lean down and untangle the rope from around his front hooves. He nudges my head, his wet breath in my ear. I do the same around his hind legs, careful not to get too close, wouldn't want him to give me a swift kick and send me clear to the other side. Once the rope is loose enough, it slides off and falls onto the ground.

I walk him across the dirt road. The last of the chickens are tucking themselves into the branches of the eucalyptus trees. The music grows louder as we approach the truck and then recedes as we walk past. I cut the donkey loose inside the corral, grab the hose, and while I'm filling the trough, El Negro comes running out of the roofless room that used to be the church, and in a single leap, he's on top of the stacked-stone wall and running along its edge. El Negro is my father's newest dog. He's a broad-shouldered black Labrador mix that seems to have a wild strand in his genetic makeup—as if he had been crossbred with a panther or a mountain lion. He usually accompanies me on my morning jogs. Crossing in front of the neighbor's house has always been an ordeal, since their three dogs are sure to come running out onto the dirt road, looking to lock jaws with whatever dog I'm with.

El Lobo had stopped jogging with me altogether, just so he wouldn't have to cross in front of their house, I assumed. But El Negro was different. The first time the neighbor's dogs had come snarling at him, he had stopped in his tracks and turned to face them, the hair on his lower back and his tail rising as if from static from a passing cloud. The three dogs carried on, but not one of them crossed over onto the road. El Negro had crouched under the barbed wire and resumed his stance inside their property. He strutted up to the dogs, one at a time. Each one barked with less gusto as it curled its tail between its legs and lowered its head, until there was silence. He ran a lap inside their enclosure and peed on the only tree on their property before rejoining me on the dirt road, tongue dangling, tail wagging. If he hadn't reeked of skunk, I would have dropped to my knees and thrown my arms around him.

A few days ago, while we were jogging on the dirt road along the mesa, I had heard some growling piercing my music. When I lowered the volume and turned around, El Negro was locking jaws with a large gray dog in the middle of the road.

"Negro," I yelled, whipping a rock at them. It had gone skidding across the road and pelted the other dog on the ribs, startling them enough that they both stopped and looked in my direction. The other dog looked like a German shepherd. He had a long snout and ears that stood straight up, and it dawned on me that he was a wild animal of sorts, as we were nowhere near any houses.

They broke into a sprint. The animal disappeared into the field, and El Negro came running up to me. I thought that was the last we'd see of him, but still, I cut my run short, turned down the music on my iPod, and started jogging back home. A few minutes later, I heard its howls piercing my music again. I pulled my headphones from my ears and turned around. There was nothing there. The dirt road stretched long and empty behind me. I continued jogging at a steady pace and again came the howling, then I saw it in the field. It was about fifteen feet away, running parallel to us and keeping at our pace.

"Chucho," I grunted, throwing a rock at it. And it fell back, but then once more it was in the field, howling and trailing us. I whipped another rock, and it slowed, fell back. Each time it got too close, I'd launch a stone, until it finally vanished into the field.

"That son of a bitch followed you?" my father said when I got home and told him what happened. He and Rosario were still in the corral, milking the cows. He said it was probably just a coyote, though Rosario insisted that it must have been a lobo, as it was unheard of that a coyote would get into it with a dog. My father shot her a look and she fell silent. "Tomorrow you should take my gun," he said, "and if that cabrón rears its head again, just blast it right between the eyes."

I laughed it off, saying that with my luck I'd probably fall down and end up shooting myself. Though after that day, my jogs were not as serene as they once had been. From then on, I was more vigilant, kept the volume on my iPod a bit lower, and looked behind me every once in a while just to make sure I wasn't being tracked.

Once the trough is full, I turn off the water and head back to my father's truck. He's still sitting in the driver's seat, pounding his chest, engrossed in a conversation with someone whom he seems to see standing there in front of him. Rosario has told me this is something he does when he drinks. He'll lock himself in his bedroom and from the other side of the door she can hear him carrying on and talking to someone.

"Apá," I say over the music. He glances at me, and I notice the tears streaming down his face. "Come on, let's go inside. Let's go eat."

He cries even harder when he sees me.

"No, mijita," he says, turning away. "You've no idea how much I've suffered."

The first time I heard him say this, I wanted to say, oh, yeah, well what about all the heartache you've caused others? What about all the families you've destroyed, all the kids you've left fatherless? My uncle alone had eleven kids, most of whom still lived in the area. And though they've always been pleasant to me, they are the reason why I don't like going into town with my father, am always wary of running into them while gallivanting around with the man who killed their father. Joaquín also had two or three kids back home. "Those poor kids," my mother kept saying. "Imagine, having their father come back to them in a body bag?" She had even collected a donation at her church to help with the shipping arrangements.

"So many cabrones have tried to take me down, but they just

haven't been able to." He raises his eyebrows and nods as if agreeing with himself. "With me, they just go round and round in circles like dogs chasing their own tails," he says. "I am Jose Manuel Venegas, El Cien Vacas, and if anyone has a problem with me, they know where to come find me. The minute any cabrón shows up here, we'll go at it, fast, and we'll see who's left standing. Right, mija?" He looks over at me, and his eyes almost look green against the red veins. There is a deeply rooted sorrow in them, and I can't help but think that perhaps his anguish is the sum of all the pain he has caused.

"Apá, it's just you and me here. Stop talking about killing people," I say, though I know it's his pride talking. The pride his mother instilled in him so long ago. I had never heard about her handing him the knife, but each time he told me about Fidel, and how she had handed him the pistol, telling him to never back down from anyone, he'd always look at me and say: "Imagine? My own mother." That had been such a defining moment in his life, and though he could look back on it now and see how twisted it was, he was unable to rescue himself from it. His stories were his identity—his pride and his pain.

"Come on, it's getting dark. Let's go inside," I say, though I can tell he's not listening. His thoughts have drifted off with the music. He can probably still hear his mother singing his praises from beyond her matrimonial grave. *You never run away from a fight. Even if you know you're going to get your ass kicked, you stay and you fight like a man.* Had we not had our mother countering his voice, who knows where we might have all ended up?

"I've taken down so many cabrones and I don't regret a single one," he says, staring at the steering wheel. "As far as I'm concerned, each one of those culeros got what they deserved. Except for my brother-in-law." He presses his lips tight, trying to dam up the impossible tears.

Each time he has a drink or two, he starts talking about my uncle, and what a fine man he was, and how he wishes he had never pulled that trigger. But no amount of regret will bring my uncle back nor restore all those hours my mother spent locked away from us, practically barricaded behind her bedroom door after she returned from burying her brother. Nor will it ease her guilt. When I was here last summer, she and I had gone to visit my uncle's widow, and my mother had broken down, saying she was sorry she had ever married that man that had ended her brother's life. Perhaps we all carry a bit of my father's guilt, but ultimately, it's he who must bear the brunt of all he's done. He may have been released from jail, but as long as he's alive, he will be imprisoned by his past. Maybe this is why he's still alive: not because he keeps cheating death but rather because life refuses to let him go—he's not finished paying his debt here yet. Perhaps only in death will he be released from his suffering. The tears are streaming down his face, and he seems so broken, so powerless to help himself, and I want to take him in my arms and hold him for a long time, as if by doing so I could untangle him.

"Manuel was a fine black bull," he says, crying even harder. "That one, yes. That one hurts. That one will weigh on me until the day I die. But other than that." He catches his breath and taps twice on the dashboard. "El que se chingó, se chingó."

23 · HAILSTORM

WE SET OUT IN THE PITCH DARK and ride in silence under the canopy of stars. It's a moonless morning, and there's nothing but the glow of my father's white shirt guiding the way in the distilled starlight. We meander up the narrow horse trail, which is overgrown with brambles. Thorny branches reach out of the darkness and scrape the top of my hat, snag my jeans as the horse's hooves slide and clack on the rocks below. The scent of wet earth hovers in the air as we ride toward the towering obscurity. Other than the sound of leather creaking and the occasional cock singing out in the distance, all is quiet and serene, and soon the stars are fading against the dawning light.

"There's a storm coming," my father says when we reach the entrance to the ranch at daybreak.

"How do you know?" I ask. The notion of a storm seems impossible, as there isn't a single cloud in the sky.

"See that turtle?" He points to a turtle that has crawled out of the river and so far up the incline that it's practically at the entrance. "When we were kids, that's how we knew a storm was coming. The turtles move to higher ground."

Must be some storm, I think, judging from the distance the turtle has put between itself and the river.

We go through the usual routine: The dogs help round up the cattle, and we hitch the horse and the donkey to a tree near the corral.

My father fills the troughs with salt, and I find a shady spot and make us tortas for lunch.

"Did you see Chupitos?" he asks, taking a seat in the shade next to me. "She's in there with La Negra." He motions to the corral, where the horns are visible above the stacked stones. Chupitos is the name he has given a calf that lost its mother when I was here last summer.

She and her mother had been grazing along the river near the house when the mother came running up the hill and ran past the small church, her head bobbing up and down as if she were trying to dislodge something from her throat. The minute she reached the house, she collapsed in front of the courtyard. Her jaw was clenched and a few long blades of grass were jutting from her mouth. I watched as my father ran his fingers along her neck and tried to pry her mouth open, saying that she may have swallowed a chapulín—a large grasshopper that, if swallowed whole, can get stuck in the animal's throat or intestines. I squatted down next to her and looked into her eyes. She looked terrified, but then a calm washed over her like a passing shadow. She inhaled and never exhaled.

That evening, when my father brought the cattle into the corral, while the other calves were feeding before being separated from their mothers for the night, I had watched the orphaned calf sneak up behind an unsuspecting cow and grab hold of an udder. She managed a few chupitos, a few little sucks, before the cow realized it wasn't her calf and either kicked or head-butted her. Eventually, she gave up and went and stood near the gate. There were three blackbirds circling above the field where her mother lay. She stared in the direction of the field, but she did not bay.

My father didn't think Chupitos was going to make it. Though Rosario was feeding her with a bottle, she had lost a lot of weight. Then La Negra, one of his best milk-giving cows, who was the descendant of one of his mother's best milk-giving cows, gave birth to a calf that died the day after it was born. He skinned the black calf, made a few holes in the raw hide, and tied it like a second skin around Chupitos. At first, whenever Chupitos approached La Negra, she was shunned, until La Negra started sniffing her and ended up adopting her.

"You should see her, she's really fat and beautiful, looks just like her mother," he says. "If you want, when we finish eating, I'll point her out so you can take a picture of her."

"Está bien," I say, handing him the first torta. Ever since she was orphaned, each time I called him, I always inquired about Chupitos, would have adopted her myself if I could have.

We chew in silence, listening to the rush of the two waterfalls, which are flowing heavy with rainwater. He pulls the binoculars out of his satchel and scans the ridge on the other side of the river.

"See that white thing over there?" he says, pointing at something among the green shrubs on the ridge. "Is that a cow or a rock?" He hands me the binoculars.

Even before I bring them to my eyes, I can see that it's a rock, but still, I have a look. The only reason I know that his eyesight is failing is because recently, when I was walking past his bedroom window, I looked in and saw him sitting on his bed in a pool of sunlight. He was going through some documents, a pair of reading glasses with thick lenses resting on his nose. It had been a while since he'd dyed his hair and mustache the usual jet-black, and they both had a silver sheen to them. He suddenly looked so very old and so calm—like he was incapable of harming even a house mouse. I knocked on his bedroom door, he called out for me to come in, and when I entered, he was still sitting on his bed, papers strewn about, but the glasses were nowhere in sight.

"It's a rock." I hand the binoculars back to him, and he slides them back into his satchel.

He finishes his torta and leans back, resting his head on a rock and saying he's going to take a quick nap before we head home.

"What if there's a reindeer under there?" I say. Two weeks before, we had come out here and had spent the morning making rock piles around the property so that the man he had hired to reinforce the barbed-wire fence would know where the wooden posts should go. "Careful," he said, watching as I slid both hands under a rock and picked it up. "There could be some reindeer under there." He rolled a different rock over with his boot, and sure enough, there were two blond, almost translucent, scorpions sitting side by side underneath it. Their pincers curled above their heads so that they looked like deer antlers. Seeing the two scorpions was as though he had hit a light switch—there were rocks scattered all over the grounds. "If one of these stings you, it will definitely be goodbye green mountaintops and goodbye blue skies," he said.

"Don't they have the antidote for it in town?" I asked.

"Eeow, by the time we make it to town, we'd be stiff as a board," he said.

He places his hat over his face and folds his arms across his chest, tucking his hands under his armpits.

"I just say a little prayer. I say, listen, cabrón, I know you're under there, but if you don't bother me, I won't bother you," he says, crossing his legs at the ankle, one over the other. "Either way, we'll wake up here or on the other side." He's snoring almost immediately.

I finish my torta and clean up, wrap the cheese in the cheesecloth, and put the leftover food away. I polish off the rest of the water and lean back, rest my head on a rock, place my straw hat over my face, and focus on the dots of dispersed sunlight that are filtering through the hat, trying not to think about the scorpions that might be lurking below, and doze off.

When I wake, my father and the sun are gone, and it seems that the sky itself has shifted. Gray clouds have moved in and hover heavy and low, though in the valley below, rays of sunlight are shining through the openings in the clouds, like waterfalls pouring from the sky.

"Vámonos porque nos agarra el agua," my father says. He's making his way back from the pools and carrying the water bottle, filled to the top. "Did you see your cow?" he asks, handing me the bottle.

"No," I say, taking a gulp. The water is ice-cold and delicious, as it always is. I can't remember when I started drinking the water, but it has yet to make me sick.

"If you want, we can walk around the corral so you can take a picture of her before we head back."

"Next time," I say, not knowing that in two weeks, my cow will be dead.

We untie the horse and donkey and sling the leather satchels over the neck of the saddles.

"Why don't you take the donkey," he says. "It'll be easier on your knee."

"Let's go back the way we came." Since his hip is still recovering, he rode the donkey and I rode the horse. "My knee will be fine," I say, stepping into the stirrup and kicking my leg over Chemel's horse saddle.

He hands me the rifle, and I sling the leather strap over the neck of the saddle. We never bring the rifle to the ranch. He usually brings his gun, tucked into the back of his belt. But on the day that he had one too many mescals, he had ended up giving me his gun and saying that I should hold on to it. I assumed he had gotten the urge to shoot it off in the house but thought better of it—what if he sent a bullet through his bedroom door and I happened to be on the other side? Since the day he handed it over, he has not asked about it, probably too ashamed that it had come to that.

On the way back, the horse and the donkey move at a swifter gait, and by the time we clear San Martín, the clouds seem to be at war with one another. From the four corners of the earth—north, south, east, and west—cloud formations have risen and are now merging overhead, snuffing out the last rays of sunshine. A rumble rips through the clouds above, and then a bright whip cracks down against the mountains as if trying to make them gallop. Lightning bolts are crashing down in the nearby ridges and fields, and each time one hits, the horse surges forward, breaks into a trot, catches up to the donkey, but soon falls behind again.

"Make that lazy horse move faster or the storm is going to catch us," my father yells back to me over the roaring wind.

I loosen the reins and dig my heels into the horse's ribs, but he ignores the soft rubber of my Merrell hiking boots. When I arrived, my father had asked if I had a different pair of shoes, something less chunky and less likely to get caught in the stirrup—just in case. Another bolt comes crashing down somewhere behind us, sending a flash across the back of my father's white shirt. Again, the horse picks up the pace, its head turning from side to side as if trying to figure out where the next bolt will hit.

"Maybe we should pull over and wait," I say when we catch up to my father.

"Wait for what?" he says, turning to shield his ear from the wind.

"For the storm to pass," I say.

He holds up his index finger and waves it back and forth. We ride on, and we are making our way along the dirt road on la mesa when two young men come riding full stride across the field toward us, the wind billowing in their button-down shirts.

"Ándele, Don Jose," one calls out over the wind. "Hay viene el agua," he yells, his eyes lingering on the rifle as they fly past.

A purple bolt snaps out of the gray clouds and spiders into five smaller threads that crack against a nearby ridge with so much force that the air itself seems to tremble. Again the horse is galloping, and I start doing an inventory of everything that might attract the lightning to me—the rifle, the bridle parts, and the stirrups—all metal.

"What if we get hit by lightning?" I ask my father, when we catch up to him.

"Pues, si nos toca, nos toca," he says, as if he's accepted his fate. If it's our turn to go, it's our turn to go. He glances over at me, and stops. "A ver ese rifle," he says, holding out his hand. I pass him the rifle and he slings the leather strap across the donkey saddle, asks if I want to throw on the poncho, but since we're almost at the horse trail that leads down to La Peña, I tell him I'll be fine.

We continue on, and when we reach the horse trail, El Negro takes off, sprinting ahead of us back to the house. Must be some storm, I think, as El Negro is not one to scare easily. Though, ever since the scuffle with the wild animal, he never jogged with me again. It was as if he knew that whatever was lurking out there was sure to take him down. I never saw the animal again, but just the other day I happened to look back, and in the distance there was a cloud of dust rising from the dirt road and a gleaming SUV was barreling toward me. A brand-new SUV on that road, at that hour, was so out of place that before I knew it I was racing along the dirt road until I reached the horse trail. I dropped down into the rocks and thorns and waited, listening to the whir of tires as they approached on the road above, and the whole time my heart was beating in time with my thoughts: Please don't stop. Please don't stop. Please don't stop. After the tires passed, I waited several minutes and then sprinted back home.

When I told my father about the SUV, he said it was probably just some norteño making his way to visit a relative farther up the mountain. Maybe it was a norteño, or maybe he was trying to downplay my fears, same as he had done with the wild animal. Still, after seeing the SUV, I stopped jogging on this road, stuck closer to home.

Soon we are descending the rocky trail and I'm relieved to be getting off the mesa, to be on lower ground.

"Here comes the rain," my father says, when we clear the back entrance to La Peña.

Even before I turn around, I hear it. All along the mesa raindrops are exploding on the dirt road where we just were, and as the wall of rain moves toward us, the water is bouncing off the trees along the ridge, then off the cornstalks in the fields, as it draws near. My father clears the gate to the corral and rides up under the aluminum shed. I dig my heels into the horse's sides but he continues to walk, taking his time along the stacked stones though the mist is already blowing past us. Just as the horse reaches the gate and turns to enter, the sound and fury of the storm overtakes us. Rain and hail the size of Ping-Pong balls come crashing down, hitting us head-on.

The horse starts jerking about, turns away from the hail, and surges, attempting to bolt for the river. He almost rips the reins from my grip, but I hold tight, and then his neck is thrashing and he's moving backward, and there's nothing I want more than to be back on solid ground—but it's too late. I think about sliding my feet from the stirrups in case he rears—wouldn't want to get dragged along the rocks like my father, who is yelling something from under the tin shed, his voice so faint it's as though he's yelling from the edge of a distant shoreline. Muddy waters are raging all around us; the minute the hail hits the ground it vanishes below the surface of the water.

"Bring him in," I hear my father yell. I pull on the reins and try to turn the horse toward the gate, but the minute he turns, hail pelts his forehead and sends him thrashing.

"I can't."

"Make him."

"You come and get him," I yell.

The horse is jerking and trying to break free, and it feels like the ground itself is moving as the brown water goes rushing by. This is how it happens, I think, this is how easy it is to slip away. I have to remind myself to breathe, to stay calm, because if I start to panic, the horse will panic, and whether I like it or not, we are now in this together. I reach out and run my hand slow and steady down his strong neck.

"O," I say, in a firm tone, as hail continues to crash down all around us. "O," I say in a voice that resonates in my chest. "O." Again I run my hand down his neck. He bows his head and I loosen the reins to give him space. "O," I say, "O."

I see my father's black cowboy boots come splashing through the muddy water. He pulls the leather strap that holds the hitching rope to the side of the saddle and the rope uncoils, falling freely, half of it vanishing into the water below. He grabs it and pulls the horse along the stacked-stone wall, through the gate, and into the corral, like a mighty ship giving us a tow. I duck to clear the tin shed and once I'm under it, the storm takes on a different sound. It's somehow louder—metallic as the hail hits against the tin roof. The minute my feet touch the ground, I want to drop to my knees and kiss the soil.

"We almost made it," I say, though I realize he had timed it perfectly. If my horse had been moving just a little faster, we would have beaten the storm. We're both soaked and stand side by side, looking out at the rain and hail.

"At least now you'll have a story to tell the others when you get back to the other side," he says, shooting me a smile, the excitement of the storm dancing in his eyes.

Two weeks later, after having spent a week in Chicago and another week in Maine visiting Abigail's mother, with whom I've forged a friendship, I'm back in New York. Since the day I left, he had been calling. It's Saturday afternoon, and I finally buy an international phone calling card, find a shady spot on a bench in a community garden in Brooklyn, and call him back.

"How was Chicago?" he asks.

"It was nice." I inform him that I had given everyone the cheese he sent. On the day I left Mexico, we had driven to the house of an elderly couple that, according to him, made the best cheese in town. He had asked me to pick out one cheese wheel for each of my siblings. "Guess what?" I say.

"¿Qué pasó?"

"Remember how you had to keep driving me into town to use the Internet?" I say. He had driven me to an Internet café a few times, and while I checked my e-mails, he had sat in the chair next to me, asking exactly how e-mail works.

"Ey," he says.

"Before leaving New York, I had submitted a short story to a

British literary journal," I say. "And while I was in Mexico, I had been e-mailing with the editor. Then, when I was in Chicago, they e-mailed me saying they are going to publish my story in their upcoming issue."

"That's good," he says. "Did you happen to see Maria Elena when you were in Chicago?"

"Ey," I say.

"Did she say when she's coming back to Mexico?" he asks.

"She was supposed to drive back down a few days ago," I say, but perhaps he should call her because she always says she's going to do one thing and then does another.

"So," I say. "Guess what the story is about."

"Sabes," he says. "What's it about?"

"Well, you know, it's kind of funny, because I never used to talk about you, or the past, but then when I got into this writing program, I started writing about it, and do you remember when everything happened with Joaquín? Well, I wrote a story about that," I say. "¿Cómo ve?"

There is a long silence on the other end.

"And guess how much they're paying me for it," I say.

"How much?" he asks.

I give him the figure.

"A jijo," he says, "that's great." I can practically hear the smile spreading across his face. "No, there are so many things that have happened to me, you have no idea. Next time you come down, you should bring a notebook, and I'll tell you some stories, and then you can go back, write them out, and make another billete for yourself."

"That sounds good," I say, thinking that when I go back down for the holidays, maybe I'll take him up on his offer. Bring a notebook and a tape recorder, even.

"¿Dónde dejó la juska?" he asks.

"You still haven't found it?" I know this is why he has been calling so much since I left—he hasn't found his gun, though I imagine he and Rosario have turned the house upside down looking for it. After he gave it to me, he never asked about it again, and when I was leaving, Rosario asked me to leave it with her, and I almost did but thought better of it. They had not been getting along, and what if she got some bright idea and turned the gun on him? Or what if he ended up doing something to her? On the day I left, I had taken it from under my T-shirt pile, wrapped it in a cheesecloth, placed it in a black plastic bag, and stashed it underneath a light-blue photo album inside one of the trunks in the storage room.

"I haven't really had time to look for it," he says.

I tell him where it is, though he will never see that gun again. Two days later, the men in the SUVs arrive and kick down his front door.

BOOK THREE

24 ◆ THE KIDNAPPING

THEY HAVE BEEN WATCHING HIS MOVES, keeping tabs on the road that runs in front of his house, and earlier that day they saw him and Rosario climb into his red truck and drive clear out of town. When he returns in the afternoon, he pulls into the dusty lot where the mercado is held on Sundays. Rosario waits in the passenger seat, while he goes into a cell phone store. He's in the store for a mere ten minutes, but by the time he steps back out into the slanted rays of the afternoon sun, everything has shifted. Blinds have been drawn in nearby stores, the sidewalks have emptied, doors have been locked, and most of the cars that were parked near his truck vacated the scene when the black SUVs rolled up.

He makes his way across the lot, scrolling through his phone when the sound of gravel crunching under his boots stops him in his tracks. It's not the rhythm of the gravel that is off but rather the absence of familiar sounds. Missing is the laughter—the shrieking and yelling of kids playing a makeshift soccer game in the lot. Gone is the rustling of bags, of people rushing along, running afternoon errands. Even the incessant bell of the paletero has been silenced. Nothing but the echo of a dog barking in the distance fills the space around him. He looks up and notices the SUVs stationed on either side of his vehicle. Though it's the sight of the man sitting next to Rosario and grinning at him from behind the steering wheel of his truck that sends the gold caps vibrating against his teeth so that he can practically taste the metal. He's standing still but hears the gravel shifting, footsteps approaching from behind, as if his own shadow had sprung to life.

"Vamos, viejo." There are two men with machine guns standing on either side of him.

They escort him into the backseat of one of the SUVs, where a woman is waiting for him.

"Hola, mi gallinita de oro," she says, her chapped lips parting in a grin and revealing her rust-colored teeth. The sour stench of alcohol exudes from her. He recognizes the rifle she's holding between her knees. It's the same rifle that has hung above his bed for years, the same rifle with which he had blown the head off a rattlesnake when he was ten years old. The woman snatches his cell from his hand and searches his pockets, pulling out his red handkerchief and his worn leather wallet. A man climbs into the seat on the other side of him and the convoy starts moving. The SUV he's riding in follows his truck onto the main road, and by the time they clear the last speed bump on the edge of town, they have already removed his boots and tied his ankles and wrists together. "Who's Norma Venegas?" the woman asks as she scrolls through his phone.

"She's a niece," he says.

"She's not your daughter?"

"No, she's a niece." They fly past the slaughterhouse where two other SUVs are sitting in the shade under the mesquite.

"A niece?" She narrows her eyes on him. She's not a bad-looking woman. Early forties, most likely, though a scar across her cheekbone, dark circles under her eyes, and her rotting teeth seem to age her beyond her years. "What's the name of your daughter, the one who owns a gas station in Jalisco?"

"I don't have any daughters in Jalisco."

She rams the butt of the rifle into his kneecap with so much force that it sends a shock through his injured hipbone.

"Don't play smart with me, viejo." She tells him they are well aware he has five daughters, and word around town is that one of them lives in Jalisco and owns a gas station, so what is her number?

"I don't know where you're getting your information from," he says, though perhaps they've gotten it from him, because even though businesses have started closing early and everyone goes home before dark, locks their doors, and stays put until morning, the taverns are still open. And though they have lost a few regulars, he has carried on as he always has. He's not one to hide from the SUVs or anyone for that matter, especially not in his own town. He has continued frequenting the taverns, and after having a few drinks, it's inevitable—he will start boasting about his five girls and how successful they are, how each one has made a small fortune, and with no help from a man at that. "I don't have any daughters in Jalisco," he says.

"What about your daughter who lives in Nueva York, what is her number?" Again she's scrolling through his phone.

"I don't have any daughters living in Nueva York."

"Who's the girl who was just down here visiting you?"

"She's just a niece," he says, bracing himself to keep the weight of his body from barreling into the woman as they fly around the only curve on that road between town and his home.

"Another niece?" The woman smirks at him before ramming the butt of the rifle into his other kneecap. "What is her name?"

"Maria de Jesus," he says, and again she's scrolling through his phone, though he knows she will never find that name, or any of their names for that matter. He has all five numbers saved under their nicknames: Chuyita, La Flaca, Chela, La Vickie, Sonita.

Up ahead his truck slows and turns left onto the dirt road that leads up to La Peña. He watches the woman go through his wallet as the SUV he's riding in also turns left, and then they're bouncing along the dirt road, over the river, up the incline, and through the entrance where the dilapidated limestone pillars still stand. She pulls out a piece of paper and a few loose bills. There's a name and a phone number scribbled on the paper.

"Sonia salon," she reads out loud, as she places the bills in her breast pocket. "Who's Sonia?"

"That's my daughter," he says.

"Your daughter?" she says, grinning so big that he catches a glimpse of the gold caps on her upper molars. "And what does she do?"

"She works in a beauty salon in Chicago."

"Isn't she the owner?"

"No, she just works there," he says, though he can tell that she's not buying it.

Even before they pull up in front of his house, he notices that the minivan he picked up two weeks before is gone, and that his house has been broken into. His bedroom door is scraped, bent, and slightly ajar. Two men help Rosario out of the truck and into her wheelchair. The woman gets out of the SUV, lights a cigarette, and walks a full circle around Rosario before stopping in front of her and asking what is the name of the viejo's daughter, the one who owns a gas station in Jalisco?

"I don't really know anything about his daughters," Rosario says.

The woman takes a long drag, narrowing her gaze on Rosario before slapping her clear across the face.

"Call his daughters," she says, throwing his phone onto Rosario's lap. "Tell them we have their father and if they ever want to see him again, they can reach us at this number." She scribbles the digits down on a scrap of paper and hands it to Rosario.

The convoy starts moving and once again the SUV he's riding in is following his truck. The woman reaches into the seat pocket in front of her and pulls out a roll of toilet paper and duct tape. She takes two wads of toilet paper, presses them to his eyes, and while she holds them there, one of the men wraps the duct tape tightly around his head. Inside that new darkness a different light snaps on. The lay of that land is practically a part of his genetic makeup, etched in his bones. He doesn't need to see when they are rolling over the river because he can hear the rushing water below, and when they turn onto the main road, the whir of the tires takes on a different sound. Again, he has to steady himself as they clear the curve to keep the weight of his body from pressing, not into the woman this time, but the man. He also knows exactly when they are passing in front of the bus depot. He can hear the engines of the buses idling, smell the diesel, and then comes the da-thump, da-thump, da-thump as they clear the three speed bumps on the north end of town before breaking out onto the open road and into the desert.

It's Monday night, and I'm out having dinner with a friend in my neighborhood.

"I'm running to the bathroom," my friend says, pushing her chair away from the table. The waiter comes by and drops off our check. I reach for my bag and notice my cell is vibrating. I have two missed calls from Sonia and a text from her: Call me 911. This can't be good,

I think as I stare at the flame in the votive, watch how it sways each time someone opens the door. *What happened now? What if he's dead? What if he killed someone? What if he shot Rosario?* It had been only two days since I told him where his gun was hidden. The reflection of the flame makes the smooth grooves in the wooden table look dark and warm, and there's a part of me that wants to crawl into one of those small nooks and stay there for a very long time.

"What's the damage?" my friend asks when she returns. There's a bounce in her platinum blonde hair, and she's wearing a fresh coat of pink lipstick.

"I just got a text from my sister," I say, clearing my throat. "And she wants me to call her 911."

"That can't be good," she says.

"I know." I tap my phone twice on the table. The bartender pours wine for a couple sitting at the bar. All the polished glass bottles are gleaming on the wall behind him.

"Well, you should probably call her back," my friend says.

"Right." I reach for my glass of red wine and down what's left before calling Sonia. When she picks up, she informs me that she just got off the phone with Mary, who received a call from Rosario, saying that my father has been kidnapped.

"Kidnapped?" I say. "How? By who?"

She doesn't know all the details, but according to Rosario, they had ransacked the whole house. The wardrobes and storage trunks had all been rifled, and they had left shattered dishes, pillows, and clothing strewn in their wake. They had given Rosario a number where they could be reached.

"And?" I say. "Did Mary call them?"

"She thinks we should stay out of it," Sonia says. When Rosario had called Mary and told her what happened, Mary had taken a few moments to let the news sink in before responding with a single knee-jerk reaction. "You know what, Rosario? For all I know, he did something to provoke this, and I'm not getting involved," she said. "You can call them and tell them that they're not going to get a penny out of me, or any of his kids, because he abandoned us when we were young." Mary had refused to even take down the number. "Did you notice anything suspicious while you were down there?" Sonia asks.

I tell her how stories of people being kidnapped were surfacing all over town and about the SUV I had seen while jogging, but other than that, I hadn't noticed anything out of the ordinary.

"How much money are they asking for?" I ask, aware of how my friend is staring at me from across the table. She's British, a fashion designer, and probably can't comprehend the words coming out of my mouth.

"They want like five hundred thousand pesos, or dollars, or something like that." She's not really certain of the amount, as Mary wouldn't even hear of it.

"Did he have his gun on him?" I ask, already feeling guilty for hiding it.

Sonia doesn't know whether or not he had his gun. We decide that until we figure out what we're going to do, it's best not to answer any calls from Rosario or any unknown numbers. She says that a woman keeps calling one of her salons and asking for her, but she's already told her employees to say she no longer works there.

My friend and I settle the tab and I go home, spend the next hour pacing around my apartment and feeling utterly useless. The first thing we do is erase our voices. We all change our greeting so that if anyone calls, they hear the automated response repeating the number they just dialed back to them. If the kidnappers call, they can't be certain of who they've reached, and if they can't get hold of us, they can't threaten us.

Rosario calls that evening and leaves several messages pleading with me to call her back, and though she sounds genuinely upset, I don't return her call. There are too many unknowns: What if we send the money and they ask for more money? What if we send the money and then they go after our mother? She had been back in Valparaíso for a week already. What if we send the money and they kill him anyway? What if Rosario is in cahoots with the kidnappers? Why had they left her as the middleman? Or worse, what if *he* had something to do with it? What if he somehow provoked this—messed with the wrong herd or owed someone money? Why had he practically insisted on knowing when Mary would be returning to Mexico?

Later that night I lie in bed, tossing and turning and wondering where he may be at that very moment. Imagining they probably have him blindfolded and tied to a wooden chair somewhere in an abandoned warehouse on the outskirts of town, and that they must be taunting him. Walking circles around the chair and asking, where are your daughters now? ¿Pues, no que te procuraban tanto? By then, the only message Mary had sent the kidnappers must have already reached them: *They're not going to get a penny out of me, or any of his kids, because he abandoned us when we were young.*

If he was within earshot of that conversation, it must have been then that he realized his past might be catching up to him—even though we had all gone back and reestablished a relationship with him, our past was still a dark line drawn between us. I assume that wherever he may be, he must already be calculating, plotting—coming up with a plan to save his hide—because by the time the sun went down that day and none of us had called the kidnappers back, the one thing that must have crystallized for him was that he may have to fend for himself.

Kidnapped. That word tumbles endlessly in my thoughts as the fan whirs in the window, providing little relief from the oppressive August humidity. What a strange word. What a vast gray space—what a relief. Dead is an infinite black hole from which nothing is retrievable. Kidnapped is good. There is hope.

First thing Tuesday morning, I e-mail my friend in Mexico City, the journalist. He puts me in contact with a friend of his, another journalist who has a direct connection to the head of the kidnapping division in the Mexican federal government.

"So your friend tells me your father isn't exactly an upstanding citizen," the fed says when I call him.

"That's true," I say, "but he's still my father."

The fed tells me that the thing with kidnappers is that they are usually after a monetary reward, and as long as we cooperate, they probably won't hurt my father.

"Have you talked to the kidnappers yet?"

"No."

"Have you talked to your father?"

"No."

"How do you know if he's still alive?" he asks. This is something that had already occurred to me, but I tried not to dwell on it. He explains that the first thing I need to do is call the kidnappers, tell them we will cooperate, but can I please speak with my father first and make sure he's okay. Once we know he's alive and well, we can begin negotiating. "I'll walk you through all the steps," he says. "And if at any point the situation escalates or the kidnappers become threatening, say, then you need to let me know and we'll proceed accordingly."

"Can't you send in the federal troops to rescue him?" I ask, imagining that the feds could somehow locate him and the soldiers would descend upon the warehouse in the middle of the night. The place would be surrounded with armored vehicles and helicopters in no time, and the kidnappers wouldn't even know what hit them.

"One step at a time," he says. "You need to call them first, talk to your father, then call me back and we'll go from there."

After getting off the phone, I call Mary. Since she lives in Mexico, I think she should be our point person, be the one to speak with the kidnappers.

"You should have never called the feds," she says, and asks if I had given them my name.

"Of course I gave them my name," I say, explaining that I trust my friend, that he would have never put me in contact with a crooked fed.

"You can't trust anyone down here, especially not the feds," she says, expressing a sentiment shared by most people in Valparaíso, and probably all of Mexico. By then, it seemed pretty obvious that the feds had been behind the jailbreak—had known about it and allowed it to happen. How else was it possible that fifty-three inmates had escaped within five minutes, and there had been no resistance? Not a single bullet had been fired.

"Maybe you should pack up the kids and get out of there," I say. "Go stay in Chicago until this whole thing blows over."

"I'm not going anywhere," she says, and tells me to stop calling her because the kidnappers are probably listening in on our conversations. She's not being paranoid—everyone knew the cartels had set up surveillance towers and had been tapping into cell phone calls.

On Wednesday morning, we hear about the latest threat. Either we send the money by the end of the day or they are going to toss his head over the courtyard wall. News of this threat sparks a frenzy of phone calls, crisscrossing over the border. Roselia calls several contacts she has in Mexico to see if anyone can help. Not only can they not help, they're hesitant to discuss anything over the phone. She calls a few private-detective agencies in Chicago, all to no avail. She contacts the

FBI, but since my father is not a U.S. citizen, there is nothing they can do. Sonia tells me to call the fed and have him send in the troops.

"Mary doesn't want the feds to get involved," I say, and though I think about calling the fed back, I know he's just going to ask why I haven't called the kidnappers yet.

When I talk to Yesenia, who's in Oakland, she says not to have the fed send in the troops because every time the soldiers get involved in these situations, it ends in a massive shoot-out, and what if he gets caught in the cross fire?

"For all we know, Dad is already on the other side," I say, and the minute I say it, I wish I hadn't.

We both fall silent for a long time.

"You really think they may have already killed him?" Her voice is barely audible.

"Think about it," I say. "With the reputation Dad has, there's no way they're going to let him walk—even if we send the money. You don't mess with someone like him and then let him go free as if nothing ever happened. I think Mary is right. We need to stay out of it. With the type of life he has lived, he's got to be okay with this. If anyone can negotiate his way out of something like this, it would be him."

Later, as I lie in bed, staring at the ceiling and listening to my neighbors carrying on in their backyard, I wish there were a way to send him a message—smoke signals, Morse code—or find him in a dream and tell him that even though we are not calling the kidnappers, it doesn't mean we aren't trying. Because what if they do kill him? What if he leaves this world thinking we had all turned our backs on him—that we don't love him? The air hangs hot and dense in my bedroom and when I finally doze off, sunlight floods my window. My father steps out of the light and stands before me. He's about the same age he was when he left Chicago—forty-five. He looks tall and strong and is wearing a black cowboy hat, jeans, and a black leather vest over a plaid cowboy shirt. He smiles at me, gives me a nod, and then turns and vanishes into the white light. I wake with an immense pressure on my chest, gasping and thinking that they must have killed him. That he had come to say goodbye.

In the morning, I check in with my sisters: Nothing has come flying over the wall—yet. By noon, still nothing—not his head nor his hand, not even a finger—nothing. The only message that reaches us later that day is that his bond has been lowered to $50,000. Cartels are not ones to negotiate—either you send the amount they ask for or you never see your relative again—it's that simple. Not only has his head not come flying over the courtyard wall, his ransom has been lowered by $450,000, and I can't help but wonder what had been that $450,000 moment. What charm had he mustered? What landscape had he painted for them—what type of deal had he struck—in order to keep his head attached?

That night, Mary wakes to loud banging, to what sounds like someone trying to break through her front gate. She makes her two teenage daughters climb the spiral staircase to the roof, telling them to go hide at the neighbor's. The noise grows louder and when it stops, there's nothing but the sounds of sirens approaching and a woman shrieking. She's yelling to someone to please look after her children. A car door slams shut, swallowing the woman's voice, then car tires are screeching past Mary's front door practically as machine-gun fire rings out. Mary is certain that at any moment they're going to come barreling into her house. But instead the blasts and the sirens pass and soon they're diminishing in the distance.

"It was the fright of my life," Mary says, when I talk to her the next day. By then she's heard that a convoy of SUVs had gone to pick up a woman from her neighborhood, but with all the banging someone had called the police and just as the SUVs were driving off with their hostage, the police descended on them and opened fire. They had chased the SUVs for several miles, forcing them to abandon two of their shattered vehicles on the main road—five people had been killed.

"Do you think it was the same guys that have Dad?" I ask.

"I wouldn't doubt it," she says.

"Why don't you go stay in Chicago until things settle down over there?" I say, but she refuses to leave.

Later that day, we receive another message. His bond has been lowered again. The kidnappers want us to send $10,000 or whatever we can afford. Roselia's partner jokes that if we hold out long enough, they might just ask us to send enough money to cover his food expenses so they at least break even.

"I'm calling the kidnappers," Roselia says. "This is ridiculous; we're not going to let them kill Dad over $10,000."

She calls Rosario to get the number for the kidnappers, but before she has a chance to say anything, Rosario informs her that she has already come up with the $10,000. She borrowed the money from Raúl, Alma's boyfriend, and says that they should be releasing my father as soon as the wire clears their account. Within the next day or two, most likely.

By Friday afternoon, the latest wave of rumors is already sweeping all over town and drifting across the border. People are saying that they saw my father riding around with the kidnappers, hanging out at the gas station in Valparaíso with them—that perhaps he was not kidnapped at all, but rather had joined them.

"When did they let you go?" I ask my father when I talk to him a few days later. Though I already know the answer to my own question, I also know that our conversation is probably being tapped, and thus I can't ask what I really want to know—about the shoot-out in Mary's neighborhood, about the rumors that people had seen him riding around with the kidnappers, and whether he had actually joined them.

He tells me they dropped him off in front of his house on Saturday night.

"Did you ever find your gun?" I ask, and he says he hadn't even had a chance to look for it, that the amigos must have found it because they had ransacked the whole house and taken anything and everything of value—his television, his stereo, his gold chains, his leather coats, and his father's rifle. Again I feel a pang of guilt for having hid his gun. Perhaps if he had had it on him, he may have been able to defend himself. Though he just as easily may have gotten himself gunned down in that dusty lot, his gun no match for their machine guns, and his corrido would have had a different ending.

"No, méndigos. There was a woman with them, and she was the mera mera. She kept ramming the butt of the rifle into my kneecaps and asking for my daughters' phone numbers," he says. "I kept telling them that they were mistaken, that I didn't have any daughters. Except for Sonia, and that's only because they found the number to her salon in my wallet. Though they seemed convinced that I had a daughter living in Jalisco, and that she owned her own gas station, even," he says. "Y a huevo, they wanted me to give them her phone number, tell them where she lived, but how was I supposed to give them information that didn't exist? Impossible, right?"

"Ey," I say, and I know he's telling me exactly what he can't say. "I'm glad you're okay," I say, though what I really want to say is, We didn't turn our backs on you. Just because we didn't call the kidnappers back doesn't mean we weren't trying. But I don't say anything, because if the kidnappers are listening, they may go pick him up again.

"I'm fine, alive and kicking anyway," he says, though later Rosario will tell me that when they dropped him off, he was dehydrated, had lost weight, and his knees were swollen and bruised. "The one that wasn't so lucky was your cow." He informs me that on Sunday, after we had last spoken, he had gone out to the ranch and she was lying on her side. Her breathing was shallow but she was still alive. On Monday morning, he had gone to the vet and picked up a vaccine for her and had planned on riding back out to the ranch on Tuesday morning. "But then they picked me up on Monday afternoon and that was that." He was just out at the ranch yesterday, and between the coyotes and the vultures, there was barely anything left of my cow.

"Maybe she went instead of you," I say. This is something he had once told me. How in Mexico, the indigenous believe that if death is coming for you, it can be diverted—tricked into taking a different soul in place of your own.

"That's the same thing Rosario said," he says. "That maybe the veinte landed on your cow instead of me." He tells me not to worry, he already has another cow picked out for me, and asks when might I be coming down again.

"Maybe I'll come once classes let out in December," I say. "For the holidays."

"I'll be here, waiting for you," he says, though he probably knows as well as I do that I won't be coming down for the holidays or anytime soon—the kidnapping has changed things.

Over the next few months, he goes through cell phones as if they were disposable. Each month, it seems, he has a new number. I keep reprogramming the new numbers into my cell, under Dad—that three-letter word no longer feels like a lie. It feels like the word itself is made of flesh and bone. Most of the time when I dial his number, my call doesn't go through because he doesn't have sufficient funds. That, or my calls go straight to voice mail, in which case I hang up, as he doesn't know how to retrieve his messages. If he does pick up, it's difficult to have a conversation with him. Not only does it feel like we're being monitored, but more often than not he's been drinking and his speech is slurred and difficult to understand.

"Who is this?" he growls into the phone.

"It's me, Dad, it's me . . ."

"Who?" he asks, and then he's gone. Either he hangs up or the call is dropped.

Mary tells me that she has called him a few times, and he'll say he's up at his ranch, but later she'll find out he had been home all along. One time he tells her he's up at La Mesa—hiding.

"Hiding from whom?" she asks. "Who are you hiding from, apá?" Before he answers, either the call is dropped or cut off.

Then he starts showing up at her house, looking wild-eyed and fatigued, alcohol fumes exuding from him. He's lost weight, all of his teeth are missing, and white stubble springs from his chin like needles. He seems so much older. It's as though all the years he managed to stave off with sheer force of will have suddenly come crashing down on him. They sit on her stoop, and though she insists that he come inside and take a bath, have a hot meal, he refuses. He puts his arms around her, pulls her close, and bursts into tears. He starts rambling on and on about those men, how they are heartless, how they do horrible, horrible things, kill innocent people—women and children even, how he had not wanted to do it, but not to worry, because as long as he's alive, no one is going to come bothering her.

"You didn't want to do what, apá?" she asks. He pulls away and stares at her as if trying to remember who she is. Red veins cut across the whites of his eyes, and she can't help but wonder how long it's been since he's had a full night's sleep. "What is it that you didn't want to do?" she asks. He pushes himself to his feet and looks around like a man that has just come to, and then he's swatting at the low-hanging fig branches in her driveway and stumbling back to his truck. He climbs in, rouses the driver, and he's gone.

He had found someone to drive him, had traveled three hours to spend a mere twenty minutes with her. It's like he had come all that way just to be held by her, as if she were his last chance—a life raft in that abysmal terrain. He shows up a few more times after that. His visits are always the same, always brief, with him weeping and saying that he hadn't wanted to do it, that those men are heartless, do horrible things, but not to worry, because as long as he's alive, no one is going to bother her.

Once he's gone, she's left with the sinking feeling that the kidnapping rattled his mind off its hinges.

"We have to help Dad," Sonia says, calling me out of the blue one day. She too has heard how he's been drinking a lot, how he's been showing up at Mary's. "We have to get him out of there."

"Where will he go?"

"I don't know, maybe he can go stay with Yesenia in Tulum," she says, because by then Yesenia was working as a massage therapist on the beach in southern Mexico. "Or maybe we can get him across the border somehow."

"How?" I ask. We had already tried getting him a U.S. visa about two years before. Sonia had filled out all the paperwork, and a few months later, he had received a letter in the mail. He had been issued an appointment. He needed to report to the U.S. consulate in Guadalajara on such and such date, and bring certain records—his birth and wedding certificates, bank statements, proof of the livestock, and land deeds. I had made the rounds around the plaza with him, collecting all the documents he would need. By then, the prison had been relocated to the outskirts of town, there were two banks in the square, and most of the government offices were in the building where the house with the pink limestone arches had once stood.

On the day of his appointment, he had really looked the part. Wearing sneakers, blue jeans, a forest-green Windbreaker from J.Crew, and a baseball cap—very believable, I thought—very American. He handed the woman behind the counter his paperwork, all neatly organized inside a manila envelope. She asked him several questions: What was the purpose of his trip? How long did he intend to stay? Where would he be staying? He answered her questions with a smile and a flutter in his eye, and she smiled back, and perhaps in trying to be convincing, he had convinced himself that it just might work, that he might be able to charm his way back into the United States, until she placed a small pad in front of him. She assured him it was no big deal, really, just a formality, and would he be so kind as to press his thumb onto the pad? Even before doing so, he knew the charade was over.

"Maybe we can drive him to Tijuana and pay a coyote to take him across the border," Sonia says. "Or maybe my tío Antonio will let him borrow his documents."

My tío Antonio, my father's older brother, had been living legally in the United States for years. They looked enough alike that maybe my father could use his papers and we could drive him to Tijuana, where he could walk across the border, but would he actually have the nerve to cross? It was no longer as easy as it once had been, back in the seventies and eighties when he had gone back and forth numerous times, treating the border the same way he had treated the law—as a mere suggestion.

He was also no longer as young and daring as he once had been. Besides, would he cross, knowing that he would be living in the suburbs, at the mercy of others to get around? There would be no way for him to get a legal driver's license, and even if he got a crooked one, would he take the chance of potentially being pulled over, questioned, and arrested? Would he go, knowing that there would be no more solitary horseback rides in the moonlight, no more horses, no more cattle, no fresh mountain air, and no vast blue skies—nothing but his body being shuffled from one house in the suburbs to another, even as the years continued to pile up on him like an unstoppable avalanche that would eventually push him into the brightly lit corner of a nursing home?

"Where would he live?" I ask.

"I don't know," she says. "With me, I guess."

"What if he keeps drinking?"

"Maybe we can take him to AA," she says.

We both fall silent.

25 ◆ STARFISH

WE'RE CONVINCED he's not going to make it. He's been drinking for days and on the day before his flight is to leave from Guadalajara, I call him in the late afternoon.

"¿Quiubo?" he yells over the music that's blaring in the background.

"Apá," I say, "are you going to come meet us or not?" My two sisters and I planned a trip to Tulum, and we bought him a ticket. It's been seven months since he was kidnapped, and none of us has been back to see him.

"Who is this?"

"It's me, apá." This is the same conversation I've been having with him for the past five days. He doesn't seem to remember that he has a flight to catch. He tells me to wait a moment, and then I hear him having a conversation with someone, yelling something over the music. "Who are you with?" I ask.

"No one," he says, and is then mumbling something incoherent about saddling up his horse and riding out to the ranch.

"Apá, if you don't sober up, they're not going to let you on the plane."

"Oh, oh, oh, okay, okay, está bien," he says, and then he's gone.

After getting off the phone, he manages to get himself into the shower and into a clean change of clothes. He shoves his toiletries, extra socks and underwear, and one change of clothes into a small beige backpack, and then finds someone to drive him to the bus depot, boards a bus to the next town over, where he sits in the station nodding off for an hour before boarding an overnight bus to Guadalajara. He arrives at Guadalajara at 6:00 a.m., and though his flight isn't due to leave until 1:00 p.m., he takes a cab straight to the airport, clears security, finds his gate, and there he sits, nodding off and watching the seats around him fill up and then empty as everyone filters through the gate and onto the plane. The young woman behind the counter asks where he's traveling to, and he tells her he's flying to Cancún, to meet up with his daughters.

"That flight is not due to leave for several hours," she says. "Why don't you go for a walk, get some fresh air, grab a bite, and then come back?"

"No, with my luck, I'll go on a walk, get lost, and end up missing the plane," he says.

He stays put; he's already made it that far.

The day after he arrives is a Sunday, and Yesenia drops him and me off at the Mayan ruins in Tulum, saying that she needs to go into town and run a few errands.

"Where was Yesenia going?" he asks, as we make our way along the path, which is covered with crushed white seashells.

"To meet up with mi amá," I say.

"Your mother is here?" His face lights up.

"Ey," I say. Yesenia and I had been traveling through Guatemala with my mother, and since we assumed there was no way he was going to make it, my mother decided to continue on to Tulum with us.

"How long is she staying?" he asks.

"She's leaving either tomorrow or the next day."

"Why so fast?"

"Why do you think?" I say, glancing over at him.

He shrugs, though he must know it's because of him. When we found out he was on his way, my mother had gone and checked into a hotel, but not without putting up a fight first, insisting that he should be the one to go stay in a hotel, and she should be allowed to remain at Yesenia's. But since we had harassed him so much about coming to meet us, we couldn't ask him to stay in a hotel.

"You see that white line out there?" I say, pointing out over the sea where, in the distance, the waves are breaking along the reef and forming a continuous line across the surface. He nods, and I tell him that there's a reef out there, brimming with all kinds of ocean life, and Yesenia is friends with a Mayan man who goes by the nickname of El Capitán, and he paddles out there in his boat around sunset and casts his net, and then returns just before sunrise and pulls in his catch. "The last time I was here, he caught a shark," I say. "He sold it to one of the fisheries in town and then took to the bottle for days."

"Pobre amigo," he says, looking out across the water. "That's rough. I'm not going to be drinking anymore. Sometimes when I drink too much, I say things, probably say more than I should, and then the next day I have no recollection of it."

"Tito always says that a man might consume alcohol his whole life, but the day comes when the alcohol starts consuming the man."

"That's what Andreita says, huh? No, caraja viejita, she always did tell it like it is." He's right. Though Tito is in her early nineties, nothing ever escapes her. "What is the world coming to?" she said when she heard about the introduction of genetically modified seeds into Mexico. "Sterile seeds?" she said. "Imagine? One day that could lead to world hunger, and possibly the extinction of the human race."

We stroll around the back of the largest pyramid on the grounds. It sits on a cliff overlooking the turquoise-blue waters of the Caribbean. Tourists smile and squint in the morning sun as they pose for pictures in front of the pyramid. I notice how their eyes linger on my father as we pass. He stands out amid the flip-flops, sundresses, and baseball caps in his black cowboy boots, jeans, cowboy hat, and burgundy-colored button-down shirt, which is lined with beige piping and has the inlay of a bull's head on the back, the horns stretching out toward his shoulders. I feel like I'm walking around with a relic from the mainland. I wouldn't be surprised if people started asking if they can have their picture taken with him.

"How is Pascuala getting back to Zacatecas? Is she taking a camión or the avión?" he asks.

"I think she's taking the camión because she wants to stop in Mexico City to visit a church where she knows some people."

"Well, I guess that's always been her negocio," he says, as we make our way along the path. "Eso sí, los hermanais have always been her priority. I think if she hadn't become a hallelujah, we might have made it," he says.

"Wouldn't it be crazy if you and mi amá had a reconciliation down here and ended up going back to Zacatecas together?" I say.

"Ouh, qué bueno fuera." He grins, and I notice his teeth, how white and perfect they are—it's an entirely new set. Gone is the gold trim that once lined his two front teeth, and the gold caps that once covered his upper molars. Though I want to ask what happened to his teeth, I don't, afraid of what the answer might be. "No, imagine the look on people's faces if we were to arrive back into town, arm in arm, after all these years?" It had been twenty-three years since they had separated, and they had recently made their separation official; they were legally divorced. Mary had gone with my mother on the day they signed the papers and told me that my father kept trying to make small talk with my mother, until she had grabbed her purse, stormed out of the room, and waited in the lobby for the attorney to arrive.

"Do you want to stop and rest for a bit?" I say, when we reach a cluster of small trees—one of the few shady spots on the entire grounds. Two large white rocks sit across from each other under the shade. We take a seat on one and he removes his hat, placing it on his knee. "The shade feels nice, huh?" I reach into my straw bag and pull out a water bottle.

"Ey," he says.

I take a sip and offer him the bottle. He takes it, drinks. We sit in silence for a while, watching couples and young families stroll by, and I feel the weight of everything I want to say to him, of everything I've been unable to say over the phone. He has another swig and passes the bottle back to me.

"You know, when you were kidnapped?" I say, turning to face him. "We were trying." I inform him that Roselia had called detective agencies, the FBI, practically everyone she knew in Mexico. That my journalist friend had put me in contact with the fed, and I thought about asking him to send in the troops, but Mary didn't want the feds getting involved, and Yesenia was afraid that if a shoot-out ensued, he might get caught in the cross fire. "One would say yes, another would say no, and by the end of the week, we hadn't moved an inch to the left or to the right," I say. "What did you think when you heard we weren't calling back? Did you think we had abandoned you?"

"No, I knew it was a tough situation," he says, glancing down the path where two kids, a boy and a girl roughly six and eight, are racing toward us. "It's a good thing you guys stayed out of it. Those people are ruthless."

"We didn't call Rosario back because we thought she might have something to do with it, found it peculiar they had left her as the middleman," I say.

"I wouldn't be surprised if she did have something to do with it," he says. "A lot of those men are from la sierra, from the same area she's from up in the mountains. That's where they grow their crops, la mota, la amapola, all of it. They grow it up there and then bring it down in truckloads." He explains how they have their lookouts stationed on either end of town. Two SUVs sit at the gas station on the north, and another two sit in front of the slaughterhouse in the south, and all day long they are monitoring the road that runs in front of La Peña as it stretches from the mountains on one end and all the way to the border, practically, on the other.

The two kids arrive screeching with laughter and throw their arms around the rock in front of us. "Chapucero," the girl yells. They're out of breath and arguing about who won and who cheated. The boy turns and shoots my father a smile—kids and dogs have always been drawn to him. My father waves at them, they wave back, and then they're off and running down the path, racing toward their parents.

"Did you think at times that might be it?" I ask.

"At times, yes." He looks across the sun-drenched grass and begins to recount the events of that afternoon. When they picked him up in the lot, they escorted him to one of the SUVs, where there was a woman sitting in the backseat, holding his father's rifle between her knees. She went by the nickname of La Mona, they all went by nicknames, but she was the main one, the one giving the orders. She blindfolded him with duct tape and toilet paper and kept calling him her "little golden chicken." "I don't know, I guess she assumed she was going to collect a fortune from you guys," he says. Once again, the two kids are throwing their arms around the rock, laughing and arguing. Their parents arrive on their heels and take a seat on the rock across from us, and though my father is looking right at them, I can tell that his thoughts are elsewhere. "There's a campground in the desert where they train their recruits, young boys mostly, some as young as eight or nine," he says. "A lot of those kids are homeless and they pick them up off the streets and offer them jobs, offer them food and money, and then they get them hooked on the white powder, until eventually the kids are willing to work for the powder alone."

"Poor kids," I say.

"No, imagine a life like that? Those kids grow up and they don't give a damn about anything," he says. "On that same campground, they have these large cylinders filled with acid, and that's where they dispose of the bodies. There's a man who goes by the nickname of the Soupmaker, and all day long he's poking and prodding inside the cylinders with a long stick, constantly stirring, and . . ."

"You saw that?" I turn to look at him.

"Ey."

"I thought they had you blindfolded."

"They did," he says, his eyes locking with mine. "They kept me in the backseat of a Suburban the whole time and sometimes they'd stop at the camp to drop someone off, and a lot of the time they left me alone in the truck or sitting under a tree and if I leaned my head back and lifted the duct tape a bit, I could see what they were doing." He wrinkles his nose as if he can still smell the stench of the acid, as if he can still see the butchered human parts flying through the air like logs. "It's horrible the things that they do. Horrible."

The family gets up and the father ushers them away, glaring over his shoulder at us as they go. My father doesn't seem to notice. A grave look has settled on his face and stayed there.

"You know, people in town were saying that they saw you driving around with them," I say. "That you must have joined them."

"People will say whatever they want to believe. Look at how many times they've said I was dead, but here we are, right?" He cocks his eyebrow. "In the end, I befriended them, but that's only because I helped them one night." He lifts his hat off his knee and contemplates the inside of it as if he can see that night unfolding right there before him. He speaks in a steady voice, recounting the details. How the SUVs had crossed the state line, gone into Jalisco to pick up a man, and they had made such a racket trying to break through the front gate that by the time they got in, the man had escaped or hidden, and because of all the noise, the neighbors had called the police and the sirens were already approaching.

They didn't bother looking for the man. They took his wife instead, and from the backseat he could hear her screaming. Car doors slammed, the screaming was gone, and soon La Mona was back on one side of him and a man on the other, and then they were moving, bouncing along a dirt road. La Mona was shouting to the driver to go faster, and all the while the sirens were drawing near. There were a few scattered blasts in the distance, and then they were overtaken by machine-gun fire. He hunched over as glass shattered all around and felt the weight of the man who had been sitting to his right slump over him. He thought for sure he'd be next, could almost feel the bullet that would crack his skull, and so he did the one thing he had always done in these life-and-death situations. He began to pray. Asking Diosito to have mercy on his soul. And then they must have made it onto a paved road, because suddenly they were moving faster and the blasts and sirens were fading in the distance. He turns his hat over in his hands, oblivious to the security guard that has made his way over to the shade and is standing with his foot propped on the rock the family just vacated.

Even through the static of their walkie-talkies he could hear the panic in their voices. Two of the SUVs had flat tires, and a few of those riding in the SUV behind theirs had also been hit. They rolled to a stop, car doors slammed, the door next to him flew open, and then the weight of the man was gone. "Vamos, viejo." Someone gripped his arm and pulled him across the slick seat. Over the wailing of the approaching sirens, he could hear La Mona saying something about just leaving the woman because she had been hit and what good was she going to do them dead, anyway.

They ushered him into a different SUV and again they were moving, flying around curves on an open road, the sirens growing louder and La Mona yelling that they needed to get off that road or they were never going to lose the feds. The driver snapped, what was he to do? This was the only road that led back to Zacatecas. They were in such a state that for a minute he thought they might turn their guns on each other, and that's when he saw his opportunity. He knew that if they were on one of the only roads that ran from Jalisco back to Zacatecas, he could help them, and he told them so.

"If we need your help, viejo, we will ask for it," La Mona said.

"Sí, viejo," the driver said, "we're near Huejúcar. Why? Is there some secret road that you know of?" He told him there was no other road. Only the terrain.

He doesn't seem to notice, or care, that the security guard is now standing with both feet planted on the ground, arms crossed, and glaring at us. I wouldn't be surprised if he came over and asked us to leave.

"They all fell silent," he says, describing how no one spoke, though their glances must have been dancing between them, and all the while the sirens were getting closer, and then he felt the sting of the duct tape practically ripping the flesh off his face. It was pitch-dark out, just before dawn. They killed the lights and he led them off the main road and through the streets of Huejúcar, turning left and right while the sirens continued to wail out on the road. Once they had crossed through town, they came to a dirt trail that wound up the mountainside. The path gave way to the terrain, they shifted to four-wheel drive, and as they swerved around nopales and ma-gueys, he tried to get his bearings. It had been years since he had ridden through those parts on horseback, and he wasn't exactly sure where he was going, but he trusted his instincts, and by the time the stars had begun to fade, the landscape was already looking familiar.

"Within an hour or so, we were in the vicinity of La Laguna," he says. "Pascuala's grandfather used to have a ranch near there, and when we were first married, we rode out there numerous times. If we set out at daybreak, we'd be arriving at his ranch right around noon." Once they reached La Laguna, he knew exactly where he was, and by the time the first light of day was illuminating the horizon, they were practically crossing right in front of the gate to his ranch. He even had the urge to say, hey, why don't you just let me out here, I've done my part, but he didn't say anything, thought it best to keep his mouth shut. And besides, he didn't want them knowing where his ranch was. He watched the entrance come and go and then they were mak-ing their way down and around the boulders near Santana. "How is it that you know this terrain so well, viejo?" La Mona asked, and he told her that in his younger years, he had crossed that terrain on horseback numerous times, had ridden as far as Monte Escobedo and back.

By early morning, they were clearing the speed bumps on the

south end of town. They pulled into the gas station and even let him use the bathroom—unescorted.

"After that day, they were a lot nicer to me," he says. "Even La Mona was nicer. She was such a harsh woman. But you should have heard her tone change whenever one of her kids called. She sounded like the pure truth, saying she missed them too and asking how they were doing in school, and were they obeying their grandmother, and had they gotten the gifts she had sent, and hee hee hee and ha ha ha. But other than that, she was heartless."

We sit in silence for a while and I try to wrap my head around his story, uncertain of what is true and what is fabricated. He seems to know an awful lot about their campgrounds and their routes, and why would he have helped his captors escape the police? Had he really guided them along the terrain or was he just trying to make himself out to be the hero? Perhaps even before he was kidnapped he had already gotten himself entangled with them, somehow. Why had he been so concerned with knowing when Mary would be returning from Chicago? Almost as soon as she returned, they picked him up in the lot.

"Did you hear about the shoot-out that happened in Mary's neighborhood?" I ask.

"Ey," he says.

"Do you think it was the same one?" I ask, thinking that it must have been.

"I don't think so," he says. "As far as I know, those people who picked me up never went near her neighborhood," he says. Though, if he were blindfolded, how would he know if they went near her neighborhood or not? Maybe if the police hadn't shown up, the kidnappers would have been kicking down Mary's front door next. But would he betray one of his own daughters like that? Guide the cartel right to her front door? Or maybe they had forced him to lead them to her front door, and he had taken them to the neighbor's door instead? *Don't worry, mijita, as long as I'm alive, no one is going to come bother you.* I'm filled with so much doubt that I start thinking he may have never even been kidnapped, grow convinced that the next time I go see him, his door will be intact and his father's rifle will still be slung above his bed. There are now two guards standing solid as pillars next to the rock.

"Are you hungry?" I ask. "There's a good seafood place just down the beach from here. We can walk there and sit with our feet in the sand, have some mariscos and an ice-cold beer."

We get up and make our way down the path. He tells me that after they let him go, La Mona and some of the others kept coming around the house, wanting him to go have a beer with them, but he didn't really like hanging around them and would usually have Rosario say he wasn't home. He says La Mona showed up one day, practically demanding to know who was watching over him, what saint was it that he prayed to? And was it true that he had a pact with the Other One?

"I don't know, I guess she heard stories around town," he says. This is a rumor that has followed him his whole life—that he has a pact with the devil, though I'm not certain where it started. "But I told her it was just Diosito that watched over me. She didn't seem convinced. Pero bueno, not long after that day, her corrido ended. I heard that her convoy had gotten into a shoot-out with the soldiers and she had been killed in the cross fire."

"Poor woman," I say, and can't help but feel for her kids.

"Poor nothing," he says. "With the way those people live, most of them don't last long."

On the night before my mother leaves Tulum, my two sisters and I meet her for dinner at La Nave, a brick-oven-pizza place in town that is run by an Italian family.

"How's your father?" my mother asks once we've settled into a table.

"He seems fine," I say, thinking he actually looks good, healthy, even though Mary had said that he had lost a lot of weight. He must have put most of it back on. "He has a new set of teeth," I say. "Maybe the kidnappers knocked his teeth out."

"What teeth?" my mother says. "Your father never had any teeth. Even before we were married he had no teeth. He got them knocked out by a mule when he was a teenager," she says. "Why? Did he tell you that the kidnappers knocked his teeth out?"

"I didn't ask about his teeth and he didn't say anything." The waitress comes by and drops off the menus. "He says he befriended the kidnappers, that they come by looking for him all the time," I say.

"Your father is such a liar," she says. "By the time he's told you one truth, he's told you ten lies. If those men are going by the house looking for him, it's because he must have joined them."

"He told me he didn't, said he befriended them, but only because he helped them escape the feds one night, guided them from Jalisco back to Zacatecas across the terrain," I say.

"That's what he said?"

"Ey."

"Who knows," she says. "Your father does know that land like the palm of his hand. My grandfather used to have a ranch out there, near La Laguna. When we were first married, we used to ride out there on horseback all the time."

"That's what he said."

"Maybe he did help them." She frowns. "Pero eso sí, your father doesn't have any friends, he doesn't trust anyone. He'll pretend to be their friend, but the first chance he sees to get even, he will."

He walks into the ocean sideways, crablike, bracing himself against the three-foot waves that are rushing toward him. The waves break and send the white water rushing above his knees. He's been here for a week and has yet to fully submerge himself in the ocean. When he first arrived, he had removed his cowboy boots, rolled his jeans up to his knees and walked to the water's edge, saying that the sand felt nice—he had never felt the sand on his bare feet before. He'd only been to the beach once, somewhere in California, but had kept his boots on and had stayed under the shade of a tree, sharing a few beers with his buddies.

"You have to come in past where the waves are breaking," I yell to him. "It's not deep, see?" I hold both my arms up so he can see that I'm standing. The waterline is just above my waist.

He holds up one finger and waves it back and forth. He doesn't know how to swim, almost drowned in the river when he was a kid. Another wave breaks and sends the white water rushing up his thigh, wetting the bottom half of the blue swim trunks that Sonia brought him from Chicago. He had arrived with one change of clothes—a pair of jeans and a black cowboy shirt, so I had called Sonia on the day before she flew down from Chicago. She brought him trunks, T-shirts, and flip-flops. I let him borrow my black baseball cap, which has STIHL written across the front in bold orange letters. He wore it into town one day and came back asking if I was aware that STIHL was a chainsaw brand. I told him a friend had given me the cap as a gift because that was the nickname my friends in New York had given me—Motosierra.

Though it was actually Martin who had come up with the nickname. He and I had gone to see a band, and were supposed to meet up with some friends at a rooftop party in SoHo afterward. I'd had one too many gin and tonics and on the way to the party had gotten into an altercation with some thugs.

"What happened to you guys last night?" my friend asked, when we ran into him the next day.

"I needed to get Maria home before midnight," Martin said, "or she might have turned into a chainsaw."

My father didn't ask any questions, probably didn't want to know how I ended up with such a nickname, though he must have understood that whatever part of me was a chainsaw was fueled by his blood. That the "nerves of steel" he had been so proud of had grown up to be a chainsaw. Another wave breaks and again the white water is rushing past his thighs.

"You need to come a bit deeper," I yell, waving both my arms above my head. "I'm standing, see?"

He takes two hesitant steps in, grabs the Santo Niño de Atocha leather necklace that hangs around his neck, and swivels it around, letting it fall onto his back. His chest and gut are riddled with scars. Each of those scars has a story behind it, though when I was a kid, I used to think that he had been born that way. I have often wondered what his life would have been like had he been born in a different time and place. Had he had a vocation or craft—music or writing—into which he could have channeled all that passion that turned to violence.

He kneels down and braces himself against the white water that is rushing toward his chest. Once it passes, he cups both his hands, scoops up some water, and douses his head, his shoulders. He waits for the next wave to break and pass, and then he holds his breath and dunks his head into the water. Just as quickly as he went under he is back up and gasping for air as if he has just plunged to the bottom of the sea and back.

On the day he leaves, I help him arrange his things in his backpack: the extra clothes Sonia brought him, the flip-flops, and all the things he's collected on his morning walks along the beach. Since he arrived, his internal clock had continued operating on the same schedule, and though my sisters and I slept until 7:00 or 8:00 a.m., he had been up at 5:00 a.m., walking down the shore, chatting with the Mayan men that rake debris from the beach in front of the boutique hotels that line the waterfront. Eventually, he returned from his walks carrying seashells and pieces of coral that he collected along the way. He laid everything out to dry on the front deck, saying he was going to bring those things back and place them on the table in front of the Virgen de Guadalupe portrait in his house.

"When you get back, make sure you clean out the starfish or it's going to start to smell," I say, placing the starfish in a plastic bag and putting it in the front pocket, apart from everything else. The starfish was still alive when I found it floating near the water's edge the night before. I had carried it back to the cabin to show it to him and he had held it in his hand and watched in awe as it curled its arms around his fingers. He had not known such a thing existed—a living star, not in the sky, but in the sea. La estrellita del mar, he had called it and said that would be a good nickname for me—the Star of the Sea. When I suggested we go throw it back in the water, he had looked confused.

"Why would you want to do that?" he had said. "What if this is the thing that's going to bring us good luck, and you go and throw it back in the water?" I told him that if we didn't, it would die. "Let's do this," he said, suggesting that we leave it out overnight, and that if it was still alive in the morning we'd throw it back in the ocean. But if it was dead, then he'd take it back home with him. "Obre Dios, obre Dios," he had said, placing it on a small wooden table near the bathroom, and all through the night I could practically hear it struggling, found myself wishing I had never found it.

I place a copy of the British literary journal where I had been published the year before on top of his clothes and zip up the backpack. When I had first shown it to him, he had taken it and flipped through the pages. It was written in English, so he didn't understand a single word. I turned to the page where my story began. There was a black-

and-white photograph of him and my mother standing in front of the house with the pink limestone arches. In the photo, it's snowing and Mary and Chemel, who are roughly two and four, stand between them. My father is wearing a large white sombrero, a black button-down, black trousers, and black cowboy boots, and there is a switch-blade and a gun slung from his belt.

"Where is your photo?" he asked, and I told him that the story was not so much about me as it was about him.

We head into town and board the Kombi to Playa del Carmen, an hour away. I had agreed to go with him to the bus station in Playa and make sure he got on the right bus back to the Cancún airport. When we arrive at the station, we're informed that the next bus to the airport doesn't leave for another hour. We purchase his ticket and go for a stroll along the promenade, find a place to sit, and have smoothies. He orders mango, I get blueberry, and as we suck them down we watch the mostly white tourists strolling by with shopping bags and Frappuccinos from Starbucks in hand. He reaches into his pocket and pulls out the small linen pouch the Mayan medicine man had given him, says that when he gets back, he's going to empty the contents all around his house; the man told him that stuff would reverse any curse.

We had stumbled upon the medicine man by accident a few days before. We were in the neighboring town, and on the way back, we noticed a handwritten sign on the side of the road, something about medicinal Mayan herbs. Since Yesenia is taking an herbology class, she pulled over. We made our way through the grounds, along narrow dirt paths that were lined with labeled plants growing out of clay jugs, plastic buckets, and old tin pots. The medicine man was at the far end of the grounds, standing under a gazebo and conducting a lecture to a group of German medical students. He looked up when he heard us coming. He was a short, solid, dark-skinned man, and when his gaze landed on my father, he stopped mid-sentence and blinked twice, as if he were seeing double. The German students moved aside and my father made his way to the front. He walked up to the medicine man as if they had an appointment, like one had been expecting the other.

"Do you have anything to break a spell?" my father asked. "Say if someone has thrown the salt on you, do you have something that will get rid of it?"

The man gave him a nod and then they were both off and walking down the path, the man pointing out and clipping leaves from different plants here and there as they went. The German students followed close behind, scribbling in their notebooks, jotting down antidotes for getting rid of the salt, notes that were probably lost in translation before the ink hit the page. My father and the man continued down the path and then were stepping into a small shack and closing the door behind them.

When my father emerged some fifteen minutes later, he was holding the white linen sack and grinning from ear to ear, saying the man had told him that the reason why no one had been able to kill him was because the spirit of a soldier was watching over him. And that wasn't the first time he had heard that. Once when he had gone up to the sierra with Rosario, a Huichol shaman had told him the same thing.

After we finish our smoothies, we meander back to the bus station and find the line for his bus.

"When we were coming here, all of a sudden the plane started shaking," he says. "Out of nowhere, it suddenly started moving this way and that and everyone sitting around me started praying and crossing themselves."

"The shaking is normal," I say, and do my best to explain how the turbulence has more to do with the clouds than with the plane, though I can tell that he's nervous about flying. "You'll be fine," I say. "They say you have a greater chance of being killed in a car accident than in a plane crash."

"Why don't you come with me to the airport?" he says as people start boarding. "What if I get lost?"

"There's no way you'll get lost," I say. "This bus goes straight to the airport."

"When do you think you'll come visit again?" he asks, when we are almost at the door.

"Maybe I'll come in the summer," I say, though I know I won't, and he must know it also. He had told his sister that the worst part about having been kidnapped was that we were not going to go spend time with him anymore. It's been seven months since he was kidnapped, and things in town have deteriorated so much that recently a young boy was gunned down by the cartel in the middle of the day and the police had never shown up. There is hardly a police force left, and of those who are left, it's difficult to know who is still straight and who is working for the cartel.

"I have a beautiful white mare for you to ride the next time you come," he says, shooting me a smile. "She's perfect for you, really nice and tame."

We reach the front of the line and give each other a hug. I give him a kiss on the cheek, and he gives me a nod and boards the bus. His chin had quivered when he had said goodbye to Sonia and Yesenia earlier today, but it's not quivering now. He's been here for two weeks and I assume he's ready to head back to his cattle, to his mountainside. The night before, while we were sitting on the beach at sunset, he pointed to the pastel cloud formations at the edge of the sea, saying that they looked like mountains.

We were admiring the violet hues when an eagle flew out of the jungle and landed on the thatch cabana next to ours. It spread its wings to their full span, revealing the black-and-white-striped feathers under the brown and beige ones. It held that pose for a long time as if wanting to make sure we grasped the full complexity of its beauty before it took flight, flew back into the jungle, and vanished.

26 ◆ BLUE MOON

IT'S WEDNESDAY NIGHT, shortly after 11:00 p.m. and I have just dozed off when I hear my phone buzzing on the nightstand. I have two missed calls from Sonia and one text: Call me 911.

What did he do now, I think. It had been eight months since we were in Tulum, and though he had stopped drinking for a while, he had started up again. He had recently called Sonia crying and saying that he was all alone down there, like a dog. "Como un pinche perro," he said. Rosario had left him for good, had been gone for three months. Maybe he shot himself. He had once told me that if he ever got to the point where he could no longer fend for himself, or no longer wanted to be here, he would put a bullet in his head and that would be the end of that corrido. I knew it was the tequila talking. He may have had the nerve to shoot himself in the thigh when he was a teenager, but he would never have the nerve to put a bullet in his own head. Though, a few years back, that's exactly what his cousin Máximo had done. It was New Year's Eve, and he and my father had been out drinking, then Máximo had gone home and blown his brains out. If there was one thing that frightened my father more than anything, it was death. He was afraid of what might be waiting for him on the other side.

"What's going on?" I ask Sonia, when I finally call her back.

"I've got some bad news," she says, and a single thought flashes through me like a sudden prayer: *Please don't let it be my mother.*

"What happened?" I ask.

"Dad died."

"That's impossible," I say. Hearing those two words used in the same phrase—Dad died—sounds like a lie. "How?"

"There was a car accident," she says.

"It's probably not him," I say, not wanting to believe it. "Who called you?"

She had thought the same thing. That the townspeople were claiming yet again he was dead when he actually wasn't, and so she had called our cousin Norma and asked if she'd go to the site of the crash and confirm that it was him.

"We just got off the phone," she says. "It's him."

"And he's definitely dead? Did she check his pulse? Did anyone call an ambulance?" I ask, aware of how my voice is already breaking. "Where's Mom?"

"She's on her way back from Mexico City."

"Where is he?"

"On the road, near the curve somewhere."

After I ask all kinds of questions for which she doesn't have the answers—was he drinking, was he driving, was he alone?—we get off the phone. I sit in bed staring into the abyss for a long time, trying not to think of him lying out there on the side of the road somewhere, two thousand miles away. I scroll through my phone and stop on that three-letter word: Dad. There he is, still wedged between Cait and Dawn. I get the urge to call him as if he just might pick up. The last time I talked to him, I told him that some publishers were interested in a book. That perhaps he'd end up with an entire book written about him and not just a corrido.

"Está bien, mija," he said, and I could practically hear the smile spreading across his face. "Sígale echando ganas a la vida, y sin mirar atrás." He told me to keep on keeping on in life, without ever looking back.

Those were his last words to me.

"You're Jose's daughter, aren't you?" a woman behind one of the counters at the indoor mercado asks me, when my two sisters and I walk in on Friday morning. The scent of freshly squeezed oranges and oregano lingers in the air, and the place is abuzz with laughter, loud conversations, and the sound of spoons hitting against ceramic plates—life as usual.

"Ey," I say, and though I want to ask how she knows who I am, I can tell by the way patrons at other counters are stealing glances that everyone knows exactly who we are.

"You're a profesora, right?" she asks, wiping her hands on her white-and-green-checkered apron.

I tell her yes, because I don't feel like explaining that the teaching was only a part of the MFA program. She offers her condolences and says that my father often ate at her counter, and that every time he came in, he would tell her that he had a daughter who looked just like her. There is definitely a resemblance.

"Your father was just in here the other day," she says. "He sat right there." She motions to the bench in front of me, and it seems impossible to be occupying the space his body recently vacated. "Where is your father now?" she asks.

"In Fresnillo," I say. The day before, after having spent the entire day traveling, I had arrived at the funeral home in Fresnillo. Mary and my mother were already there, along with my father's younger sister. When they rolled his coffin in, his mustache was jet black, recently dyed, and his head was covered with a white linen cloth in order to conceal his skull, which had been severely fractured in the accident. We had stayed up all night, taking turns nodding off in foldout chairs, and the whole thing felt off—the stale air in the place, the glare of the fluorescent lights, the cold coffeepot in the corner—not what he would have wanted. "We're having him transferred back to La Peña today," I say.

My aunt had tried to protest, saying that we shouldn't take my father back to La Peña, that we shouldn't be going there ourselves—it was too dangerous. Rumor had it that he had something hidden in the house, drugs or weapons, or both, and what if whoever that stuff belonged to came looking for it? We assumed she was being overly dramatic, or that perhaps she had an ulterior motive for wanting us to stay away from his house. She was the one who had nearly sold off all of their inheritance when he was in prison.

"That's good that you're taking him back to La Peña," the woman says, looking not at me but at something or someone behind me. "That was his home. That's what he would have wanted." She smiles politely and goes back to stirring the giant pot of menudo in front of her.

After eating, we make our way back to the rental car and run into Rafael, the young man my father had hired to fix the barbed-wire fence posts on his ranch. He offers his condolences, asks when my father's funeral Mass is going to be.

"Tomorrow at noon," Sonia tells him. "At the cathedral in the plaza."

"Good to know. People have been asking, but no one seemed to know anything." He removes his baseball cap and cocks his head to the side, squints in the sun. "I went looking for him in La Peña yesterday, a few others did as well, but he wasn't there. Rosario and Miguel are there, inside the church," he says. Rosario and Miguel were with my father on the night of the accident—all three had died. Both Rosario and Miguel were also from La Peña. I had never met Miguel, as he had recently moved back to La Peña from elsewhere. And though Rosario lived in Texas, I had met him once, briefly, during the annual Día Tres de Mayo festivities, which had been held inside the church where his body now lay. When I first heard that two others had gone with my father, I couldn't help but think that he had taken them with him so that he wouldn't be alone when he crossed over to the other side. "Where is your father now?" Rafael asks.

Sonia tells him that his coffin should be arriving at La Peña by early afternoon.

"That's good, that the three of them are going to be together," he says. "They went together, so it makes sense that they should be together." He cranes his neck to the side and it seems he's trying to look over his shoulder without actually looking. "Can I ask you something?" he asks.

"Sure," Sonia says.

"How well did you know your father?"

"Pretty well, why?"

"No reason." He places his baseball cap back on his head and pulls it down tight over his ears.

"Listen, there is nothing about my father that would surprise us," Sonia says.

He takes a deep breath and then he's speaking rapidly, as if he's being timed.

"I was with your father two weeks ago and he told me to tell you to pray a lot for him. He said he had done some very bad things, and to tell you to ask God to have mercy on his soul." He scans the sidewalk behind her. "There's a red poster in his house, perhaps you've seen it? It has the portrait of a Spanish pirate or conquistador on it?"

She knows the one—we all do.

"He told me to tell you to take that poster down and burn it." He looks off to the side, toward the gravel lot where the outdoor mercado is held every Sunday. "You know your father had a pact, not with God, but with the Other One."

"Okay," she says, "we'll burn it."

He gives her a nod, says he'll see us later at La Peña, at the wake, and turns to leave, but stops as if he suddenly remembered something, as if there is just one more thing he wants to say. He looks at her, presses his lips tight, gives her a nod, and walks away.

"That was strange," Sonia says, once we're all back in the car and driving to La Peña. She says she had called my father a few days before, and had told him that we might be coming down for the holidays, which were only six weeks away. None of us had been back since he had been kidnapped. But she, Yesenia, and I had been egging each other on, saying, I'll go if you go, practically daring each other to enter together into that new and uncharted territory where norteños were no longer arriving in shiny new trucks—they were hardly arriving at all. Even the locals seemed to have bets on who could drive the most beat-up car, because the last thing anyone wanted was to call attention to themselves—to become a target. By then most of the SUVs had been replaced with bulletproof Hummers, which belonged to a different cartel, and it had become increasingly difficult to know who in town was still straight and who was working for the cartels. When Sonia told my father that the three of us might be coming for the holidays, his response had not been the usual "My home is your home" or "I'll be here waiting for you." "We'll see if you catch me," he had said. She hadn't thought much of his remark at the time, but now it seemed to take on a whole new meaning. "It's like Dad knew he was going to die," Sonia says as we clear the last speed bump on the edge of town.

"He probably did know," Yesenia says. "A lot of people know. They have dreams—premonitions. That's kind of crazy about that red poster, though."

"That poster always gave me the creeps," I say, thinking how not once but twice I had found a black scorpion lurking underneath it. Maybe he did have a pact with the Other One after all, and I can't help but wonder what would be worth trading his soul for. A reconciliation with each of his kids in this lifetime, perhaps? We drive past the yonke and soon we are flying past the slaughterhouse, and the curve, where there are a few people milling about.

At the entrance of La Peña, one of the original limestone pillars is gone, has been demolished and replaced with a cement replica. There are cars and trucks parked haphazardly all over the grounds, and people are lingering in the courtyards of homes that are usually locked year-round. I've never seen so many people in La Peña, and yet it feels dismal—empty. Smoke smolders in a fire pit in front of the small church. Its tall wooden doors are wide open, and inside, two coffins sit side by side, flanked with fresh white flowers and waiting for my father's to arrive.

Chickens scatter when we pull up in front of his house. The old blue Ford truck is parked in front of the eucalyptus trees, and three dogs crawl out from under it and come up to the car, growling and barking at us. I've never seen any of them before. There's a tall Doberman, a yellow-colored mutt with black stripes running across its back so that it looks like a miniature tiger, and a German shepherd puppy, but there's no sign of El Negro.

"Do you think they'll bite?" Sonia asks, as she rolls down her window a bit. The puppy starts wagging its tail. I push my door open, just a crack. The Doberman sticks his snout in, barking and sniffing, and soon his tail is also wagging. Slowly, I step out of the car and make my way to the courtyard. I pull the gate open, chickens scurry away, and his yellow cat and a white cat with sky-blue eyes crawl out from under the slate sink. They meow as if voicing some deep complaint.

"Poor animals," Yesenia says. "They're probably starving."

We look for the key, checking the usual hiding spots: inside the plants that line the cinder-block wall, under the slate sink, and behind the slab of limestone that sits next to his bedroom door.

"That's probably from when they kidnapped him," Sonia says, staring at the door. It's bent in several places and has rusted where the blue paint was scraped away. A new deadbolt lock has replaced the old one, and the sheen of the brass keyhole seems to glare at me, and there's nothing I can do to douse the sudden flash of guilt I feel for having doubted him.

We find the skeleton key, and inside the spare bedroom the red felt poster hangs on the wall above the bed where it has always been. I stare at the man in the portrait and for the first time notice the slight resemblance between him and my father. The Virgen de Guadalupe portrait is flanked with faded plastic flowers, and the green wooden table in front of the frame is covered with all the seashells and pieces of coral that he had collected on his morning walks along the beach in Tulum. Tucked behind the plastic flowers, on the bottom edge of the frame, is the starfish. I pick it up and turn it over in my hand. It's been dead for eight months, and there is still a slight odor emanating from it.

I place it in my bag and make my way to his bedroom, crossing through the storage room where Yesenia is filling up several tin cans with corn kernels and dog food. I pull open the shutters in the kitchen and can see the door to the corral is unlatched. Though El Relámpago and his other horse had gone missing within hours of the crash, in his house everything seems to be as he left it. The pine bowl sits on the kitchen table and is filled with a few Granny Smith apples, two overripe bananas, three potatoes, and one yellow onion. In the fridge there's an orange plastic pitcher filled with milk; a thick layer of cream has solidified on top. Next to it is a white plastic pitcher filled with pinto beans. The freezer is packed with fresh red meat, which is not fully frozen yet.

In his bedroom, too, everything seems to be as he left it. His bed is made, and his gun is in the same place where he had always kept it, the same place where his father had kept it, and his father before him—under his pillow. It's a gun I've never seen before. A handsome .357 Magnum and it's fully loaded and cocked. His cell phone sits on a chair at the foot of his bed, charging. I had called him on Tuesday and my call had gone straight to voice mail. Then I found out that on Tuesday, he had been up at the ranch branding all the new calves that had been born during the rainy season. Service up at the ranch was always spotty. The rusty nail on which his father's rifle once hung juts out of the wall above his bed, and I wish there was a way I could find him and tell him I was sorry I had ever doubted him.

At the other end of the room, on the spare bed, all of his hats are laid out in a row. Though he had always kept them either in their box or hanging on the wall and wrapped in a plastic casing, now they are all seemingly on display. Next to the hats are two framed prints of the black-and-white photo that had always hung on his bedroom wall. In the photo, he sits atop El Tapatío, the black horse he had owned in his younger years. He once told me that he had taught that horse how to dance. He had taken the photo down, had two prints made and framed, and had laid them out on the bed along with the original. The hats and the photographs are neatly organized in two rows that seem to say, "Pick one."

Sonia stares at the display on the bed and seems to be thinking what I'm thinking—my father knew he was going to die. It wasn't a mere premonition, but something more concrete—a threat or a warning. Maybe he had seen the chance to get even, had gone for it, and he knew it was only a matter of time before they came looking for him, before they arrived and kicked down his front door yet again. And perhaps he knew that the second time around he might not be so lucky, the second time around there wouldn't be enough charm on the planet to save him. Be that as it may, he was not going to run away. It's as though he had accepted his fate.

We head back outside and one of the neighbors makes her way over. She offers her condolences and says they've already made a space for my father inside the church, next to the other two.

"Who could have foreseen such a thing," she says, and tells us that just a week ago, two men from a ranch that sits a bit farther down the road had also flipped their truck at that curve and died. And only a few days before, a van with five students had also gone off the road at the curve, and how strange it is that people who grew up here, traversing that stretch of land their whole lives, would all come to die at the same spot.

She had seen my father on the day of the accident. It was about three in the afternoon and he had just fed his horses and was coming out of the corral when he ran into Miguel and Rosario. They were already in Rosario's Suburban, heading into town to run a few errands, and he had asked them for a ride. His compadre, a mechanic, was doing some work on his black Bronco, and he wanted to see if it was ready. She had seen the three leave together, and then it was just after nine when the news reached her. Someone from Tejones, the small ranch that sat near the curve, had called—the people there had heard the noise when the Suburban went flying off the shoulder. The vehicle had been going about ninety miles an hour, and it had rolled some six or nine times as it went thrashing along the side of the road in a fury of spinning lights and crushing metal, sending each of its passengers soaring into the moonlit night. The music was still blaring from the mangled mess after it stopped, the drums and horns of some corrido sounding out as if serenading the men—bidding them farewell.

"The police turned off the music," she says and explains how she, her husband, and a few others from La Peña had gone out to the site and waited with the three bodies until they were picked up. It was a frigid night, and the moon was shining bright, as it would be a full blue moon in a few days. Its rays were illuminating the three white sheets under which the bodies lay. All three of the men had landed facedown. Miguel was missing an arm. My father's legs were crossed at the ankle, he wasn't wearing any shoes, and his skull was caved in. Had his Bronco been ready, he wouldn't have been with the other two. "It was nearly three in the morning when the vehicle of the coroner in Fresnillo arrived to take them away," she says, and it breaks my heart to hear that my father had lain on the side of the road for six hours before being picked up. I thank her for having waited with him and she says it was no bother, it was the least she could do—they were neighbors, after all. "People in town often asked if I wasn't afraid living next door to that neighbor of mine," she says. "On the contrary," I told them. "Having him for a neighbor was like having a security guard in La Peña. Who knows what will happen now that he's gone."

She tells us that the musicians who usually play at all the events in La Peña called and offered to come play at the wake in the evening for a few hours—free of charge, as they knew all three of the men. She's making a large pot of coffee and asks if we can pick up some cookies and bread from the panadería in town, since it's going to be a long night and there will be a lot of people coming to pay their respects. Just yesterday, a bus with about twenty people, most of whom were originally from La Peña, arrived from Texas.

"There will probably be people coming just to see if it's true, if Jose is really dead. Your father was famous for cheating death," she says. "Pero bueno, se nos fue el héroe del valle." She jokes that people will have to find something else to talk about now that he's gone, as he was the one who was always out there causing trouble and creating stories. She's right. There was a long list of stories, myths, and rumors that had surrounded him his whole life, and though he was gone, his stories had not died with him.

"Which one of you is the writer?" asked a woman who had come to the funeral home the night before. She and her husband operated a tavern on the edge of town, and my father had been one of their regulars. "Just two weeks ago, he brought me a book, saying that his daughter had written one of the stories in it, and could I please translate it for him." She was fluent in English, as she and her husband had lived in California for several years before returning to Valparaíso. And so in between pouring drinks and busing tables, she had begun to relay bits and flashes of his life back to him.

Over the next few days—and years, even—people will share stories about him. My tío Antonio will tell me the story about the shoot-out with Fidel, how it had all started because of a misunderstanding over a bull. For the most part it will be the same story my father had told me. Though in my uncle's version, it was Salvador who was twelve years old and my father was a bit older.

I lock up his house, drop the skeleton key in my bag, and we make our way back into town. People are still lingering near the curve. We pull over and park next to the cars and trucks that are stationed on the dirt road that runs parallel to the paved one. Red and orange bits of taillights and shattered glass are strewn about. The windshield is still lying on the shoulder, and though it's completely shattered, every shard of glass is still in place, held together by the black rubber lining around it. Someone has made the sign of the cross with stones, marking the spot where each body was found, and just off the side of the road, two stone crosses lie side by side. Next to the crosses is the sideview mirror. Red and blue wires reach out from the base where it was ripped clear off the door. Half the mirror is still inside the frame, and in it I see the reflection of my black motorcycle boot and the vast blue sky behind it.

"Do you know where they found Jose?" I ask a man who is roughly my father's age and is wearing a straw cowboy hat and has a leather cell phone case slung from his belt.

"Jose was all the way over there," he says, pointing to the barbed-wire fence that runs along the side of the dirt road. On the other side of the fence there's an open field with dried cornstalks, and just beyond it is the river that runs between Tejones and La Peña. From where I'm standing, I can see the entrance to La Peña. "He was the one who got thrown the farthest," the man says. "You see those skid marks?" He points toward the road, and just before the curve there are two sets of long black lines that snake into and away from each other before disappearing into the tall grass. "The truck started rolling from where those lines end and it took out that sign." He motions to a slightly bent green road sign that has TEJONES written across it in white letters. "But the people of Tejones already stood it back up. They say they heard when the truck hit the curve, heard the metal grinding and the voices of the men crying out as it rolled over a span of about twenty-five meters," he says, and while he speaks I can practically see the truck thrashing along the expanse, like a mighty bull bucking, refusing to go down, and yet it went.

"They must have been flying," the man says. "No, pobres, the truck landed right about here." He is standing near the two crosses. "Rosario and Miguel were right next to it, practically, but Jose was about twenty meters away from where it landed." He starts walking across the dirt road, toward the barbed-wire fence, and stops in front of a slanted wooden fence post. "Jose landed somewhere around here and then he either crawled or dragged himself, I don't know, I guess with the anxiety of death upon him, he started pulling himself across the ground. You can see the trail he left."

The man makes his way along the barbed-wire fence, pointing to the flattened grass, which is streaked with dried blood. There are imprints in the dirt, not from a shoe but from something smaller, an elbow or a knee perhaps. The arms of a nopal are reaching through the barbed wire, and one of them has a dark-brown streak where the thorns have been wiped clear off it. I had heard that my father had a few thorns in his face when they found him. The tracks continue on in a straight line along the fence, moving in the direction of his home. Hurt as he was, his instinct had not been to hold steady and wait for help to arrive this time but rather to keep on moving. What was he trying to get away from?

The movement comes to a sudden stop at the foot of a huisache, and there, next to the third stone cross, is a dark pool of dried blood. A few leaves are caught in the grass blades around it and are fluttering in the breeze. I squat down and pluck one of the leaves from the grass and run my thumb over the dried blood on its surface.

"That is where they found Jose," the man says, and I'm vaguely aware that he's standing somewhere behind me. "As you can see, that's where he left his blood. How did you know him, anyway?"

I stare into the dark pool where life had drained from him. It's like staring into a black hole—a space so dense that nothing escapes it, not even light.

"He was my father."

EPILOGUE: EL CORRIDO DEL CIEN VACAS

MY FATHER had already written his own corrido. A few days after we buried him, we found it inside the green trunk that sat in the corner of his bedroom, along with his will, old land deeds, court documents, letters, and newspaper clippings. My sisters had each taken one of his hats, and I took the original black-and-white photograph, the newspaper clippings, and several old documents. I placed everything inside the same beige backpack he had in Tulum and brought it back to New York. The backpack sat at the foot of my bed for weeks, as I had intended to go through everything. Eventually, the sight of it became unbearable—a constant reminder that he was gone. I finally shoved it under my wardrobe, behind a row of shoes, and it sat there for three years before I worked up the nerve to go though it. I had not been back to Mexico since we had buried him, though I had heard about the roadside memorial the people of La Peña had erected at the curve in memory of the three men.

I poured myself a glass of wine, placed my father's photograph on a wooden shelf in my kitchen, next to a small cactus plant, and spread all the documents out on my living room floor. He had saved everything—newspaper clippings for each time he had made the paper, the court documents with all the testimonies for when everything happened with my uncle and my brother, and love letters that women had sent him while he was in prison. I started reading through the testimonies, and stumbled upon that of the man who had killed my brother. Up until then, I had never known what his name was because everyone had always referred to him as the handicapped bastard. His name was Herman Sinmental and in his testimony he stated that on the day he shot my brother he had not been drinking, though he had been very anxious and that he had been hearing voices all day, as he often did. Sometimes he'd have visions as well, visions of naked women and children playing in a lake of fire. He stated that his brothers had given him the gun and later that night, when his father told him that he had shot Chemel Venegas, he had no recollection of it.

"Your brother was pure life around here," Jose, a man that I met at my father's wake, told me. He had been one of the twenty that had gone down in the bus from Texas, as one of the other men who died with my father was his brother. Jose had lived in La Peña back when my brother was there; they were the same age and went everywhere together. I asked if he knew the man who had killed my brother. "Sí, cómo no, méndigo cojo," he said, yelling over the music, while we stood outside the church, warming our hands near the fire pit and sipping coffee with tequila from Styrofoam cups. "Your brother was always giving him lifts, we all were, but your brother would drive him to his front door. Though it was really his two brothers that had it out for Che," he said. "One time we were at a rodeo and the two of them showed up with a few others. They started taunting your brother, saying things to him, but he ignored them. Che was really calm, never went looking for trouble, pero eso sí, if it came looking for him, he didn't back down either. We were leaving the rodeo when one of them threw a bottle and it hit your brother in the back. We all stopped, wanted to jump in, but he told us to stay out of it. He turned around, and there must have been about six or seven of them, and one by one, they came at him, and believe me when I tell you that just as they came, so, too, did they fall," he said. "You know Che was a karateka?"

My brother was a black belt in karate. He had always loved those old Bruce Lee movies, and while Jose spoke, I could practically see my brother standing in the field, the dust rising around him as he sent them reeling to the ground—a black belt cowboy.

"Well, ever since then they had it out for him, but it had really started long before then, because Che and one of the brothers both liked the same muchacha, and she liked Che," he said. "Incluso, on the night they killed him, he had gone to say goodbye to her. To tell her that even though he was leaving for the other side, someday soon he'd be returning, because he had decided he wanted to stay here," he said.

"He did?" This is something I hadn't known, I had always thought my brother didn't like living in Mexico, assumed the last two years of his life had been miserable. Though it made sense that he would have wanted to stay—what was the point of going back to the other side, to pick up his day shift at the factory, where he would be breathing toxic fumes day in and day out for years to come.

"Told me so himself," Jose said. "Even his corrido was written that way, don't you remember?" There was something about the way he asked this question that made me feel as though we had known each other for years. My father had played my brother's corrido night after night and though I had memorized all the other ballads, I could not remember a single word of my brother's. "It's hard to believe that your father is gone," he said. "When he was ambushed I stepped out of my house in the morning and his truck was still pressed up against the wall across the dirt road, and on the driver's-side door alone I counted forty bullet holes."

The morning after the wake, the red poster had been reduced to ash in the fire pit in front of the church. Rafael telling us to take that poster down and burn it had been the first of my father's messages to reach us—he had left messages with others, including Doña Consuelo.

"When you take your father away from here, tell the músicos to play 'Las Golondrinas,'" she said. She had been in her courtyard hanging laundry when she heard the music coming from my father's house, and so she set out across the dirt road to find me. The white truck that would be taking his coffin to the cathedral in town was already stationed in front of his courtyard, his coffin resting on the truck bed, while the musicians played from under the shade of the mesquite—a final send-off. "Two weeks ago, your father came over, he had been drinking, and I made him a sandwich," she said. "And while we sat in my kitchen, he told me to tell you that when you took him away from here, to take him with that song."

"Las Golondrinas" is a ballad about the final flight of the swallow that speculates where the swallow that has left this place will find its new home. While it played, the procession made its way out of La

Peña. I sat next to his coffin and the noon sun shone strong and bright while the drums and horns echoed off the distant ridges. A few people were milling about at the curve, and in front of the slaughterhouse, under the shade of the mesquite, were two Hummers, parked side by side, like two scorpions nestled under the cool dank of a rock.

"You and your sisters need to be careful of who you talk to and what you say," one of my father's acquaintances told me when he came by the wake. I looked at him and asked if he thought we were in some sort of danger by being there, though it's not like we could have left town and abandoned my father's coffin. "No, nada de eso," he said. "It's just that there are going to be a lot of cabrones coming around here tonight. Some of them you may know, but others you probably don't. And you and your sisters just need to be careful, that's all." He suggested we stay in a hotel, or with relatives in town, while we finished putting all of my father's business in order, saying we should do what needed to be done and leave town as soon as possible. "You and your sisters have a reputation for having money, and now that your father is gone, some imbecile might start getting bright ideas," he said.

After we passed the slaughterhouse, I kept looking back, wouldn't have been surprised if the Hummers had come after us. No one would have stopped them. It had been a year and a half since the jail break, since the SUVs had arrived in town like a plague, like a swarm of moths that had begun to eat away at the fabric of the community, leaving holes where so many had been killed or disappeared. It started with kidnappings, though eventually people were simply vanishing. Someone would go missing and there was no phone call, no ransom to be paid—there was nothing but the growing sentiment that the government had turned its back on the people, that the cartels and the government were the two sides of the same coin.

Before the procession reached town, we could already hear the drums and horns thundering in the plaza. The music overtook ours as we pulled into the square. It seemed the entire town was there, like everyone who had claimed that my father was dead, time and time again, had come to see him off. One of my cousins had approached me at the wake and told me about the first time that the town had claimed my father was dead.

"When your father was still a teenager, fifteen or sixteen, he was at a rodeo, pulled out his gun, and unloaded it into the sky, as he always did," my cousin said. "Two feds rode up to him. 'Jose,' they said, 'we already warned you. Hand over your gun. You can go pay the fine and pick it up on Monday morning.' And what do you think your father did? He made his horse rear and took off at full gallop. The two feds went after him, shooting at him from either side. Up ahead, the road was barricaded. Someone had parked their truck across it, and the feds stopped, thinking your father would have to stop. Well, believe me when I tell you that his horse leaped clear over the truck and disappeared into the desert. A few hours later, when he hadn't resurfaced, everyone started saying that he was dead—shot by the feds. The feds themselves swore that they had been aiming for his horse, but they had seen the dust flying off your father's back where the bullets hit. So, imagine everyone's surprise when a few days later he was hanging out in the plaza as if nothing had ever happened? It was from then on that people were afraid of your father, started saying he must have a pact with the devil."

The procession pulled up in front of the cathedral as the first bell rang out. Its tall wooden doors were wide open, and six men carried my father's coffin up the stairs as a parade snaked around the square. Young girls in floor-length dresses and ribbons in their hair twirled round and round with their partners, who wore cowboy hats and handkerchiefs around their necks. Behind the dancing couples was a marching band, and behind the band were teenage girls dressed like Adelitas. They too wore long dresses and the iconic revolutionary bullets across their chests—it was Saturday, November 20, 2010, the centennial anniversary of the start of the Mexican Revolution. It was on that same day, one hundred years ago, that the people of Mexico had taken up arms and risen against an oppressive government.

The second bell rang as the men steadied my father's coffin at the front of the altar—this was the same cathedral where he had been baptized and married. The third and final bell sounded out as I took a seat in the front pew, next to my sisters. When the priest was about halfway through the sermon a woman entered through the side door and sat down at the foot of the pulpit. Though she was facing us, her gaze was on the coffin. I had seen her around town several times and, no matter the weather, she always seemed to be wearing the same dark polyester slacks and navy-blue sweater. Her hair was boy short and looked like she may have chopped it herself using a machete. Had it not been for her full breasts, which practically rested on her stomach, obvious through her bulky sweater, one might have mistaken her for a man.

"No, no, no, no, no," she started chanting, as she rocked forward and back. The priest paid her no mind. He was saying something about how each one of us had our designated hour with God. "No, no, no, no, no." Her chant grew louder and all the while she kept her gaze on the coffin. The priest adjusted his tone to overpower hers, and soon both their voices were echoing off the high ceiling and being amplified by the acoustics of the cathedral, so that they seemed to be arguing with each other, and I got the feeling that I was not in a church, but a courtroom, and it was my father's soul that was on trial. And what if he did have a pact with the Other One? The love I felt for him was so overwhelming I was convinced it might be the antidote—the one thing strong enough to break any spell.

The woman rose to her feet and slouched over to the coffin, craning her neck this way and that, like some prehistoric bird. She walked in a semicircle around the coffin, keeping her ear close to it, as if she were whispering or listening for something. She then reached for the lid, though her fingers stopped short of touching it. Her hands hovered there for a bit, she seemed to be negotiating something, and then she turned and went back out the way she came.

After the service, the men hoisted the coffin onto their shoulders and went out the side door. The musicians played softly as we made our way across the river and up the hill to the cemetery on the edge of town—the same cemetery that had lived in my memory for years. The house my brother had built for my mother still sat next to it; she had never lived there and probably never would. Before we reached the cemetery, I saw her standing at its iron gate. She was wearing a long, light-blue dress that was fluttering in the breeze, a white wide-brimmed hat, and she was waiting for my father at the entrance. Later she would tell me how when she had received the call, they told her there had been an accident and word had it that the man she had been married to for a number of years had died in the crash.

Bajaron al Toro Negro. This had been the one thought that had flashed through her—they have taken down the Black Bull. The Black Bull was immortalized in a corrido that told the story of a notorious black bull that no one had been able to take down, though many had tried.

On the day after we buried my father, the last of his messengers found us.

"Your father had a lot of money in that house," the man said. "Just two weeks ago, we were having a few drinks at his house, and he took me into the storage room and moved an old wooden trunk away from the wall, and in the wall there was a large hole that was filled with weapons and money," he said. "He had a great deal of old silver coins, and he told me to tell you to look for them. To search the house, search everything."

My sisters and I had ransacked his house but found nothing. Though by then, the only thing I wanted more than anything was to get out of town, thinking that whoever that stuff belonged to might come looking for it. For days after returning to New York, the minute I fell asleep, my mind raced back to his house and searched in vain for the hidden treasure. I climbed into the chimney, which led to a labyrinth of rooms from which there was no exit. Other times, the limestone floor would turn to dust beneath my feet, and I'd fall into a sinkhole that was infested with rattlesnakes.

Eventually, Rosario told me that those things belonged to my father. That he still owned several of the weapons he had driven down from Chicago, including a machine gun. If there was some hidden treasure, it's possible that Alma and Rosario found it. They had both come back for the funeral, and we told them they should stay and live in La Peña. Perhaps that was their inheritance—the house and the treasure—though my father also had a life insurance policy on which he had named Rosario as the beneficiary.

I poured myself another glass of wine and continued sifting through the documents, and stashed between the birth and death certificates there were old land deeds dating back to the late 1800s, along with several rough drafts of his corrido. Traditionally, a person doesn't write his own corrido. It's usually written to commemorate a life after the person has died, but my father had hired some musicians to compose one for him. It was titled "El Corrido del Cien Vacas," and the final copy was inside a plastic sleeve—it had even been notarized. His corrido was incomplete, of course, as he had no way of knowing how his life would end. He may have known his days were numbered, may have even accepted his fate, but he didn't know what the last verse of his ballad would be.

When he died he had made the newspapers yet again, and I had stored a copy of the article in the backpack. According to the report, on Wednesday night, just before 9:00 p.m., a blue Suburban that had been traveling south on Rural 44 had gone off the road and rolled several times, killing all three of its passengers. Miguel García, forty, Rosario Bueno, fifty-eight, and Jose Venegas, sixty-nine. Ever since the first time he had made the headlines, when everything had happened with Joaquín, I never trusted the newspapers, as more often than not they only scratched the surface of the real story. I could still practically hear my father laughing. *Imagine? Killing a man over a goddamn beer?*

There was a knock at Tito's door on the morning after the funeral. It was a man who had known my father since they were kids, and he had come to tell us the one thing the whole town must have been aware of but wouldn't dare utter. The fear the cartels had instilled had silenced the community. The man was good friends with a couple from Tejones, and on the night of the crash, they had seen that when the Suburban went flying off the shoulder, practically traveling on its tailwind were two Hummers. My father had survived the crash and one of the men in the Hummers had hit him on the back of the head with the butt of a rifle—that was how his life had come to an end.

I placed all the newspapers in one pile, court documents in another, birth and death certificates in another, as if by organizing everything, I might start to make sense of what was fact and what was myth. My father's life story was written within those piles of paper, and the stories they contained were my patrimony. This was what I had inherited from him—not the hidden treasure, his cattle, or his ranch, but his stories.

On the day we brought his herd down from the ranch, I stood on the plateau where I could still do a three-sixty and see the horizon all the way around. My mother was standing next to me and we were watching his cattle filter into the corral, and as the dust rose up around them, I could already feel his world receding from me. He was the doorway through which I had entered that terrain. Bringing his cattle down felt like the end of an era, like the mountain itself had been dismantled. He had no son to take over the livestock or the ranch. Chemel would have been the one, and now they both lay under the same headstone, under the same name, behind the gates of the cemetery that had haunted me for years. Where there was one cross, there were now four.

"Look," I said to my mother. "That's Chupitos." My mother had already heard all about the orphaned calf that had been adopted by La Negra. The last time I had spoken to my father, he had told me that Chupitos was pregnant. And now there she was in the corral, and trailing close behind her was a newly branded calf that looked just like her.

ACKNOWLEDGMENTS

According to Virginia Woolf, "A woman must have money and a room of her own if she is to write." In an ever-changing cityscape, coming across either of these has become increasingly difficult. Thus, I feel the need to acknowledge the two individuals who provided me with ideal living situations while I was writing this book. George Wanatt, thank you for keeping my rent stable throughout the years, even as the towers on the Brooklyn waterfront went up, the rents soared, and the neighborhood shifted—you are the most generous landlord on the planet. Elspeth Leacock, thank you for sharing your cottage over the summers, and for saving me from the city (and often from myself).

This book would not have come to fruition without the encouragement and support of numerous friends and colleagues who read the manuscript and provided invaluable feedback along the way. Thank you to all at Hunter, especially Colum McCann, Vanessa Manko, and Peter Messina. I'm forever grateful to *Granta* and John Freeman for being the first to publish my work. My deepest gratitude to all at the Wylie Agency, especially Sarah Chalfant, for the guidance and all the hard work on behalf of this author. Many thanks to Kate Guiney, as well as to Gabriella Doob and everyone at Farrar, Straus and Giroux. I'm beholden to my brilliant editor, Eric Chinski, whose patience, encouragement, and keen edits made this a much stronger book.

In the end, no one deserves more recognition than my family, especially my mother and my grandmother, both of whom helped me fill in the gaps. I'm also deeply grateful to my siblings for being there while we were going through the trenches, and once again while I was rehashing our lives. Cualita, Nena, Chavo, Chela, Sonia, Jorge, and Yesi: it's your love and support that keeps me grounded. And finally, Chemel, my beloved brother, thank you for keeping watch from the other side. You may be gone, but your influence lives on.